Aging and the Digital Life Course

Life Course, Culture and Aging: Global Transformations
General Editor: Jay Sokolovsky, University of South Florida St. Petersburg

Published by Berghahn Books under the auspices of the Association for Anthropology and Gerontology (AAGE) and the American Anthropological Association Interest Group on Aging and the Life Course.

The consequences of aging will influence most areas of contemporary life around the globe: the makeup of households and communities; systems of care; generational exchange and kinship; the cultural construction of the life cycle; symbolic representations of midlife, elderhood and old age; and attitudes toward health, disability and life's end. This series publishes monographs and collected works that examine these widespread transformations with a perspective on the entire life course as well as mid/late adulthood. It engages in a cross-cultural framework to explore the role of older adults in changing cultural spaces and how this evolves in our rapidly globalizing planet.

AGING AND THE DIGITAL LIFE COURSE

Edited by

David Prendergast and Chiara Garattini

berghahn
NEW YORK · OXFORD
www.berghahnbooks.com

Published in 2015 by
Berghahn Books
www.berghahnbooks.com

Library of Congress Cataloging-in-Publication Data

Aging and the digital life course / edited by David Prendergast and Chiara
Garattini. -- First Edition.
    pages cm. -- (Life course, culture and aging: global transformations; 3)
    Includes bibliographical references and index.
  ISBN 978-1-78238-691-9 (hardback: alk. paper) -- ISBN 978-1-78238-692-6
(ebook)
  1. Older people. 2. Technology and older people. I. Prendergast, David, 1973-
editor. II. Garattini, Chiara, editor.
  HQ1061.A42724 2015
  604.84'6--dc23

                                                              2015006169

British Library Cataloguing in Publication Data

A catalogue record for this book is available from the British Library.

ISBN 978-1-78238-691-9 (hardback)
ISBN 978-1-78238-692-6 (ebook)

CONTENTS

ILLUSTRATIONS

Figures

Tables

ACKNOWLEDGEMENTS

WE WERE FIRST INVITED TO prepare a book on the subject of ageing and technology in 2011 to talk about our experience working as ethnographers at Intel, researching, designing and critiquing technologies for supporting ageing-in-place and independent living. By this point, we had worked together for several years on projects ranging from platforms for reducing social and emotional loneliness, the reinvention of retirement, peer learning and behaviour change and opportunities for telehealth. With every research study we undertook, it became more apparent that there was a need for a book that would attempt to reveal and unravel the complexities surrounding the emergent technologies and socio-technical practices encountered within the later life course. Such a book, we felt, needed to embrace and represent perspectives and insights from the plethora of providers and recipients of services across the later life course whilst allowing space for critical questions such as 'how can technology support caregivers?' or 'what happens to our data after we die?'

Many of the authors who contributed to this collection have worked with us in the past as we have attempted to navigate, explore and sometimes invent the embryonic landscape of gerontechnology. Others, whose research offers original, exciting insights and fills gaps in our evidence base, we pursued with vigour. We would like to thank all our authors for the contributions they have made towards seeing this project to completion, and also to express our deep appreciation for the warm encouragement and guidance of Jay Sokolovsky, General Editor of Berghahn Books' 'Life Course, Culture and Aging' series, and friend and colleague Dawn Nafus for her precious input.

We have also benefitted greatly from the wisdom and advice of colleagues and friends at Intel and would particularly like to acknowledge the support of Intel Labs, the Health Strategy and Solutions Group and, previously to this, Intel's Digital Health Group, the Technology Research for Independent Living (TRIL) Centre, as well as the many organizations focused on ageing that have worked with us.

Finally, we wish to thank our families for their love and forgiving patience as we repeatedly disappeared into our offices on evenings and weekends to work on this book. Kim, Harry, Beth and Kate Prendergast, Gianni, Liliana, Michele Garattini and Davide Giovanardi, we dedicate this collection to you.

INTRODUCTION
Critical Reflections on Ageing and Technology in the Twenty-First Century
Chiara Garattini and David Prendergast

BETWEEN 2006 AND 2008, SHORTLY before the global economy was turned on its head, we were engaged in a large-scale, long-term ethnographic research project designed to develop a global, comparative understanding of the practices and meanings associated with growing older (Plowman, Prendergast and Roberts 2009). This study, funded by Intel, the technology company, focused on the experiences and expectations of ageing with a view to help frame the questions being asked to imagine new technologies for supporting independent living. It aimed to analyse, among other things, the multiple meanings of 'home' for older people and the implications for those seeking to deliver services, technology or other interventions.

Dozens of households in many countries each generously gave two days of their time to allow researchers into their lives, sharing their health stories, personal and family histories, social activities and ambitions for the future. Many extraordinary insights emerged from that wealth of data, some of which are covered in this introduction. Certainly any lingering reifications about the homogeneity of older age cohorts, or assumptions about the dependencies of old age or universal technological illiteracy, were quickly exploded. The broad comparative 'Intel Global Ageing Experience Study' later led the team to both directly conduct and sponsor deeper, more focused research projects on a variety of themes around the subject of independent living. This programme of activities brought us into contact with some amazing projects and researchers in many contexts and cultures. It explored how technologies, sensitively designed with social, personal and institutional practices in mind, can help contribute towards building positive experiences in the later life course.

This edited collection is designed to provide a platform for some of the promising and insightful work in this emergent and exciting domain that is taking place internationally. The chapters in this book cover a wide range of subjects such as social media, robotics, chronic disease management, caregiving, gaming, migration and data inheritance, to name a few. This complex diversity itself reflects the richness of the research on later life. We have organized them into three sections: Connections, Networks and Interactions; Health and Wellbeing; and Life Course Transitions. These themes address some of the major trends in ageing and technology research, but also highlight some obvious limits. Many topics discussed by the chapters overlap across the different fields. Is telecare about health or social connectedness? Can we confine civic engagement through Information and Communications Technology (ICT) in later life to social networking and not to wellbeing? Is e-learning about social interaction, health, or transitioning into the community of ICT and technology users? Can we really separate these domains? We think not. The concepts of 'being old' and 'technology', albeit very complex and nuanced, are sometimes flattened in easy explanatory categories. In this introduction we would like to unpack both concepts and to start what the rest of the volume will continue to do: highlight the complex relationship between ageing and the use of technologies. The chapters cover a great deal both in terms of technology and social practice. Yet, as we witness rapid developments around how data is collected, analysed, visualized and put into action, it is only the start of a much larger and very important conversation about what we need to consider when designing technologies across the landscapes of the later life course.

Global Ageing in Perspective

In recent years, there has been a great deal of discussion about global ageing. Many consider it to be one of the megatrends of this century alongside rapid urbanization and climate change. The United Nations (UN), in a now famous 2001 report, described the situation as unprecedented, 'without parallel in the history of humanity', pervasive, 'a global phenomenon affecting every man, woman and child', profound, 'having major consequences and implications for all facets of human life', and enduring, with the trend of proportion of older persons expected to continue to rise in the twentieth-first century (United Nations 2001: xxviii passim). According to the World Health Organization (WHO) 'the proportion of the world's population over 60 years will double from about 11% to 22%' between 2000 and 2050, with the absolute number of people aged 60 years and over expected to increase from 605 million to 2 billion (WHO 2014: passim).[1]

This phenomenon, often described in apocalyptic terms in media, government and even academic literature, is the outcome of people living longer combined with a decrease in the number of children they have. While the reasons for having fewer children are complex and highly debated, the reasons why we live longer are easier to agree upon. Amongst others, these include improvements in nutrition and food supply, in public health and hygiene, especially in terms of the way we live and work, and in the advancement of medicine with the introduction of vaccines, antibiotics, and the control of many infectious diseases.

Despite sensational labels such as 'the ageing time bomb' and the 'demographic tsunami', the fact that we live longer and healthier lives is a great achievement of humanity that should be celebrated. It is wondrous to consider that the first child to live to the age of 150 has probably already been born and that in certain societies, one in every two girls born today can be expected to reach their centenary. It is even more incredible to reflect that human life expectancy has increased by approximately two years for every decade since the start of the twentieth century, and that the additional time, on the whole, involves 'healthy life years' for most of the population.

Ageing demographics, of course, do carry great consequences for the way in which complex organizations and societies structurally organize themselves at the macro level and for the dynamic configurations of relationships between individuals and groups at the local level (Vincent et al. 2006). A rapidly ageing population has critical impact on, for example, family structures, intergenerational relations, the length and options for working life, not to mention the financial stability of citizens and economies alike. In the UK, many of the policy commitments and labour expectations agreed as part of the post-war 'Beverage Reforms' originally helped to shape perceptions of later life, starting with official retirement at 60 for women and 65 for men. In the UK, as in many other countries, once established boundaries around retirement age and pension rights have been challenged and renegotiated in the panics, contractions and shockwaves generated by the 2008 global economic crisis. To varying degrees throughout Europe and the world, experiments with alternative forms and scenarios for welfare provision are also taking place with targeted eligibility schemes, layered payment options, public-private hybrid models of funding, and initiatives to drive and support the growth of volunteering and collaboration. In patrilineal South Korea, the government has formally overhauled the family law system and attempted to reshape inheritance practices in order to encourage married daughters to become involved in the care of their aged natal parents as the number of sons available, able or willing to take formal responsibility dwindles (Prendergast 2005). Similarly in China, concerns over the erosion of family values and caregiving practices as a result of rapid uneven urbanization and industrialization is a common topic in the national media. At the time of writing China has 221 million people over the age of 60; one-third of whom are living below the poverty line. Legislative initiatives such as the 2012 'Law of Protection of Rights and Interests of the Aged' are attempting to force offspring to take financial responsibility for their parents whilst limiting and punishing elder abuse. The new law gives aged parents the means to prosecute their own children and, despite much local scepticism, the first court case took place on 2 July 2013 where a 77-year-old woman from the Jiangsu city of Wuxi sued her daughter for neglect. The court ruled in favour of the plaintiff and ordered the daughter to provide financial support and visit her mother in person twice a month.

Also in question is the ability of many of the world's health and social care systems to cope with the dramatic increase in numbers of often manageable but expensive, multiple 'non-communicable diseases' and chronic conditions that often accompany the process of growing old. For healthcare specialists and policy makers alike, this issue becomes greatly amplified when discussed in relation to older adults aged 80 years or more. Often referred to as the 'oldest old', this is the fastest growing segment of the population, so much so that it is expected to quadruple in size in many countries by 2050 (WHO 2014). This is a major concern as costs and requirements of care associated with frailty, critical health events, falls, social isolation and cognitive decline increase exponentially for this group. A recent OECD report on emerging trends in biomedicine and health technology innovation argues that chronic brain disorders are set to become the number one public health problem worldwide during the twenty-first century. Alzheimer's disease alone affects one in eight people above the age of 65 and approximately half of those over 85 (OECD 2013).

In such contexts, older people are often explicitly or implicitly represented as non-productive recipients, a 'burden' from both an economic and a healthcare system point of view. Even though we acknowledge the challenges that are part of the phenomenon of an ageing population and the frailty that often accompanies those who are older, it is equally critical to recognize that growing old can be an active, healthy, happy, productive stage within one's life course. As the World Health Organization says, 'how well we age depends on many factors' (WHO 2014). There are risks involved in using terms such as 'old age' and 'elderly' as it can lead to a tendency to misleadingly homogenize and reify a very large diverse population with myriad variegated expectations, resources, and life course experiences (Blaikie 1999; Arbor and Evandrou 1993).

Perceptions of Ageing

Ageing in medical terms has been described as 'bio-chemical explanations of the pathological deterioration of the human organism' (Turner 1989: 595). In social sciences however, ageing is understood as the 'cultural and sociological process by which humans are classified and ranked by reference to their chronology' (Turner 1989: 595). From this perspective, Turner continues, age and ageing are 'socially constructed categories for the classification of persons'. Turner is not the only one that has considered 'old age' as a problematic category on which many quick decisions are taken every day (Degnen 2007). First of all, as Catherine Dengen noticed, it is broad: it covers a long lifespan with very little internal distinction, unlike other categories of the life course, such as 'childhood', that are conceptualized with a more nuanced approach (e.g. 'infants', 'toddlers', 'pre-school', etc.) (Degnen 2007: 69).

Secondly, there is problem of identification: who can be said to be old? People identified by others as old often do not see themselves as such, and being old becomes something that other people are. Degnen defines oldness as 'relational', struggling between epistemological ('old age exists') and pragmatic (being able to call somebody old) categories of 'old', and encourages social scientists to avoid talking about 'old age' as a category, and to discuss instead the context of ageing (Versperi 1985, quoted in Degnen 2007: 71). In this sense, '[t]he experience of "becoming old" [...] is not "unidirectional", nor is it distinctive of people who are old. Rather it is intergenerational and reflexive: "the individual moves ... through a spectrum of emotions in which the past, present and future are in essentially unstable combination"' (Hepworth 1998, quoted in Williams 2000: 61).

Thirdly, 'old age' is often charged with negative connotations. Becoming old is broadly considered to be associated with losing strength and independence from a physical, social and financial point of view. There is a danger, for example, in describing older people always on the verge of losing independence, making them into personifications of risk (Lee and Dey 2010).

Even though we do not argue that some of these elements are part of the common process of becoming old, what we contest is the stigma that in our youth-oriented society is applied to the idea of being old. The problem, for example, of associating old age with illness is that it creates a situation where the individuality and uniqueness of a person might be pushed into the background, dominating somebody's perceived social role. As Graham Scambler famously noted in his discussion of stigma, an assigned 'label' can become a 'master status' (Scambler 2008: 207).[2]

There is considerable literature on how stigma impacts people. Yang and colleagues define stigma as situational (e.g. emerging from the interaction around a situation), as part of a process of 'cognitive categorization' (e.g. stigma occurs when the 'mark' of an undesirable characteristic is attributed to an individual), and via collective representations (e.g. when cultural stereotypes, local hierarchies, values, etc. are used cognitively to label somebody with undesirable traits) (Yang et al. 2007: 1526). Stigma therefore does not emanate from an individual and is not inflicted on an individual, but instead is the outcome of complex social processes.

Besides the issue of physical frailty, it is also a mistake to characterize those in later life as passive recipients or consumers of resources. In Europe, the population over the age of 50 controls approximately 75 per cent of the wealth, more in the UK and Japan. As Jones et al. (2008) put it,

> The cohorts of people retiring now are those who participated in the creation of the post-war consumer culture. These consumers have grown older but have not stopped consuming; their choices and behaviour are the products of the collective histories of both cohort and generation. People approaching retirement, entering retirement, or currently living in retirement will have very different experiences of later life to those of their predecessors. (Jones 2008: 11)

Similarly, it is a significant error for policy makers, academics, marketers, or indeed older people themselves to correlate later life with powerlessness. In terms of the former, older population segments form an increasingly large portion of the electorate and are the most likely age category to actually exercise their right to vote. Lobby groups for and by older people are proliferating and associations such as the AARP (formerly the American Association of Retired Persons) or Age Platform in Europe are deeply involved in central and local politics. In Ireland, various campaigns spearheaded by the Older and Bolder Campaign in 2010 successfully averted substantial budget cuts in basic supports and the state pension proposed as part of the national austerity measures.

Perceptions generated by apocalyptic labels or burden models can also lead to simplistic and often erroneous assumptions about later life as unproductive. The anthropological record is littered with historical and contemporary examples of the economic and social roles played by older people in cultures throughout the world (see for example Spencer 1990; Keith et al. 1994; Sokolovsky 2009). As noted above, people will be increasingly expected not only to work longer into the life course (and many are willing to do so) but also to volunteer and participate in their communities more as welfare and health systems and services adjust to new demographic realities. In practice, many older people continue to work far beyond the statutory retirement age whether in formal employment and consultancy roles or as community volunteers, childcare providers, or family caregivers. It is difficult to classify as taxpayer burdens the approximately 6 million unpaid and largely invisible carers, many of them older adults, who save the British NHS an estimated £119 billion per annum.[3]

Downward transmission of resources to younger generations seldom happens in one post-mortem inheritance transfer. Throughout the later life course, wealth and social capital are invested in adult offspring and their families by older people by way of wedding contributions, mortgage guarantees, multigenerational living arrangements, cost of living subsidies and gifting, and looking after grandchildren to enable dual partner income streams.

It is similarly easy to gather examples of older people as community champions, activists and social entrepreneurs. Across Ireland, a programme organized by the Third Age Foundation has seen hundreds of older people flock to sign up as conversational English teachers for immigrant workers and their families. In Australia, a scheme called 'Men's Sheds' was created to provide a venue and reason for older males, some of whom would be otherwise socially isolated, to gather and teach construction skills to younger generations. The products of some of these sheds, such as recycled bicycles, are then sent to low-income countries. In the US, many capable older drivers volunteer for a not-for-profit organization called Independent Transportation Network America (ITNAmerica). This organization was set up to provide a dignified 'arm-through-arm, door-through-door' transport option for adults with mobility issues and an affordable flexible alternative that encourages and enables older people, who feel it is time to give up driving for safety reasons, to maintain independence. This is especially important in areas with underdeveloped public transport systems. To cover costs such as insurance, vehicle maintenance and fuel, the programme, now running in at least twenty-one states across the country, charges transport recipients a basic fee per mile which, providing they book well ahead, is considerably cheaper than private hire alternatives. A technology layer underpins the scheduling, payment and innovative cashless microcredit scheme. Volunteer drivers are awarded mileage credits for their contributions. Likewise, older drivers who wish to give up their cars can donate them to the organization which reciprocates by providing the equivalent value in credits into their personal transportation accounts. In addition to direct purchase of credits, members of the scheme can accumulate credits in a number of other ways including co-payments from participating merchants and healthcare services and through gifts from friends and relatives.

As discussed, ageing has biological, social and, because it happens at a particular point in history, 'generational belonging' dimensions to it (Hagberg 2012). A study of ageing has to be a study of the life course, of generational cohort relationships, domestic cycles, definitions of middle and late adulthood, and meaning making rather than the study of an entity, 'the old', as a fixed, romanticized body (Cohen 1994: 148). It is our aim to be part of the literature on ageing that counteracts stigma and problematic simplification of 'old people'. Instead we want to conceptualize ageing as a diversified process that does not bend to superficial definitions. It is within the context of this complexity that we want to situate this book on the interaction of ageing people with technologies. But technologies themselves do not escape the trap of simplification, something we will discuss in the next section.

Technologies in Perspective

Across the entire life course new forms of community, methods for keeping in contact, and ways of engaging in work, healthcare, retail, learning and leisure are evolving rapidly with developments in smart phones, web 2.0, cloud computing, the internet of things, online social networking, big data, mobile broadband, and vast gaming universes. Opportunities and forums for social participation are proliferating and content is becoming more visual, interactive, and frequently community or peer led.

Many of the technologies that we are so familiar with today, to the point that we can hardly imagine our life without them, are recent developments. On 30 April 2013 for example, the World Wide Web celebrated its twentieth birthday,[4] and it was only in 1994 and 1995 that Amazon and Google, respectively, were founded. In comparison, Facebook is even younger, only ten years old at the time of writing. Yet, it is reasonable to say that these technologies have significantly changed the way in which we work, communicate, interact, purchase and access information. It is also reasonable to say that technologies as we know them today have the potential to support us in those areas where it is most needed, such as living healthier, longer, happier lives.

Certain population categories, especially the oldest old, frequently lag behind in adoption and uptake of these new possibilities, and are often perceived to be at risk of becoming marginalized by digital exclusion. Beginning in 2009 the UK's Race Online programme, later rebranded 'Go ON UK', set itself the task of creating a truly networked nation. The campaign argues that despite 90 per cent of jobs in Britain requiring some level of Information Communication Technology (ICT) interaction, 16 million people do not have basic online skills such as emailing, using a search engine and filling out an online application form. Of these, they suggest that around 3 million people should be classified as active resistors to technology adoption. The first iteration of the campaign suggested in 2010 that 5.7 million people over the age of 65 were offline and estimated that savings of around £1 billion would accrue from moving online just two of the contacts a month this cohort has with government bodies. On the other hand, the 4 million older people that do use the internet spend longer online that any other age group – an average of forty-two hours per month (Race Online 2010, 2012). Likewise in the US, figures from April 2012 suggested that for the first time more than half of all older American adults now have access to the internet. Of these, 70 per cent use it on a typical day and 34 per cent have signed up to social networking sites (Zickuhr and Madden 2012).

When considering ageing and technologies, however, we need to think in terms of complex interactions. Often things appear simple when they rely on social and cultural assumptions that serve as a form of shorthand. These assumptions can be problematic. For example, technology is often conceptualized in opposition to 'nature', which implies associations with ideas of 'progress' and 'tradition', 'efficient' and 'inefficient', 'new' and 'old'. In this sense 'older people' are often represented as 'not interested' in technology, within an almost irreconcilable opposition such as in the discussion of the supposed 'digital divide' between young 'natives' and old 'immigrants' (Prensky 2001a; 2001b). The problem, as discussed elsewhere, is that both categories – 'young' and 'old' – are flattened in this process (Loos, Haddon, and Mante-Meijer 2012). As Eszter Hargittai and Gina Walejko pointed out, not all youth are equally digitally adept (Hargittai and Walejko 2008). Attitudes, education, aptitude, socio-economic background, gender, ethnicity, personality, generational cohort and age all arguably contribute to the diverse ways in which people interact with technologies. Every person has to judge whether learning to use a new technology is worth the effort (Hagberg 2012: 97). We have to balance the right to be included with the right of being excluded.

Also, while technologies carry potential for great benefits, they can carry downsides that people might want to consciously resist. For example, in the area of health they tend to increase a trend, which follows a centuries old thread, of medicalizing every aspect of life. Technologies involve techniques of enumeration and as such carry the risk of what has been called *data-ism* and data-centric biology: people can get caught up into the over-importance of data and what it says about people (Leonelli 2013: 470). They can enable a 'tyranny of numbers' that creates 'risk' categories and brings forth a potentially problematic biological reductionism of 'decontextualized probabilities' (Lock and Nguyen 2010: 26).[5] The importance of numbers in Western society is rooted in the scientific ethos characteristic of Enlightenment thinking and positivism, whereby 'the world is made known through systematic investigation and transformed for the better by means of the application of technologies' (Lock and Nguyen 2010: 19). Technologies are a key component of this process.

Technologies are therefore not neutral, but at the same time we believe it necessary to avoid easy simplification of them as being intrinsically 'good' or 'bad'. Technologies are powerful, and they mediate (and augment) relations and imbalances of power. They often channel and, in our society, embody authority, and because of that it is very important to enable people to have a choice about using technology rather than be used by it.

As well as avoiding the assignation of values to technologies as either 'good' or 'bad', we also want to steer clear of another dichotomy. Technologies are often conceptualized in opposition to people, as being completely separated from them. However, technologies and humanity have a much more complex interaction and nuanced distinction. People have been making tools to solve problems and enhance their lives since the very beginning of their existence, by mastering fire, stone and wood. Part of the issue is that in Western societies, for example, people tend to be imagined as subjects performing actions and things as objects passively receiving them, but this idea can be, and has been, challenged. For example, Material Culture scholars have suggested that, thanks to their materiality which can be experienced through the senses, objects produce effects on people (Tilley 2007: 259). In this sense, they may be attributed what is generally referred to as agency (see Gell 1988), which in simple terms means they are attributed with the capability to perform actions. The idea that things are not merely the recipient of actions that people enact upon them, but instead have agency of their own, blurs the boundaries between subjects and object, things and people (Miller 2005; Tilley 2006). Science and Technology Studies (STS) scholars have also pointed out that objects, including technologies, influence our actions and therefore can be treated as subjects and 'social actors', gaining a status of quasi-objects (see also Latour 1993).[6]

The chapters in this volume discuss technologies in all the complexities highlighted above, for example by exploring robots as social actors, by looking at the effect of telecare devices on people's perceptions of themselves, by investigating the bending of time and space which occurs through digital social media's asynchronous and co-present (and yet distant) interactions, and by considering how fragments of ourselves continue to exist beyond physical death. Different contributions consider the risks of being excluded by the ICT society we live in, and look at ways in which better design of technologies can enable people to find the right information to change or make their lives better, if they wish to do so.

In essence, technologies cannot be understood or treated separately from society, people and politics, or what Dourish and Bell (2011) aptly refer to as 'the everyday messiness of lived experience'. Much of the discussion on new technologies today revolves around the idea that they produce 'revolutions' and 'unprecedented change' to society. In this book we wish to acknowledge the novelty of recent developments, and yet avoid tendencies towards technological determinism. We would rather consider technologies as part of the broader social, economic and cultural landscape. People have always created new technologies, and technological innovations, whether it be irrigation, gunpowder, the computer chip or the invention of glass, all of which have had a great impact on people and societies throughout history (Macfarlane and Martin 2002). This is one more, very interesting, chapter that we are living through.

Conclusion

With this in mind, we would like to conclude as we started with some guiding themes and insights distilled from many older voices and accounts from eight countries as part of the Intel Global Ageing Experience Project (Plowman, Prendergast and Roberts 2009). Initially developed for the inventors, engineers and designers of independent living technologies, the six principles below now perhaps serve as a useful reference and critical reflection points for readers exploring the chapters in this collection.

> *1) People want to focus on what they can do, not what they cannot.* Many older adults are reluctant to accept a perception of themselves as being or feeling sick or old regardless of their chronological age. Many seek out physical and mental challenges within the parameters of what they can do, pushing boundaries and shunning assistive devices. Whether they use or need assistance, it is essential to develop technologies that help people to do what they want to do, rather than act as reminders, or create real or perceived stigmas of disability, restriction, dependence and lack of control.

> *2) Ageing in place means more than staying at home.* Independence for many does not refer to merely dwelling in a private residence, but to being able to prepare meals, shop, work on the garden, take part in community life and remain socially active. Technology can assist in many ways such as enabling mobility, identifying and coordinating trusted providers of home services and helping secure peace of mind both inside and outside of the physical house.

3) Health perception is not an objective quality. It is defined collaboratively through social interaction, personal and cultural history and is often the outcome of complex negotiations between all manner of stakeholders, including medical professionals, family members, informal caregivers, peers, friends and neighbours – all of whom may differ in their assessments of the older person's health issue; sometimes with implications for access and control of resources. Cultural, social and political systems also shape attitudes and behaviours related to health.

4) People often mark the progression of ageing by watershed events such as falls, change of residence, or loss of a loved one. Monitoring, assessment and early intervention are useful, but people often are in a state of healthy denial about ageing and thus may not be willing to adopt technologies that are not aligned with their desired ways of living. Technologies should be designed to adapt to emergent needs and ability levels.

5) Healthy aging is inextricably linked to social participation. Social relationships benefit health. Beyond simple contact and companionship, a sense of belonging to a larger group or community can provide psychosocial security, especially if it is linked to opportunities to be useful, productive and engaged. Nobody of any age likes to feel they are a burden.

6) Healthcare networks are large and increasingly complex. Many of the households visited had been forced to learn how to navigate the healthcare system, often during a period of intense pressure due to a critical health event. Several noted that it was unfortunate that they had no place to share their hard-won knowledge. Collaborative user-based technology system should enable sharing and promote peer learning and supports. Homecare technologies of the future should look beyond the vertical relationships between doctor and patient and focus more holistically across the many partners and stakeholders involved in the care relationship.

As we move to explore these issues through a wide variety of contexts it is important to remember that ageing is a complex concept that classifies people relationally from a chronological, generational and cohort perspective. Yet, when interviewed, it is surprising how people seldom admit to feeling old until challenged by critical life course events that have eroded resiliency. Drawing from insights provided in the chapters, this book critically explores how positive ageing might look in the future, if sensitively supported and enabled by appropriate ICT frameworks, and what technological, social and cultural pitfalls are to be avoided as we design for ageing.

Notes

1. http://www.who.int/ageing/en/ (accessed April 2014).
2. Yang et al. discussed several definitions of stigma (Yang et al. 2007). For example, they reported how for Goffman (1990 [1963]) stigma is an attribute that is deeply discrediting and transforms the person from a whole to a 'tainted, discounted one'. Jones et al. (1984) built on this example to argue how it describes 'a deviant condition identified by society that might define the individual as flawed or spoiled'. Link and Phelan (2001, 2004) proposed a more sociological definition of stigma, whereby stigma is a process that influences and is influenced by the role played by social, economic and political powers (all from Yang et al. 2007: 1525 passim).
3. See http://www.carersuk.org/news-and-campaigns/press-releases/unpaid-carers-save-119-billion-a-year.
4. Following a statement by CERN, 30 April 1993 is selected here as the date of the birth of the World Wide Web, as the day on which the technology was made available on a royalty-free basis. See http://home.web.cern.ch/topics/birth-web.
5. See also, for example, Greenhalgh's brief discussion of the challenges in fitting the language of Evidence Based Medicine (EBM), defined as 'the use of mathematical estimates of the chance of benefit and the risk of harm, derived from high-quality research on population samples, to inform clinical decision-making', to the complexities of most medical cases encountered in real primary care practice in the UK (2012: 93–95 passim).
6. In his sophisticated discussion on modernity, Latour problematizes, among other things, the (supposedly) Western conceptual dichotomy between Object and Subject/Society. For Latour these concepts are just 'partial and purified' ideas resulting from modernity's attempts at classifying entities. He proposes instead to consider mediators (e.g. agents between the two 'pure forms'), suggesting that we move from discussing a world of objects and subjects to one of quasi-objects and quasi-subjects (Latour 1993: 76–79 passim).

References

Arbor, S. and M. Evandrou. 1993. *Ageing, independence and the life course*. London: Jessica Kingsley Publishers.

Blaikie, A. 1999. *Ageing and popular culture*. Cambridge: Cambridge University Press.

Cohen, L. 1994. 'Old age: cultural and critical perspectives', *Annual Review of Anthropology* 23: 137–58.

Degnen, C. 2007. 'Minding the gap: the construction of old age and oldness amongst peers', *Journal of Aging Studies* 21: 69–80.

Dourish, P. and G. Bell. 2011. *Divining a digital future: mess and mythology in ubiquitous computing*. Cambridge: MIT Press.

Hagberg, J.-E. 2012. 'Being the oldest old in a shifting technology landscape', in Eugène Loos, Leslie Haddon and Enid Mante-Meijer (eds), *Generational use of new media*. England: Ashgate, pp. 89–106.

Hargittai, E. and G. Walejko. 2008. 'The participation divide: content creation and sharing in the digital age', *Information, Communication & Society* 11(2): 239–56.

Gell, A. 1988. *Art and agency – an anthropological theory.* Oxford and New York: Oxford University Press.

Greenhalgh, T. 2012. 'Why do we always end up here? Evidence based medicine's conceptual cul-de-sacs and some off-road alternative routes (guest editorial)', *Journal of Primary Healthcare* 4(2): 92–97.

Goffman, E. 1990 [1984]. *Stigma: notes on the management of spoiled identity.* New edition. Penguin.

Jones, E.E., A. Farina, A. Hastorf, H. Markus, D. Miller and R.A. Scott. 1984. *Social stigma: the psychology of marked relationships.* New York: W.H. Freeman & Co Ltd.

Jones, I.R., M. Hyde, C. Victor, R. Wiggins, C. Gilleard and P. Higgs. 2008. *Ageing in a consumer society: from passive to active consumption in Britain.* Bristol: Policy Press.

Keith, J., C.L. Fry, A.P. Glascock, C. Ikels, J. Dickerson-Putman, H.C. Harpending and P. Draper. 1994. *The ageing experience: diversity and commonality across cultures.* Thousand Acres, CA: Sage.

Latour, B. 1993. *We have never been modern.* Cambridge, MA: Harvard University Press.

Lee, M.L. and A.K. Dey. 2010. 'Embedded assessment of aging adults: a concept validation with stakeholders', *Pervasive Computing Technologies for Healthcare (PervasiveHealth) IEEE*: 1–8.

Leonelli, S. 2013. 'Centralising labels to distribute data. The regulatory role of Genomic Consortia', in Paul Atkinson, Peter Glasner and Margaret Lock (eds), *Handbook of genetics and society. Mapping the new genomic era.* Oxford: Routledge, pp. 469–85.

Link, Bruce G., and Jo C. Phelan. 2001. 'Conceptualizing stigma', *Annual Review of Sociology* 27(1): 363–85. doi:10.1146/annurev.soc.27.1.363.

Link, Bruce G., Lawrence H. Yang, Jo C. Phelan and Pamela Y. Collins. 2004. 'Measuring mental illness stigma', *Schizophrenia Bulletin* 30(3): 511–41.

Lock, M. and V.-K. Nguyen. 2010. *An anthropology of biomedicine.* Oxford, UK: Wiley-Blackwell.

Loos, E., L. Haddon and E. Mante-Meijer. 2012. *Generational use of new media.* Farnham, England: Ashgate.

Macfarlane, A. and G. Martin. 2002. *The glass bathyscaphe: how glass changed the world.* London: Profile Books.

Miller, D. 2005. 'Materiality: an introduction', in Daniel Miller (ed.), *Materiality.* Durham and London: Duke University Press, pp. 1–50.

OECD. 2013. 'Emerging trends in biomedicine and health technology innovation: addressing the global challenge of Alzheimer's', *OECD Science, Technology and Industry Policy Papers*, No. 6, OECD Publishing.

Plowman, T., D. Prendergast and S. Roberts. 2009. 'From people to prototypes and products – ethnographic liquidity and the Intel Global Aging Experience Study', *Intel Technology Journal* 13(3): 20–39.

Prendergast, D. 2005. *From elder to ancestor: old age, death and inheritance in modern Korea.* Folkestone, Kent: Oriental Press.

Prensky, M. 2001a. 'Digital natives, digital immigrants', *On the Horizon* 9(5) (October): 1–6.

———. 2001b. 'Digital natives, digital immigrants, part II: do they really think differently?', *On the Horizon* 9(6) (December): 1–9.

Race Online. 2010. Manifesto for a networked nation.

———. 2012. *Getting on. A manifesto for older people in a networked nation.* http://www.go-on.co.uk/wp-content/uploads/2013/12/Getting_ON_August_2011.pdf.

Scambler, G. 2008. 'Deviance, sick role and stigma', in Graham Scambler (ed.), *Sociology as applied to medicine*, 6th edn. Philadelphia: Saunders Elsevier, pp. 205–17.

Sokolovsky, J. (ed.). 2009. *The cultural context of ageing: worldwide perspectives.* 3rd edn. Westport, CT: Praeger Press.

Spencer, P. (ed.). 1990. *Anthropology and the riddle of the Sphinx: paradoxes of change in the life course.* London: Routledge.

Tilley, C. 2006. 'Objectification', in Christopher Tilley, Webb Keane, Susanne Kuechler-Fogden, Mike Rowlands and Patricia Spyer (eds), *Handbook of material culture.* London; Thousand Oaks, CA: Sage, pp. 60–73.

———. 2007. 'Ethnography and material culture', in Paul Atkinson, Amanda Coffey, Sara Delamont, John Lofland and Lyn Lofland (eds), *Handbook of ethnography.* London: Sage, pp. 258–72.

Turner, B.S. 1989. 'Ageing, status politics and sociological theory', *The British Journal of Sociology* 40: 588–606.

United Nations, Department of Economic and Social Affairs – Population Division. 2001. 'World Population Ageing: 1950-2050'. ST/ESA/SER.A/207. New York. http://www.un.org/esa/population/publications/worldageing19502050/pdf/62executivesummary_english.pdf.

Vincent, J., C. Phillipson and M. Downs (eds). 2006. *The futures of old age.* London: Sage.

Williams, S.J. 2000. 'Chronic illness as biographical disruption or biographical disruption as chronic illness? Reflections on a core concept', *Sociology of Health & Illness* 22: 40–67.

Yang, L.H., A. Kleinman, B.G. Link, J.C. Phelan , S. Lee and B. Good. 2007. 'Culture and stigma: adding moral experience to stigma theory', *Social Science & Medicine* 64: 1524–35.

Zickuhr, K. and M. Madden. 2012. 'Older adults and internet use', *Pew Internet Report.* http://www.pewinternet.org/~/media//Files/Reports/2012/PIP_Older_adults_and_internet_use.pdf.

PART ONE
Connections, Networks and Interactions

WE OPEN THE BOOK WITH a section discussing digital and technologically mediated ways of connecting and interacting with people. There
are two main reasons for this choice. Social media and ICT have changed
modes of interaction at many levels in our daily lives. We keep in touch
with friends and families, get updated with events and news, create and
connect with people through diverse social networking sites, and address
diverse communication needs via the internet. We therefore wanted to
launch the volume with chapters that explore these new media and the
way in which older populations are engaging with them. This brings us
to the second reason for beginning with this topic. As discussed in the
introduction, when exploring the interactions between older people and
technologies, it is often easy to fall into stereotypes and simplifications. We
want to challenge these assumptions and present research based work that
examines, as Phil Stafford puts it, communal and interactional models of
ageing rather than merely individualistic ones.

The first chapter in this section, by Stafford, begins from this position
by exploring technologically mediated political engagement (e.g. electoral
behaviour), and civic participation (e.g. voluntarism and voicing opinions).
He does this through two examples: the Tyze Network, a social networking
site originally developed from an offline group created by parents of adults
with developmental disabilities; and the AdvantAge Initiative, a project
originally born from the idea of engaging people to age as, and within, a
community as opposed to within an individual trajectory. He highlights
the importance of the inclusiveness of ICT given that the statement 'information is power has never been more true'. In this sense, he suggests that
age-friendly communities should shift from focusing predominantly on the
built environment and transport to include a serious discussion on the
inclusiveness of ICT.

Even though adults over the age of 65 are one of the fastest growing groups using ICT and social networking sites, at the time of writing, this cohort still lags behind in terms of overall online presence. Access to ICT and technologies through different forms of e-learning are the theme of the second chapter in this section. Great attention has been paid in recent years to this topic, but the article by Josie Tetley and colleagues explores the issue by looking at e-learning through peer-to-peer playful engagement rather than through self-learning or class based training. The empirical basis of the chapter is a project called Opt-In, a European wide study that investigated older users' e-learning by collecting feedback via qualitative interviews and diaries. Here again, communal rather than individual modes of learning provide a new way to introduce technologies to an older audience who might be unfamiliar with them.

As increasing numbers of older users go online, many are positively and comprehensively embracing emergent and newly available forms of sociality. Rachel Singh's chapter discusses her ethnographic research on older people's use of Constant Contact Media (CCM).This term refers to technologies and online platforms that encourage a variety of frequent personal and group interactions, which, whilst often seemingly minor and undemanding, can act to enhance perceptions of co-presence regardless of physical proximity.

In this sense, through her case studies of older CCM users, Singh erodes 'the idea that technology keeps people distant' and rather proposes that these virtual interactions frequently strengthen those in the physical world. While bringing us closer and giving us a constant sense of co-presence with people we know, as hinted at in Singh's first portrait, CCM and other ICT can also increase distance from those in close physical proximity (e.g. in the same village) if they are not part of the social network. In any case, Singh's excellent examples do not allow us to flatten older users into easy categories of ICT usage; rather, they enable us to resist stereotypes of older adults as passive recipients of technologies.

The last chapter in this section discusses a fascinating and emerging topic within technology design for ageing in place: that of companion robots. The chapter treats robots as social entities and as potential 'problem solvers', either in a functional or emotional and cognitive way. Neven and Leeson touch on the underlying worry, partly rooted in Western approaches to conceptualizing technologies, that the interaction between people and machines might be less satisfying than that between two people. This implies a divide between people and technology that serves visions of the future as either utopian, with technology solutions resolving all problems, or dystopian, with technologies taking over our lives and transforming them in a dehumanized nightmare. The authors move away from this trap and from deterministic ideas of technology and society, and instead discuss these technologies as social phenomena. They do so through two examples from ethnographic studies of design and use of social robots, in the Netherlands and Japan respectively.

1. SOCIAL MEDIA AND THE AGE-FRIENDLY COMMUNITY

Philip B. Stafford

MUCH OF THE EDIFICE OF ageing services and our overall orientation to issues of ageing in society is based on a model of ageing as an individual challenge. This has an atomizing effect, and has led to the neglect of the community and environmental context in which disability and old age emerge. A rapidly growing public health movement is paying more serious attention to the person-environment relationship as the locus of health and wellbeing, as well as the locus of illness, disability and age (Verbrugge 1994; Stafford 2009; WHO 2011). The concept of the age-friendly community has emerged as a framework for planning places that address the needs and support the aspirations of older adults. The WHO Age-Friendly Community model is being employed worldwide as communities begin to address the serious issues around the changing age-demographics. In 2010, three US communities were organizing to respond to these changes employing the WHO blueprint. In 2012, thirty-three cities and towns had taken up the effort. They join the large number of municipalities that have initiated a variety of similar efforts under different rubrics: fifty cities have employed the AdvantAge Initiative elder-friendly model;[1] twenty-three communities have become Communities for all Ages;[2] fourteen communities joined an Administration on Aging project entitled Community Innovations for Aging in Place;[3] and several communities in Indiana have become Lifetime Communities.[4] Whether they are called age-friendly, inclusive, lifetime, or elder-friendly, they share the goal of creating places that work well for all ages and abilities.

Access to information and community participation are frequently cited as key elements of an age-friendly community. Logically, this suggests that digital information technologies are accessible to all older adults, to enable them to meet their needs as well as to foster civic engagement. A recent Pew

Internet study indicates that the 50 per cent threshold of computer use by persons aged over 65 had been reached by the end of 2012.[5]

This is good news. But it also suggests that half of the older adult population in the USA does not employ or have access to a technology that has revolutionized communication, learning, work, leisure, family life and civic participation. This chapter addresses the issue of internet use and civic engagement by and for older adults. It provides a brief review of what is known about how older adults engage through technology and provides insights drawn from two case studies to offer recommendations for increasing civic engagement in the future.

Older Adults and Civic Engagement: Definitional Issues

In the well-received book *Bowling Alone* (2001), Robert Putnam refers to the current oldest cohort as the 'civic generation', so as to highlight its extraordinary level of participation in community organizations and politics. Putnam is not alone in pointing to high levels of civic engagement within the cohort. He emphasized membership in civic associations and political engagement as two primary indicators, along with participation in clubs, church and unions, philanthropic giving, time spent with family and friends and even trust in others. This broad ranging, if somewhat nebulous, definition leaves much to be desired if we are to discuss the concept of civic engagement with some precision. Moreover, Putnam attributed much of the decline he observed in civic participation over recent decades to private media consumption, especially television, and in a later work (2000: 234), the internet, which he described as a 'flawed medium for creating social capital', while acknowledging the potential value of online groups such as Craigslist. org. This is particularly relevant here, for the chapter focuses specifically on the relationship between older adults' use of new media and civic engagement.

Typically, engagement with a church or religious organization is not included within the definition of civic engagement. Also excluded, and quite relevant here, would be engagement with friends, families or social pursuits such as sports, recreation, culture, etc., Putnam notwithstanding. To be fair, Putnam's focus is social capital and, practically speaking, one can build social capital through connections with any fellow human being, thus blurring the boundary between social capital and social networks, between civic engagement and social engagements. One useful review, published by the Pew Charitable Trust (which supports on-going research in civic engagement and new media), clarifies the differences among voting (more precisely, 'electoral') behaviour, civic participation, and the expression of voice and opinion (Keeter et al. 2002: 9):

- Electoral behaviour includes voting, persuading others, displaying buttons/signs/stickers, making campaign contributions and volunteering for political candidates or organizations.
- Indicators of civic participation include community problem solving (whether informal or not), regular volunteering for a non-electoral organization, active membership in a group or association (including donating money), or participating in fundraising or other forms of charity.
- Expressions of voice include contacting public officials, contacting print or other media to express an opinion, protesting, signing petitions (including electronic), boycotting, buycotting, and canvassing on behalf of a cause, group or candidate.

Civic Engagement as Political Engagement

As noted above, political engagement has been seen as one facet of the broader notion of civic engagement. Political engagement, however, is not synonymous with simple voting behaviour. Voting merely represents one form of political engagement and there is neither a consistent nor agreed upon definition or measurement of the concept in the sociological or political science literature. When it comes to electoral behaviour, there is little doubt that older age is positively associated with higher levels of voting.

Using presidential election voting rates as an index of civic engagement, according to the US Census, the voting rates of the 65+ population passed that of all other adult age groups in 1988 and have, in every election since then, far outnumbered rates for the 18–44-year-old age group. In the 2008 election, voter participation among the 65+ age group was 68.1 per cent, compared to 44.3 per cent for the 18–24 age group, which was the highest for that group since 1972 (US Census 2012). The Pew Study cited above, based on an extensive national survey, clearly documents generational differences in electoral behaviour. 'Matures' (born before 1946), when compared to other generations, exhibit the highest rates of voter registration (89 per cent) and the highest report of 'always voting' (72 per cent). The registration rate for boomers (born between 1946 and 1964) is 83 per cent, GenX (born between 1964 and 1976) is 70 per cent, and Millenials (born after 1976) is 60 per cent. 'Always voting' rates for the three latter groups are reported as 53 per cent, 34 per cent and 24 per cent. In other arenas of political behaviour – displaying campaign literature, contributing money to political groups and volunteering for political groups – similar trends are observed. Matures and Boomers are equivalent in making contributions and volunteering and all four groups are equivalent in 'trying to persuade' others on political issues. The Pew Study was published in 2002, prior to the full employment of digital information technologies in politics. The national election of 2008 has been seen by many as the watershed event: the entry of politics into the digital age. One might predict change in the rates of political engagement as alternative, digital opportunities become increasingly available. Indeed, a recent Pew Study (Rainie et al. 2012) of social media and political engagement found that the youngest group (aged 18 to 29) exhibited the highest levels of social media use for political engagement and the 65+ age group the lowest. The landscape of political engagement is changing rapidly so it is worth asking whether the generational 'lag effect' of computer use is leaving older adults behind in the new digital politics.

Civic Engagement as Voluntarism

As mentioned above, much of the literature on civic engagement among older adults focuses on non-political, especially volunteer, activity. Acknowledging the diffuse nature of the definition of engagement (Kaskie et al. 2008), much of the literature on voluntarism comes at the issue from one of two directions: research on the individual benefits of voluntarism (usefully reviewed by Morrow-Howell et al. 2003, and Lum and Lightfoot 2005); and assertions regarding the significant societal benefits of voluntarism by the increasingly large older adult population (e.g. Freedman 2007).

That older adults volunteer in significant numbers is rarely questioned, though rates of voluntarism by adults in the 65+ group are lower than in other age groups. Yet, while the percentage of older adults who volunteer is less than the average rate for all ages (24 per cent compared to 27 per cent, according to the Bureau of Labor Statistics 2012), the amount of time spent volunteering by each individual is significantly greater than with other age groups (Morrow-Howell 2010). As health status and educational attainment are typically seen to be important predictors of volunteer activity, this is often taken as a reason for lower rates among the 65+ population (Tang et al. 2012). Overall, the average number of hours per week spent volunteering by older adults is approximately two: as proponents of the community benefits might point out, this is over 14 million hours per week! Cross-national studies suggest that in continental Europe, rates of voluntarism are much lower, averaging 10 per cent of the population aged 50 and over, only approaching US rates in Denmark, Sweden and the Netherlands (Hank and Erlinghagen 2010).

The Boomer boosterism that points to societal benefits and the more academic model of 'successful aging' (Rowe and Kahn 1999) that points to individual benefits have been subject to critique by feminist and critical gerontologists (Martinson and Minkler 2006; Minkler and Holstein 2008; Netting 2011). These scholars point out that there may very well be structural explanations for lower rates of voluntarism by certain populations (Musick, Wilson and Bynum 2000; Tang, Copeland and Wexler 2012). Why would we find it surprising that lower income individuals, individuals with less education, and individuals who are frail or in poor health are less likely to volunteer? The flag-waving associated with voluntarism can be seen as an indirect slap at those whose circumstances may limit their opportunities to contribute. As formal studies and official surveys about voluntarism typically limit their definition to 'volunteering through an organization' (Bureau of Labor Statistics 2012), an incredible amount of productive labour represented by informal family caregiving and neighbourly assistance by the latter group is not counted as civic engagement at all. One study has argued that employment itself, during the normal retirement period, should be counted as civic engagement (Kaskie et al. 2008). Kaskie differentiates between those who continue or return to work out of necessity and those who work in civic organizations, acknowledging that social benefits to society accrue from both endeavours. He and his co-authors point to the prospect of re-thinking civic engagement as a 'role' rather than a behaviour, which ties their research into the broader discourse concerning the development of a new or remodelled stage of human development, harking back somewhat to the phrase *Third Age* (Freedman 2007; Bateson 2010).

Older Adults and Internet Use

Use of the internet by older adults, while still lagging behind that of younger populations, has grown faster in this age group than in any other. According to the Pew Internet and American Life Project, as of April 2012 over half of the 65+ population (53 per cent) were online. Ironically, as mobile computing becomes ubiquitous, many online seniors are likely working from desktops and fewer use broadband services (39 per cent). Will this generational lag effect continue into the future or will the rate at which seniors pick up new technologies also rise? Whatever the case, internet use among older adults has risen dramatically and has the potential to rise even faster and further in the coming months. In the period between August 2011 and April 2012 alone there was an increase of 12 per cent among those aged 65 and older. (Rates of use in the population aged 50 to 64 have also risen steadily but less dramatically.) The Pew Study also notes some interesting patterns associated with daily online activity. Overall, 82 per cent of all adult internet users go online daily, and among those aged 65 and over, 70 per cent use the internet daily. This suggests that, once seniors are connected, they become avid users of the technology.

What is the attraction of the online world for older adults? This question has driven much of the research around the age of users. A 2009 AARP-sponsored nationally representative sample of internet use by adults aged 50 and over found that the use of the internet to conduct research into a topic of interest (57 per cent), send or receive email (56 per cent), to do shopping (44 per cent) or to make travel reservations (41 per cent) led, by far, uses associated with participation in affinity groups such as political organizations (8 per cent – at the bottom of the list of options). It is perhaps notable that the patterns of internet use reflect a broader stereotype about what interests consume older people in our society (family and medical issues). It is fair to ask whether the internet market has responded to their authentic interests or to the stereotype. What options are truly available to engage older adults in other potential forms of digital social participation? I will return to this question following a discussion of two projects that can be considered as case studies in digital inclusion for older adults.

The Tyze Network: Older Adults and Social Media

For social networking sites (SNS) such as Facebook, age is perhaps the most significant variable in identifying user groups. A second survey by the Pew Internet Project[6] revealed that traditional distinctions around the digital divide fade somewhat with respect to social networking sites. For example, there is little variation according to annual household income. Among internet users with an annual income of less than $30,000, 73 per cent use social networking sites. Among internet users with incomes above $75,000, 74 per cent use social networking sites. The differences are also relatively small with respect to race/ethnicity, political ideology (with liberals slightly more likely to use SNS), education level and geographic location. Seventy-five per cent of women internet users participate in social networking compared to 64 per cent for men. Age, however, reveals large differences: of internet users aged 18 to 29, 92 per cent use social network-ing sites, while only 38 per cent of those over 65 who are internet users use social networking sites. The use of Twitter is even more divergent. Thirty-two per cent of users aged 18 to 29 use Twitter. Only 4 per cent of internet users over 65 use Twitter.

Clearly, age is a key variable in identifying areas for growth in consumer usage. The Pew Study itself does not explore the entire range of uses of SNS and Twitter by different groups, but does offer insights into civic engagement. The survey identifies eight different ways in which social networking sites and Twitter might be used for civic activities, ranging from 'liking' or promoting political material (most frequent use) to following officials or candidates on social media (least frequent use). For all eight uses, the 18–29-year-old group exhibits the highest percentages, the 65+ group the lowest. For the most frequent use, promoting political material, there is a twenty point spread for the youngest (44 per cent) to the oldest group (24 per cent). Of those older users of social networking sites, only 8 per cent belong to a political group through SNS.

In the offline world, older adults are much more likely to be politically engaged than younger adults. In the online world, the situation is reversed, though with other forms of civic engagement, the numbers are drawing closer. The development of the Tyze™ social networking site provides some clues as to how online political engagement might grow in the coming years. The evolution of the Tyze network, it is important to note, did not grow out of a desire to expand the political engagement of older adults. As the reader will see, the network started as a support network for caregivers which led, as a consequence, to a greater awareness of the social and political context in which care is embedded.

Tyze is a social networking platform that is used to organize support around an identified individual who may have a disability or some other personal need that can be met through their social network. Tyze has its origins in the offline world. It is the digital sequel of a Canadian organization called PLAN (Planned Lifetime Advocacy Network). PLAN was initiated in 1989 as a grass-roots organization of parents of adults with developmental disabilities asking the question 'who will take care of our children when we are gone?' It had been observed that traditional approaches to care and support of people with disabilities were organized around a personal or individual model of care – based on identifying deficiencies and treatments, and supported through a bureaucracy (and science) of assessments, diagnoses, prescriptions and interventions (Cammack and Byrne 2012). In short, care for people with disabilities (and older people) was, and still is, based on a medical model. Originators of the PLAN approach (including Vickie Cammack) believed that a model of support that acknowledged the actual and potential role of members of the individual's social network (including family members) would revolutionize the support system, or at least complement the individualized model of care. As a practical strategy, PLAN began developing and training 'connectors' who would assist persons with disabilities and their key family members (often a parent) in developing, expanding and nurturing their social networks of support. Twenty years of 'social capital' building taught PLAN leaders that a network-centric approach can bring about significant improvements in health, wellbeing, self-determination and even collaboration with the formal system of care. In 1999 the PLAN Institute was developed to better understand and support the development of caring citizenship.

More recently, it has been a natural progression for the PLAN Institute to take advantage of social networking technologies to expand the programme and take the model 'to scale'. In 2007 Tyze was born as a private, personal social networking platform that 'uses technology to engage, connect, and inform the individual and their personal network members to co-create the best outcomes' (Cammack and Byrne 2012). They have developed a strategic 'social technology' that moves people from isolation into community and have trained hundreds of community connectors in the art and science of network facilitation. The PLAN Institute is a recognized social innovator and its staff has been invited to share their model and approach with a wide variety of audiences including international foundations, federal and provincial government departments and community coalitions. There are 8,000 Tyze users across Canada, the USA, the UK and Australia and 30 affiliated organizations offering Tyze to their clients/customers. In 2012 alone, the Tyze network grew from 5,000 to 8,000 users. The Tyze network advertises itself in the following manner on its website:[7] 'Tyze creates personal, private, secure, online networks that strengthen relationships and address isolation. Our primary beneficiaries are people with disabilities, seniors and people experiencing life challenges, as well as the agencies, businesses, and governments who provide support for them'. Tyze networks are created around a specific person so that his or her caregivers and a larger circle of friends can be invited to support the desire for greater independence.

People who care for and about someone can be invited to join a private, that is, secure, online network centred on that individual or family. Without the need for face-to-face meetings, these people can easily and efficiently share personal, logistical, or clinical information, discuss issues that arise, share stories, identify and assign needed tasks, and/or make necessary decisions. The Tyze system is family and person-centred, and is designed to foster family and individual choice and decision-making around planning and carrying out activities related to their individual networks. A Tyze network can not only empower the family member with a disability, but also support the family as caregivers, strengthen family unity, and help the family access needed resources, services, and support. The unique feature of Tyze is that it can bring in natural and informal supports to supplement or complement supports typically available from the traditional formal service systems. Paid providers of care can join a family network and assist in care planning and delivery as a member of a broad team.

With the goal of expanding to the US market, Tyze received funding to work with community based organizations in northern California, with the San Francisco Community Living Campaign (the Campaign) as the provider of training, technical assistance and programme development. Marie Jobling, a veteran community activist around issues of ageing and disability in San Francisco, provided the leadership and many of the insights offered in this section. From the beginning of the project, Jobling saw the potential for connecting the 'service' (building relationships within caring networks) to the broader social and political issues that affect the context for care and support (Jobling 2012).

The isolation of many seniors and people with disabilities in community life makes their needs and priorities invisible in the public life of a community. Tyze networks encourage older individuals and those with disabilities to enter into online relationships, no matter how small, to help a friend in need.

Jobling notes that attracting non-computer-literate elders, people with disabilities and family members to the platform by offering the service was not compelling enough a reason to get online. What prompted people was the opportunity to commit oneself to making another's life 'less isolated and more valued' (2012). In retrospect, Jobling sees the project through a developmental lens, though its evolution was organic and emergent, with a lot of learning along the way. Despite the obvious importance of providing computer classes at convenient times and places, the most favoured 'portal' to get seniors online was the 'magic' Google search engine, which provided a new world of fascinating options for retrieving information, shopping, genealogy, Wikipedia, and other interests.

The Tyze programme itself was a building block, erected from the personal concerns that seniors had for one another. Providing computer training was, of course, the first step, and this required community-based locations where the training could be provided, senior centres for example. It also required the collaboration of professional service-providing organizations that would support their personnel to be trained as connectors to assist the social networks. That was, in fact, the toughest sell, and Jobling and her team discovered that it was easier to go straight to community institutions such as churches, neighbourhood groups, senior leaders and families themselves. A Senior Summit organized around new technologies drew large numbers of seniors to try out fun new activities, several of which resulted in engaging YouTube productions; these featured seniors discussing how they learn and use computers,[8] and seniors rapping about surfing the web.[9]

According to Jobling, the potential to get involved with social media was not the magnet which drew seniors to these events. Seniors were aware that social media such as Facebook put one's life into a very public space and so assurances about privacy were necessary and needed to be demonstrated in the training. Political engagement and advocacy, however, proved to be a door opener. The energy around the 2008 presidential election itself was a major catalyst to get seniors online.

The local Gray Panthers organization wisely saw the opportunity to employ the new technologies for expanded political advocacy. Jobling notes that, indeed, the influence of the senior community has waned with the expansion of the new technologies for communication and advocacy. The prospect of having a key issue, and the potential for tapping youth expertise in line with the Gray Panther mission, reflected in the phrase 'age and youth in action', proved irresistible. The Gray Panthers and the Campaign organized an 'on-line day of action' to be held at University of California San Francisco. After commandeering a large room with many computers, the programme organizers took a group of seniors through the process of setting up a Facebook profile, writing calls to action, posting on other people's sites, and signing and circulating petitions. Those who had the computer skills could also participate in the event from their own homes.

The technical assistance needed to build community networks no longer came from the disability service organizations but from the advocacy groups themselves (also supported by a grant from the SCAN Foundation). Basic computer training was and is still essential and a two-tiered scenario developed. It was discovered that local senior centres would be an effective starting place for providing basic computer training, including non-English-language training, but that these would only be the spokes on more major hubs where public computing could be made available (libraries and large community centres). Taking this more inclusive approach allied seniors with other marginalized groups in the community who could benefit from the computer hubs. One of the very first networks in San Francisco was organized around 'Tricia', a woman with cerebral palsy who was subject to multiple hospitalizations and who experienced co-occurring cancer (Jobling 2012). Initially, she was assisted and later became adept at using the site to plan, organize and disseminate photos through Tyze and Flickr from a monthly party at her home. As a civic-minded community member she next learned how to use tele-conferencing to join board meetings of two non-profit organizations she followed. When her health began to deteriorate, her network discovered and connected Tricia to one of the few local physicians who made house-calls. She was admitted to a hospital facility and became disenchanted with the care, which led the network, and the physician, to establish a complicated but effective web of in-home support. When invited by Jobling to provide a quotation for her story here, she responded: 'Tyze has opened up many doors that I thought were closed in this area – the support I've received since it started has been wonderful, remarkable and truly unbelievable'.

Tricia's story indicates how important it is to place new technologies within the immediate domain of the needs of the individual user. Whether those needs are recreational, family oriented, or even concern 'life and death', as in Tricia's case, the effect spreads beyond the individual. Tyze undoubtedly facilitated the development of the helping network and, moreover, contributed to Tricia's continued civic participation.

Over time, social networks engaging seniors and families in the San Francisco project expanded through the leadership of individuals who were passionate about specific causes and issues. One woman who had experienced TBI (traumatic brain injury), while being an advocate offline for some time, found the internet to be a remarkable tool for building awareness about TBI. As Jobling reports, much of her advocacy took place 'in the middle of the night', which says something important about the role of asynchronous interaction for those with conditions that limit mobility and who might otherwise have difficulty fitting in with the schedules of existing bureaucracies. She also used her growing social media network to great effect to organize offline events, such as a successful picnic for families affected by TBI. Another social media novitiate trained in the Campaign employed her new influence to advocate for the humane treatment of animals.

As seniors indicated an interest in what was going on in their community, specialized training to view blogs was created, with a link to the ever-popular Linda Post blog San Francisco FYI Net: http://sanfranciscofyi.blogspot.com/. This user-friendly blog provides a wealth of information for any senior interested in following or participating in civic affairs. The blog for 13 November 2012 alone had information and links to a park groundbreaking, a town hall meeting on Criminal Justice Reform, meetings of the Port Commission, School District Board, and a 'happy hour' get together of the League of Pissed-Off Voters. As senior engagement with computers became 'institutionalized', clubs were formed and seniors themselves joined the community of bloggers: http://bropete7.blogspot.com/.

AdvantAge II: Online Surveys for Community Planning

The AdvantAge Initiative, like PLAN, emerged from the sense that ageing and disability are issues that concern the collective, and not merely the individual. In 1999, a small group of colleagues convened around the notion that communities could be designed (or retrofitted) to be more elder-friendly. Not discounting the value of medical and social services to individuals, it was argued that the goal of many older people is to age within a community. Unfortunately, there were few models around that provided guidelines for planning communities that work for all ages and abilities. With the aim of developing a set of 'benchmarks' or community indicators to measure a community's elder-friendliness, the AdvantAge Initiative, as it came to be known, organized a series of focus group discussions throughout the US to engage older adults (of all ages) and community leaders in defining the elements of an elder-friendly community. That research led to the identification of four key 'domains' of an elder-friendly community, reflected in Figure 1.1.

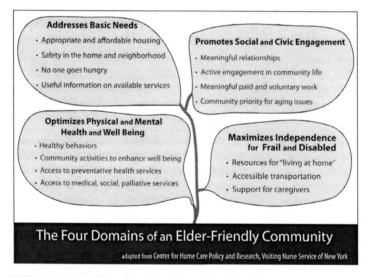

FIGURE 1.1 The four domains of an elder-friendly community.

As the group could find no extant survey tools that would provide comparative community-level data, the AdvantAge Initiative survey instrument was developed and piloted in ten US communities over the period 2000–2003. The survey instrument was a randomized telephone survey, taking on average about twenty-eight minutes and targeting thirty-six indicators of elder-friendliness embedded in the four domains. In subsequent years the survey was conducted in an additional forty communities around the country. In 2008, the first state-wide use of the instrument involved a random sample of 5,000 older residents of Indiana, sorted into sixteen planning and service districts (the 'Area Agency on Aging' districts).

The comprehensive chart-book of results that was produced for every community provided baseline data for subsequent community participation activities to create local strategic plans to address the changing age demographics. Communities also employed local or project-provided consultants for the technical assistance that was helpful in facilitating community progress. Research associated with local projects and the national experience resulted in publications that introduced the planning model to a wider audience (Feldman and Oberlink 2003; Oberlink and Stafford 2009; Emlet and Moceri 2012; Hanson and Emlet 2006; Stafford 2009).

While, in 2012, one community was currently employing the randomized survey model for strategic planning (Memphis, Tennessee, with funding from the Plough Foundation), many communities can no longer afford the expense of randomized telephone surveys. Survey companies themselves are everywhere struggling with diminishing response rates due to lower public trust and lower rates of landline telephone use. The recent telephone survey in Memphis saw a response rate of 23 per cent for a $49,000 investment. While the data from a randomized survey is not comparable in validity to a self-administered convenience sample, there have been some advantages in moving towards an internet survey model.

In order to accommodate to these changes in the research climate, the AdvantAge group sought and received funding to explore the development of an online version of the AdvantAge survey. Thus was born AdvantAge II, developed and piloted in three diverse communities: Toulemne and Calaveras Counties, California; Georgetown, Texas; and New York City (Manhattan). The California counties are extremely rural with limited broadband service. Georgetown, Texas is a rapidly growing community near Austin, with a large population of older adults and a continuing care retirement community within the city limits. The New York sample was drawn from the Chelsea/Hell's Kitchen and Clinton Hill neighbourhoods, in a partnership with the Actor's Fund service organization. In respect of non-computer-literate elders, a paper and pencil version of the survey was also used. The online AdvantAge survey taps the same range of issues – all four domains cited above – although local communities can add or subtract questions which are not pertinent to the local setting. Because it was self-administered, the survey was shortened to eliminate questions that, in the past, were not deemed useful. In the end, the new survey was closer to twenty minutes, eight minutes shorter than the standard telephone interviews. It was discovered that the rate of computer use in the communities did not correlate very closely to the use of those computers for taking the survey. In California, while 78 per cent of the respondents indicated they use computers, only 27 per cent took the survey online (83 per cent and 33 per cent in Texas; 73 per cent and 50 per cent in New York). Hence, it cannot be assumed that the mere possession of a computer guarantees that it will be used for this purpose.

Despite a similarity in outreach efforts to increase the sample numbers, the rural community found it most difficult to achieve high numbers. Nevertheless, the California survey yielded 429 respondents, compared to 1220 in New York and 1820 in Georgetown, Texas. The data from the surveys is currently being used by the communities for strategic planning to address the changing demographic character and needs of each. In the end, despite the loss of scientific validity (which is becoming ever more difficult anyway as response rates decline), the online survey process revealed some advantages. Beyond the significant cost savings associated with an online survey ($8,000 vs. $49,000), there have been two important community benefits:

1. In order to achieve good samples, a high degree of community mobilization is required to develop, advertise, and recruit respondents. In each location, this meant that multiple community-based organizations had to 'buy in' to the process in order to assist with outreach to the populations they serve or engage with. Doing this from the beginning had the very useful consequence of securing local ownership of the results and subsequent commitment to action in response to identified needs and issues. Each community established a very active and wide-reaching advisory group to assist with conducting the local survey and analysing the survey results. Advisory groups engaged not only with service providers but also with older adult leadership in community groups and advocacy organizations.
2. Unlike the telephone survey and, to a lesser degree, the paper and pencil survey, the online survey enabled open text responses and comments around several key issues. In New York City, one open-ended question – 'If you were the leader of this community, what changes would you want to make to improve conditions for older people living here?' – yielded thirteen pages of commentary.

Lessons Learned

Current research continues to affirm that older adults lag behind in access to the new base of knowledge and influence that has come about through the digital revolution. The cliché 'information is power' has perhaps never been more true and there has been a troubling diminution of influence by people who are structurally marginalized from this new world. This is especially true for older adults who are less privileged – for example, in the US, African-Americans, newly arrived residents, people with lower incomes, those with less education, and those in rural areas poorly served by broadband. As government agencies and healthcare organizations move towards online methods both to qualify individuals and to provide services and public information, the risk of not being served increases for those on the wrong side of the digital divide. There is certainly room for optimism, given the increasing utilization rates among older adults and given the astounding increase in mobile phone usage (mobile computing) through-out the world, including in developing countries. Based on a limited review of pertinent literature and two important case studies, some observations suggest there are ways of expanding access to and use of the internet by older adults for the purpose of civic engagement.

Since the first and most frequent use of the internet by older adults may involve connecting with family and friends, on the one hand, and commerce, on the other, these uses can and do serve as gateways to civic engagement, both online and offline. A study of older Chinese new users of computers and the internet found that the excitement associated with computer salons as social environments led to greater advocacy for munici-pal support of improved technology for seniors (Xie 2008). A study of an online breast cancer support group discovered that the most common use of the site was not for emotional support but for fundraising for research (Perkins and LaMartin 2012). The San Francisco case study started with the creation of online environments for family support and evolved towards the creation of politically engaged advocacy groups. Recreational use of the internet may not be a gateway to increasing social capital, however, as suggested by Shah, Kwak and Holbert (2001).

Secondly, while not focusing on seniors, online civic engagement-pro-moting projects that bring forth a connection and commitment to friends and family, to the neighbourhood and to the local community itself seem to be useful ways of pulling in users who do not necessarily want to con-nect with the global internet community. Privacy and simplicity are key to attracting new users, despite the fact that this personal practice can lead to greater social visibility. This was certainly true in the San Francisco case study and was found to be relevant in a project to develop hyper-local news media in diverse Los Angeles neighbourhoods (Chen et al. 2012) and in an Israeli project organized around local online bulletin boards (Mesch and Talmud 2010).

Finally, online democracy provides a new world of opportunities for citi-zen participation and it is imperative that marginalized groups be involved. Online polling and surveys represent an increasingly important avenue for government and other decision-makers to retrieve opinion and per-spectives from individuals who are not usually engaged (Solop 2001). The AdvantAge II online survey process demonstrates that it is possible to reflect the experiences and opinions and assess the needs and contributions of older adults. Participation by the numbers required for public policy decision-makers to take the survey seriously requires a significant mobilization effort, itself a generator of civic engagement. Multiple vehicles for participation are required: computer training for new users, public computing sites, events at kiosks, paper and pencil surveying with individuals and in group settings. The buzz required to generate enthusiasm for the survey has the effect of elevating public awareness about the needs and contributions of older adults in the community. A strategic communication and marketing plan helps to create the buzz. A clearly established time frame for the survey creates a 'need' for people to get involved and not procrastinate in taking the survey.

Much of the discussion of age-friendly communities centres on the built environment and the infrastructure of services associated with mobility and housing. It is time for a serious discussion of the basic information technologies that need to be in place in an age-friendly community. Successful practices can now be found and the next step involves scaling up those ubiquitous 'pilot projects'.

Notes

1. AdvantAge Initiative elder-friendly model available at www.advantageinitiative.org.
2. Available at www.communitymatters.org/communities-all-ages.
3. http://www.ciaip.org/.
4. www.lifetimecommunities.org.
5. http://pewinternet.org/Reports/2012/Older-adults-and-internet-use.aspx.
6. http://pewinternet.org/Reports/2012/Older-adults-and-internet-use.aspx.
7. www.tyze.com.
8. http://youtu.be/fBh1WgntN2E.
9. http://youtu.be/rygOJvSPvcE.

References

Bateson, M.C. 2010. *Composing a further life: the age of active wisdom*. New York: Random House.

Bureau of Labor Statistics. 2012. 'Volunteering in the United States – 2011', USDL-12-0329, US Department of Labor, Bureau of Labor Statistics.

Cammack, V. and K. Byrne. 2012. 'Accelerating a network model of care: taking a social innovation to scale', *Technology Innovation Management Review* July: 26–30.

Chen, N-T.N., F. Dong, S.J. Ball-Rokeach, M. Parks and J. Huang. 2012. 'Building a new media platform for local storytelling and civic engagement in ethnically diverse neighborhoods', *New Media and Society* 14: 931–50.

Emlet, C.A. and J. Moceri. 2012. 'The importance of social connectedness in building age-friendly communities', *Journal of Aging Research* Article 173247, accessed 15 November at http://www.hindawi.com/journals/jar/2012/173247/abs/.

Feldman, P. and M. Oberlink. 2003. 'The AdvantAge Initiative: developing community indicators to promote the health and well-being of older people', *Family and Community Health* 26(4): 268–74.

Freedman, M. 2007. *Encore: finding work that matters in the second half of life.* Perseus: New York.

Hank, Karsten and Marcel Erlinghagen. 2010. 'Volunteering in "old" Europe: patterns, potentials, limitations', *Journal of Applied Gerontology* 29: 3–19.

Hanson, David and Charles A. Emlet. 2006. 'Assessing a community's elder friendliness: a case example of the AdvantAge Initiative', *Family and Community Health* 29(4): 266–78.

Jobling, M. 2012. Personal communication.

Kaskie, B., S. Imhof, J. Cavanaugh and K. Culp. 2008. 'Civic engagement as a retirement role for aging Americans', *The Gerontologist* 48(3): 368–77.

Keeter, S., C. Zukin, M. Andolina and K. Jenkins. 2002. *The civic and political health of the nation: a generational portrait.* New Brunswick, NJ: The Center for Information and Research on Civic Learning and Engagement.

Lum, T. and E. Lightfoot. 2005. 'The effects of volunteering on the physical and mental health of older people', *Research on Aging* 27: 31–54.

Martinson, M. and M. Minkler. 2006. 'Civic engagement and older adults: a critical perspective', *The Gerontologist* 46(3): 318–24.

Mesch, G.S. and I. Talmud. 2010. 'Internet connectivity, community participation, and place attachment: a longitudinal study', *American Behavioral Scientist* 53: 1095–110.

Minkler, M. and M.B. Holstein. 2008. 'From civil rights to ... civic engagement? Concerns of two older critical gerontologists about a "new social movement" and what it portends', *Journal of Aging Studies* 22: 196–204.

Morrow-Howell, N. 2010. 'Volunteering in later life – research frontiers', *Journal of Gerontology: Social Sciences* 65B(4): 461–69.

Morrow-Howell, N., J. Hinterlong, P.A. Rozario and F. Tang. 2003. 'Effects of volunteering on the well-being of older adults', *Journal of Gerontology: Social Sciences* 58B(3): 5137–45.

Musick, M., J. Wilson and W.B. Bynum. 2000. 'Race and formal volunteering: the differential effects of class and religion', *Social Forces* 78(4): 1539–70.

Netting, F.E. 2011. 'Bridging critical feminist gerontology and social work to interrogate the narrative on civic engagement', *Affilia* 26: 239–49.

Oberlink, M. and P. Stafford. 2009. 'The Indiana AdvantAge Initiative: measuring community elder-friendliness and planning for the future', *Generations* 33(2): 91–94.

Perkins, E.A. and K.M. LaMartin. 2012. 'The internet as social support for older carers of adults with intellectual disabilities', *Journal of Policy and Practice in Intellectual Disabilities* 9(1): 53–62.

Putnam, R.D. 2000. *Bowling alone: the collapse and revival of American community.* New York: Simon and Schuster.

Putnam, R., L. Feldstein and D. Cohen. 2003. *Better together: restoring the American community*. New York: Simon and Schuster.

Rainie, L., A. Smith, K. Lehman Schlozman, H. Brady and S. Verba. 2012. 'Social media and political engagement', Washington, DC: Pew Research Center's Internet and American Life Project.

Rowe, J. and R.L. Kahn. 1999. *Successful aging*. New York: Dell.

Shah, D., N. Kwak and R.L. Holbert. 2001. 'Connecting and disconnecting with civic life: patterns of internet use and the production of social capital', *Political Communication* 18: 141–62.

Solop, F.I. 2001. 'Digital democracy comes of age: internet voting and the 2000 Arizona Democratic Primary Election', *PSOnline*, at www.apsanet.org.

Stafford, P.B. 2009. *Elderburbia: aging with a sense of place in America*. Santa Barbara: ABC-Clio.

Tang, F., V.C. Copeland and S. Wexler. 2012. 'Racial differences in volunteer engagement by older adults: an empowerment perspective', *Social Work Research Advance Access*. National Association of Social Workers.

Verbrugge, L.M. and A.N. Jette. 1994. 'The disablement process', *Social Science and Medicine* 38(1): 1–14.

WHO. 2011. *World Report on Disability*. New York: World Health Organization.

Xie, B. 2008. 'Civic engagement among older Chinese internet users', *Journal of Applied Gerontology* 27: 424–44.

2. EXPLORING NEW TECHNOLOGIES THROUGH PLAYFUL PEER-TO-PEER ENGAGEMENT IN INFORMAL LEARNING

Josie Tetley, Caroline Holland, Verina Waights,
Jonathan Hughes, Simon Holland and Stephanie Warren

RECENT YEARS HAVE SEEN A proliferation of technologies aimed at improving the independence of older people, for example assistive technologies and monitoring devices, and increased attention is being paid to age-friendly and disability-friendly design. In the UK, use of the internet is well established in the general population with 80 per cent of households having internet access in 2012 (ONS 2012). Although older people on the whole use the internet less and for fewer purposes than younger age groups, people in their 50s and 60s are increasingly closing the digital gap (Ofcom 2012; McNair 2012). Despite this, older people remain less likely than the general population to use new technologies such as smart phones and tablets that are not specifically designed as 'assistive technologies'. Indeed, a survey conducted in the US in 2012 showed that only 12 per cent of people owning eBook readers, and just 7 per cent of tablet owners are aged 65 or over (Rainie et al. 2012). The reasons are many and complex, but include: computer jargon; the cost of acquiring devices, maintaining and up-dating them; age related changes; a lack of access to information about what is available and what might be useful; and an absence of opportunities to try things out (Charness and Boot 2009; Hakkarainen 2012; Hill et al. 2008). Also some older people are reported to be 'just not interested in owning a tablet' and not 'know (or want to learn) how to use one' (Rainie et al. 2012).

Alongside the developments of new technologies, initiatives aiming to introduce adult learners to ICT and the internet have generally taken the form of classroom-based training programmes (Cody et al. 1999; Gorard and Selwyn 1999) and are still advocated as beneficial training for older adults, aiming at improving their computer self-efficacy and increasing their engagement with ICT (Woodward et al. 2011). While this approach works for many, it does not suit everyone all the time. In the case of older people for whom it might be many years since they were formally taught in this way, it does not even have the benefit of familiarity. Some of the barriers identified generally in this classic teacher/learner 'instruction' approach include a lack of flexibility in courses, a focus on awards and certificates (which may be irrelevant to the learner) and a fear of not having basic skills (Gorard and Selwyn 1999; 2008). In the context of specifically older adult learners there have been many formal classroom-based courses for the 'Silver Surfer' aimed at helping them to develop the skills, knowledge and confidence to use computers and the internet (Cody et al. 1999; Woodward et al. 2011) but there is evidence that here too this approach can be too inflexible for some people. For example, some evaluations of Silver Surfer initiatives have identified that people withdrew from formal training programmes when they found the content too difficult or were not able to commit the time needed to follow the course (Cody et al. 1999; Woodward et al. 2011).

There are alternatives to formal classroom-based teaching, and a European Union evaluation of EU-funded adult e-learning projects (Commission of the European Communities 2008) concluded that self-learning and informal peer-learning also provide important and effective mechanisms through which people can develop and obtain skills and competences in using new technologies. But that review also identified the need for new and innovative pedagogical approaches that recognize adult learners as knowledge builders and creators, not just recipients of transmitted knowledge. The role of play in adult learning was highlighted by Harris and Daley (2008), who identified that play is creative, active and enjoyable, and that when used in an adult learning environment it can support the group as they collectively discover and make sense of experiences. When they evaluated the impact of play in an adult learning environment Harris and Daley found that this approach alleviated pressure, brought creativity to the fore and enabled people to make connections between their learning and the real and imagined world (Harris and Daley 2008). Unstructured play with tablets and laptops has also been shown to enhance adult learners' development of ICT skills (Kennewell and Morgan 2006) and therefore this approach may have value in engaging older adults with new technologies.

This chapter is based on Opt-in, a recently completed study of how older people's engagement with new technologies is affected by the context of learning informally and alongside others in a sociable environment. Five authors of this chapter are academics who led and facilitated the project work and the sixth is an older learner (Stephanie Warren) who helped to recruit other older learners to the project, as well as participating in the local and international project activities. The chapter starts by describing the aims of the Opt-in project and explains how the project introduced a group of older people living in a range of Europe countries to new technologies through local and international interactive 'hands-on' workshops. These project participants' past and present experiences of using technology are then discussed, drawing on data from both individual interviews and the workshop evaluations gathered during the course of the project. Thematic analysis of the interviews produced five core emergent themes: in discussing these, the participants' own experiences are compared with the experiences of others as reported in the wider UK and international literature. The outcome of a broader evaluation of Opt-in is presented, followed by a discussion of the main project findings and a summary of key learning points from the Opt-in study.

The Opt-in Project

The workshops, on which the Opt-in project was based, were funded by the Grundtvig Lifelong Learning programme. Building on EU guidance about the role of informal peer-to-peer approaches in learning,[1] the Opt-in project set out to explore the potential use of play and creative learning as a way of enhancing the experience for older adults with an interest in getting to know about technologies. The main aims of Opt-in were to increase the:

- confidence of older people and workers to use diverse technologies in daily life;
- opportunities for older people and their supporters to engage with existing, new and emerging technologies;
- use of technology as a medium that enhances older people's opportunities to be fully engaged citizens in local, national, European and global society.

The Open University (OU) academics acted as overall coordinators for the project, working locally in England with the older people's organization AgeUK, and with Senior Voice, an independent group of older people which provides a platform to raise issues of concern and represents the voices of older people to service planners and providers. The project also involved partner organizations in Germany, the Netherlands, Slovenia and Scotland. The Grundtvig funding provided resources for twenty-four trips for learners from the UK (older people and academics) to take part in exchanges to meet other older learners in the other project partnership countries. Each partner country also engaged larger groups of older people in local workshops where play and interaction were used as the main method of enabling people to engage with new and existing technologies. From each of these groups some of the older learners undertook travel to one of the other partner countries to take part in shared workshops. The older learners in England taking part in travel between partner countries were risk assessed and briefed before their trip, debriefed afterwards, and travel insurance was arranged for them. Ethical approval for the project was granted by The Open University's Ethics Committee. Although, as academics, we had a responsibility to manage the overall project, we were also involved as learners, wanting to find out how local and international interactions impacted on the project participants.

Engaging with Technologies via Opt-in

Locally, joint work between The Open University academics, Senior Voice, and AgeUK (the 'Opt-in Group') included facilitated play with touch screen technologies using tablets and mobile phones. These sessions were informal with an emphasis on shared learning in an attempt to move away from traditional teacher-student distinctions. One session took place in the Digi-Lab at The Open University where people played with the Nintendo Wii, portable reading and music technologies and a range of mobile telephones. A second session in OU laboratories introduced a problem-solving game with which participants interacted using a touch table and iPhones. Further interactive workshops included activity sessions with Nintendo Wii, Xbox Kinect, and dance mats. Learners were also given demonstrations of devices and systems in development by members of the staff of the OU Centre for Research in Computing, and encouraged to handle and comment on the experimental equipment. For example, they used an early version of a haptic in-the-dark navigation system; a bespoke touch table with activities under development; and a prototype music composition programme utilizing physical movements to control harmony. The aim of these sessions was to familiarize the older learners with a range of devices, as well as to introduce some of the possibilities offered by emerging ubiquitous technologies. The interactions and knowledge shared in these sessions were not unidirectional as older learners brought their own technologies to sessions and told computer scientists about features of new equipment that had not been previously understood. Some of the participants also took part as co-presenters in hands-on demonstrations of technologies (Kindle, iPad and iPod, smart phone, Wii, Xbox Kinect, and iRobot vacuum cleaner) at a local stadium in support of two consecutive International Days of the Older Person.

The European exchanges took place between 2009 and 2011. The Opt-in Group in England hosted two visits involving groups from the partner countries, with some Group members taking part in three exchanges: two to the Netherlands and one to Germany. These exchanges included:

- presentations and joint activities to introduce the national groups to each other;
- a visit to a centre promoting independent living for people which allowed practical interaction with modern and assistive technologies based on a 'design for all' philosophy;
- exploration of web-based developments that aimed to promote social contact with peers and reduce risks of social isolation;
- visits to local museums or areas of particular cultural interest (these included a coal mining museum in Dortmund, an interactive miniature park in Holland, and a music box museum in Utrecht).

There were twenty-five older people involved in the Opt-in project in England, of which fourteen took part in the local activities only, and eleven took part in both local activities and an international visit. Stephanie worked as the Chair of a local group that campaigned for the rights of older people and in this capacity she facilitated access to a group of older people who had a range of views about the potential use of new technologies in everyday life. The ages of these participants ranged from 61 to 78 years, and after screening for suitability and availability to take part they were recruited to the project; they included people with a range of previous experience of technology and attitudes to new technologies, as well as a range of general health conditions such as high blood pressure and disabilities, including sensory and physical impairments.

Data Collection and Analysis

Consistent with a mixed methods approach, the investigation of the English learners' attitudes to technology, before and after taking part in the workshops and exchanges, was undertaken using a range of data collection methods that included:

- a semi-structured evaluation pro forma, developed by the project partners for use across the whole international project partnership;
- unstructured diaries which participants from England completed during the international exchanges;
- semi-structured interviews with participants from England who took part in local workshops and/or international project workshops and exchanges.

A thematic analysis was conducted on the data from the interviews which covered the participants' whole-life experience with technologies, and we will reflect on these next, before considering their comments about taking part in the project, taken from the diaries and evaluation pro forma documents. Quotations from participants have been purposefully selected to demonstrate how people's experiences related to the emergent themes and categories, and all participants have been given pseudonyms to protect their identities. From an analysis of the interviews we identified six core themes:

- the context of 'daily life' – with an emphasis on electrical and labour saving equipment, and technologies for personal safety and security;
- lifelong experiences – including working lives and changes in technologies over time;
- experiences and perceptions of technologies – whether positive, negative, or mixed, scepticism about technologies and using them in some sense to 'cheat';
- communication with others – an incentive to use new technologies;
- barriers to using technologies – especially costs;
- ways of learning about technologies – including collaborative and peer-supported learning.

Technologies in Daily Life

When talking about technology generally in their daily lives most of the Opt-in participants focused on electrical/labour-saving equipment such as televisions, radios, audio equipment, washing machines, ovens, microwaves and vacuum cleaners, and devices for personal security. For the most part the development of these was seen as positive, but even here, with commonplace and familiar devices, there were sceptical viewpoints and discrimination about which technologies were used and which were not:

now with our machine, washing machine, what I do, I think, 'Oh, this is dirty.' Chuck it in the washing machine. You find you're using it more than you did before when you did once a week. Things like that. The vacuum cleaner, that comes out every day. It didn't before. You had for the table – we had a table cloth on – you had a little brush to brush up the crumbs. So you didn't... you don't... I mean I just go like that and it goes on the floor, you know, so you bring out the vacuum cleaner. I think, yes, I think it's... I don't think it's made life easier. I think it's made life more demanding. (Maud, aged 78)

Another participant described how his personal interests and preferences had influenced which technologies he chose not to use:

> I've never been interested in personal Hi-Fis, Hi-Fi equipment and stuff like that, no. Microwave, we don't actually have a microwave, I mean I know how to use a microwave, I've used one in the past in various places. My house doesn't actually have a microwave. (James, aged 73)

James' and Maud's comments reflect some of the differences in personal experience of commonly available technologies that people bring to their encounters with new technologies: thus exposure to specific technologies can be selective, and the manner of their use and ideas about their appropriateness are influenced by many factors not related to the technologies themselves. These very personal positions can have an important impact on long-term engagement, or not, with potentially useful technologies. Swedish studies working with people both with and without cognitive impairment have found that personal interests and frequency of use, together with simple design, have an impact on older people's motivation and continued use of technologies (Patomella et al. 2011; Rosenberg et al. 2009), resonating with the general Technology Acceptance Model (Davies 1989) of technology adoption behaviour. Moreover, Nehmer et al. (2010) note that as the range of modern technologies that support tasks in daily life increases, those technologies designed to fit in with the everyday lives of older people are more likely to be used and thus more likely to make a real contribution in supporting older people to lead independent lives.

Lifelong Experience with Technologies

The types and forms of 'everyday' household technologies that people had used had clearly changed over the course of their lives, but in the context of this study participants tended to reflect on the impact of obvious change mainly while thinking about computers and technical equipment that they had used as part of their paid employment. For example, Ellen had worked as a teacher and, towards the end of her career, as a Head Teacher. Throughout this time she had experienced computers and the use of technology in education from its very embryonic development:

> the first computers we had really were the little BBC ones that were put in and the [local university] did a lot of that, did a lot of work with that in [name of town], especially with local system at one time, it crashed so you had to be very careful and very aware that the class, you either did it before your class

came in, you put them all on which was not the point of teaching because they should have done that themselves, but if you didn't do that, your computers were going to crash so when you had got a good class you let them do it four at a time and that was it. (Ellen, aged 73)

James and Harry had both worked in the forces and similarly experienced developments in technology from very early stages through to more sophisticated and robust systems. Harry described the roles that technology had played in his earlier life:

I mean it really started way back with the Royal Air Force. I wanted to work on aeroplanes and they said no, no, no, Radar so I thought oh it's the clean end of the aeroplane. No, no, no, ground Radar, big Radars and so in the early days of computers and certainly the last job I had in the Air Force which was the twelfth year I was there and I was coming out and I was working on satellite tracking systems and that was using paper tape and a 128K of memory and we had seven of these little units trying to tell it to turn, look where the rockets or missiles or whatever were being tested or looking for satellites and so on and they'd tear and you'd have to keep putting it inside. I come from the one end where technology was very basic in its way, you know, through to when you got the first mobile telephones, I remember seeing those big blocks with a little phone on the top. (Harry, aged 67)

These accounts by Ellen and Harry of their use of technology across the course of their lives highlight how in their experience early technological developments were difficult and not necessarily reliable. These experiences are similar to those reported by Buse (2010), whose study of older people's use of technologies identified that changes from manual to computerized processes were initially difficult to grasp. However Buse's participants reported that initial misgivings were overcome when they discovered that new technologies could make manual tasks quicker and easier. Despite the early difficulties reported by both Ellen and Harry, they too had persisted and had become keen IT users in later life. Their accounts of learning to use technology 'on the job' are an example of 'learning by doing'. This further resonates with the findings reported by Buse (2010), where after the initial reservations that many participants felt towards computing, progression towards competency was described as something that they only achieved through practice or use. As a result Buse concluded that:

If computing can only be learned through practical experience, this may help explain why previous studies have shown that many older people find computer training courses or manuals unhelpful. (Buse 2010: 1005)

Experiences and Perceptions

As participants described their use of a broad range of technologies in their daily domestic and working lives, their perceptions of them as good, bad or indifferent emerged, revealing attitudes to the wider range of technologies, including those that they had not (yet) used. In-car Satellite Navigation (SatNav) proved to be a case in point: Julia described how she had used a SatNav locally and it had been helpful, but she could not fully trust it:

> I had a tutorial in [name of city] once and I used it [SatNav] and it nearly gave me a nervous breakdown because [name of city] ... on a Saturday is closed [to traffic] but they didn't know so I haven't used it since. (Julia, aged 73)

In contrast Harry had used SatNav all over the world:

> I wasn't persuaded until one day someone said to me, you know, I bought this SatNav and it did help me out a hell of a lot so I thought no I won't and then I left it and left it and they had a deal on or something when I was buying something else so I thought well I'll buy one and I got it and I must admit – but I went for a high spec one which was very useful in Australia – it covers Australia, all of Europe and America – so I took it with me and when we hired cars it was in there and it did make a hell of a difference. (Harry, aged 67)

While such experiences can exemplify how positive or negative early experiences may play a role in individuals' on-going use or uptake of new technologies, further analysis of these participants' accounts identified that the multiple and mixed experiences they had registered with technology could engender feelings of ambivalence. Indeed, despite Julia's bad experience with the SatNav she also described some forms of technology as 'enabling, enabling, going way back I could not live without my washing machine'; however, for her technology in general was 'A mixed blessing. Mainly a blessing, I've spoken about surfing, that is a mixed blessing but it is so much easier to look up something than have to make a phone call'. It was also of interest to note that where technology was helpful in her everyday life she considered that this may also be a form of 'cheating': 'And I've just, this is naughty but I've just started using a bread machine so I don't have to remember to buy bread' [Julia, aged 73].

James also expressed scepticism about the development of technology and its use in everyday life, reflecting that the impact of trade in technology was 'not necessarily for the benefit of mankind I am afraid'. Although he had worked with technology throughout his life he said:

There's also been a measure of scepticism about its use and its application and because it was... it didn't take long for the marketing bits, guys to get involved in it and a profit motive to come in. and now a lot of technology people have been persuaded that you've got to have it otherwise you're nobody and it isn't necessary in a lot of the cases. (James, aged 73)

He used emails as an example:

Communication nowadays is infinitely inferior to what it was twenty years ago and that is down to technology. Typical example, the person I worked with in the [Primary Care Trust] PCT recently, she went away for thirty-six hours, came back and she had 286 emails. Nobody, I don't care who they are can handle 286 emails efficiently, okay, that is if the emails are accurate and correctly written and of course most of the time they aren't. So they are always open... emails and things like that are always open to misinterpretation, that's if they get read at all. (James, aged 73)

As a result James refused to have email at home and only accessed emails through an account at the local library.

The experiences of Julia, Harry and James illustrate how their individual experiences could both motivate and de-motivate them to use specific technologies. While the older people that took part in Opt-in tended to be mainly positive about the use of technology, James was the most reluctant user, both in and out of the home. His take on the interplay between wider social issues (marketing and communication), which he saw as negative and resulting in an unnecessary use of technology, ultimately shaped his decision to limit how and where he used technology. This response is not unique: a Finnish study of older people who were non-users of computers and the internet found that a strong influence on continued non-use was negative perceptions, shaped in part by cultural and social attitudes to technology (Hakkarainen 2012). It is therefore important to recognize that people's views of technology are shaped by wider social influences beyond immediate practical use and user interface issues. These influences are strong intrinsic factors that will not be easily overcome simply by redesigning or simplifying technological innovations. This needs to be taken into account as efforts are made across Europe and elsewhere to promote digital inclusion. Hakkarainen (2012) concluded that for some people it will not be easy for these particular barriers to be overcome, to promote inclusion: 'older people should also be provided with the opportunities for ageing actively without using the computer' (Hakkarainen 2012: 16).

Clearly as access to many services, consumer products, and information moves towards exclusively online presentation life can become increasingly difficult for the non-users of computers and there needs to be clarity about the different implications of non-use by choice, accessing computers via proxies, and digital exclusion caused by barriers to access.

Communication with Others

Wanting to communicate with others emerged as an important influencing factor in using new technologies, to an extent not originally envisaged at the start of the project. Many participants had a mobile telephone, although in some cases they were seldom used. However, several also reported using Skype, or wanted to learn how to use it to keep in contact with friends and family, particularly younger family members who lived overseas: for example, Skype enabled Ellen (aged 73) to keep in touch with her grandchildren in Canada. Having picked up on other people's use of Skype, Maud (aged 78) asked the project team to show her how it worked so that she could keep in touch with her relatives in Prague, particularly a young cousin.

The project team had not initially expected social media to be of primary interest to the participants, but having family abroad was also identified as a motivating factor for a wider use of technologies as media for communication:

> I've got a Facebook, I haven't used Twitter. I'm not too sure about Twitter, it's another form of texting to me and you know, one goes on about Twittering well people have dropped themselves right in it on the (-) ... It doesn't really appeal to me Twitter but Facebook I actually use between relatives like the one in Hawaii and some of the ones in Australia we Facebook backwards and forwards. (Harry, aged 67)

Harry was the only Opt-in participant to use social media, specifically in his case to communicate with family. Yet this is an area of technology use that is increasing with people aged over 50 (Housing LIN 2012). A US study of social networking found that, like Harry, older people used social media to communicate with others (Ancu 2012). However, this online survey of 218 people aged over 50 also found that older people more commonly used Facebook for mood management, which included having fun and overcoming boredom and social isolation (Ancu 2012). One of the concerns about social media is the charge that they diminish face-to-face contact, to the detriment of real relationships. While this is contested (Ballantyne et al. 2010), for many older people it remains a real worry and constitutes an additional barrier to their exploration of social media along with unfamiliarity and poor access to information. This is another example of the drag effect of culturally influenced perceptions of how technologies can affect everyday life, but one where incremental acceptance by peers could shift individuals' opinions about utility and benefits.

Barriers to Use

While participants described using a range of equipment and the way in which their personal experiences had affected their decision to use, or not use, specific devices, when it came to talking about newer technologies a number of barriers were identified which affected ease of use and access. In particular, costs and the need for upgrading equipment affected people's ability to continue using new and developing technologies. For example Nancy felt the new technologies changed too quickly, and somewhat unnecessarily, especially for older people:

> I feel there should be a sort of basic, reasonable level PC and equipment. We don't want all this, unless you are working in a field, it really doesn't matter if it's high D or [...], it really doesn't matter, you just want to be able to use it and all this constant upgrading is more than pensioners can afford. (Nancy, aged 78)

Nina (aged 78) was blind and was dependent on the use of technical adaptations such as screen readers to continue using her computer, but she described how she had made the decision to stop paying for upgrades:

> Nina: I had lots of problems with Window Eyes, my screen reader, but now it is better, it is getting better, technology is improving the system.
> Interviewer: Do you keep getting updates for the Window Eyes?
> Nina: Yes I do.
> Interviewer: And do you have to pay for those updates?
> Nina: Yes I have to pay for them.
> Interviewer: So how much does each upgrade [cost]?
> Nina: I think it was £250 I paid. It allowed me four updates and that has just run out. I don't intend to get any more updates really because it serves the purpose, like Windows 7, I haven't got Windows 7, I still have 2003 Word because it does the job I want it to do.
> Interviewer: So there is a point in which you wouldn't necessarily keep upgrading technology?
> Nina: Yes.

The barriers to using technology identified by our participants, such as rapid change and cost, have been identified elsewhere as contributing to a social digital divide (Millward 2003), reducing opportunities for older people to access important sources of information, services and other activities that could benefit them. Our participants' responses illustrate that individual factors contribute to the digital divide in older populations, at least as much as the properties of given technologies. Overcoming barriers becomes even more complicated when an older person has a disability. In this study, Nina had paid for the software and some of the upgrades that enabled her to use a computer and the internet, but Watling (2011) notes that the majority of people with disabilities are on fixed incomes which restrict their ability to afford the cost of technologies as they cannot use 'off the shelf' solutions unless they also pay for expensive hardware and software add-ons. Hill et al. (2008) therefore note that initiatives aimed at moderating the digital divide are more likely to be successful if they take account of a wider range of factors such as perceptions, skills, social networks, culture, habits and economic circumstances.

While it was important for the Opt-in project to understand what older people saw as the barriers to using new technologies, we were also interested in understanding how they learned to use the technologies that they did use.

Learning Styles

Given the developments that participants had experienced throughout their lives and the ubiquity of technologies in the world around them it was probably not surprising that they were still interested in seeing how technology was continuing to develop. We were interested in understanding how the participants preferred to learn about technology. Intergenerational and peer-supported learning were commonly reported as positive ways of getting to grips with new technologies, even before the participants' involvement with Opt-in. For example Mary, having tried to learn Excel via a formal training scheme but never quite mastering it, described how she had mastered her new smart phone: 'I have played with it, I couldn't possibly not play with something new, but my son in law, my esteemed son in law, has shown me lots of bits on it' (Mary, aged 68).

Nancy (aged 78) also described how her family had been more helpful than formal training when she wanted to develop her skills in using new technologies. She described taking one formal class, 'but it was a waste of time because I already knew that basically. I found when I went to the beginner's course, that it was too basic'. However, when she was learning to use an iPad, she found it quite helpful to consult her grandson and his girlfriend.

These two examples illustrate the importance of practice and 'everyday' learning that works with the person's individual current state of knowledge and learning pace. Here, (non-competitive) 'play' and intergenerational learning more naturally and positively supported learning how to use new technologies more appropriately than formal or instructional ways of learning had done. This finding is supported by the work of Khoo et al. (2008) and Druin et al. (2009) who found that as well as allowing learning about new technologies intergenerational play and family interaction improved skills and confidence for those involved.

However, not all participants had family or family nearby and in these instances peer support was particularly important as one of our older participants said:

> I suppose finding your way round it really, because I'm trying to find my own way round it. I've got a friend who does help in some respects, but there's some of it I just cannot do, because I haven't got a clue how to do it. (Maud, aged 78)

When asked for an example she said: 'Getting onto the website. Now I know how to do that now, but it was because Patrick [her friend] told me'. Despite her reservations about constantly up-grading, Nina, who was visually impaired, found out about new developments in technology through news items and articles. However, she did not use manuals when she was learning to use the technology itself:

> I'm not very good in manual books. You see that is one of the things I find for older people, I think one way of making it more popular is RNIB have computer volunteers you see. If I am stuck I can always email them and they will send some local person to help me with my problems so they could have that sort of volunteer. Age Concern [Now known as Age UK] could have for all older people you see. (Nina, aged 78)

The support of peers and family reported by the participants clearly came across as one of the most important forms of support for learning to use new technologies and getting onto the internet. Our participants' descriptions of the support they found useful here is reflected in other studies and literature reviews of technology use and older people (see for example Broady et al. 2010; Eisma et al. 2004; Godfrey and Johnson 2009). This helped us to understand that working with their peers might enhance the participants' confidence to have a go in the workshops and interact with the technologies that we aimed to introduce to them.

Having reflected on the themes emerging from the biographical experience interviews with Opt-in participants, we now turn to a consideration of their experience of taking part in the project. There were as many different prior experiences of technologies as there were participants, and different expectations of being involved in a project with a focus on technology. For the most part the participants enjoyed the experience, though not without certain criticisms, which they were invited to share.

The Opt-in experience: Technologies, Connections, and Confidence

A specific aim of the project was to understand some of the factors that affected older people's confidence in using or at least considering using diverse technologies in daily life. This was seen as particularly important as psychologists argue that attitudinal and cognitive barriers can significantly affect older people's confidence in using new technologies (Charness and Boot 2009). Although Opt-in was a small-scale project it gave people the opportunity to be collaborative. As one 78-year-old participant noted after taking part: 'I have the capacity to learn new technology and not to be afraid of it'.

Confidence has been identified more generally as a factor affecting older learners' use and uptake of new technologies, as for example in a study by Hamilton (2011) who worked with a Senior Learners Group to explore their everyday encounters with communication technologies. Using group discussions, interviews and photographs Hamilton identified lack of confidence, knowledge and support as barriers to older learners' wider engagement with ICT. The cost of equipment is another limiting factor: Holland (2012) argues that older people can be open to using and trying new technologies, but when 'faced with an apparent unending stream of new devices, some of which are costly, unproven and liable to be superseded in a short time, older people are justifiably wary of committing time and resources to getting involved' (Holland 2012: 152).

The Opt-in project activities were therefore designed as a way of giving participants opportunities to handle, play and interact with tablet and touch-screen technologies that they may well have otherwise rejected on cost grounds alone. In evaluations learners noted that they had enjoyed engaging with a range of technologies. Indeed, an issue in the feedback on one of the international exchange visits was that, if anything, there was still too much emphasis on demonstrations and presentations by the host organization at the cost of further hands-on play: 'I expected to have some time for an opportunity to play with some innovative gadgets which, with the time constraints, did not materialize'.

However, an interesting use of technology arose during the visit to the interactive miniature park where one participant realized that another with visual impairment was unable to see the detail of exhibits that were not within a few feet of her. She took photographs on her phone that she was then able to share, enlarging sections of each photograph to enable closer inspection, greatly enhancing the enjoyment of the person with visual impairment.

The workshops initially appeared not to have motivated any of the participants to invest personal resources in expensive equipment outside of the project workshops. However, several months after the final project workshop, a female participant who had taken part in the second learner exchange to Utrecht emailed the project to say:

> Just wanted to let you know I now have an i-Pad and am delighted with it. It is so wonderfully easy to have with one anywhere. So light and quick to use. I am still discovering all it can do. It is just so amazing this touch screen response in so many different programmes. I can see it will give me hours of delight and entertainment... [I] have loaded books to read and photos to show. GREAT. (Personal email April 2012)

In this case her old computer at home had started to fail and rather than invest in another PC or laptop she had decided to buy the tablet because it was lighter and easier to use but still met her needs – yet still an expensive solution for her, and meant she had to use savings.

Since Opt-in was an EU-funded lifelong learning project, there was also an expectation of cultural exchange and fostering communication between the partner countries. The interactive international exchanges gave learners an appreciation and awareness of how their peers in other countries were using new technologies within their own cultural contexts. While some members of Senior Voice had previously found some interest in gaming technologies, real enthusiasm was triggered by a project exchange to Germany. On the first day of the exchange to Dortmund, the German learners set up an interactive session for all the learners using the Nintendo Wii. This was an enjoyable competitive session which brought together the learners from all five countries. As participants helped each other to play, language barriers became less important. In this day centre, the Wii club had been established by older people themselves, who had sourced the equipment and games and organized the session. This had an impact on the older learners from England who noted how this relatively inexpensive technology for play could help to develop social interactions and also introduce a benign non-sedentary activity. Participants who were no longer able to engage in outdoor activities such as bowls found that virtual gaming 'brought back memories' and they really enjoyed trying new games, in particular the ski jump. Previous studies have shown that game-playing on the Wii improved older adults' cognitive and physical skills (Maillot et al. 2012), thereby bringing real benefits to their everyday living. On our return to the UK one of the participants introduced the gaming station to the wider membership of Senior Voice as an entertainment at their Christmas meeting. Other members attending that meeting though that this had potential for the social aspects of their luncheon clubs, and as a result another older woman started taking a gaming station and equipment out to the luncheon club that she supported.

Some of the participants were particularly interested in having a role in disseminating their own knowledge and experience more widely among the older people they were in contact with. The Opt-in experience gave them the confidence to think beyond 'PCs and laptops' and begin to think (or think again) about the potential relevance in their own lives of different forms such as mobile and gaming technologies. In addition to introducing new possibilities, being involved in Opt-in also highlighted the work that still needs to be done to familiarize many older people with these possibilities. One of the participants explained:

> As a volunteer for the blind association, I find loneliness among the elderly especially those with disability, has grown into epidemic proportions. Modern technology could be the key to empowering them with independence. However, speaking to my fellow older learners from Germany and Scotland, I found that motivating and supporting the elderly to use modern technology is a challenge facing all societies. Local events and get-togethers sponsored by websites like Beppie's [friendship finder] could prove a conduit to finding an answer to this challenge.

She went on to say:

> On the whole it has been a very enjoyable and educational visit to the Netherlands which has inspired me to hatch-up two campaigns. One to gather enough support from my Sagazone friends to get Sagazone involved in joining hands with local organizations to start Internet cafes for the older people; and secondly, to get Age UK [local] to use their high profile to get some of our large companies to sponsor a SeniorWeb on the Dutch model.

Yet it must be said that even though most of the participants appreciated the opportunity to explore some new technologies, certain reservations and some scepticism about them still remained, for some more than others. One participant, talking about the range of technologies that had been explored, from demonstrations of assistive devices to working with tablets and smartphones, commented that:

> I felt that able bodied but elderly people were being placed in the same category as the disabled and one solution for both will not suffice. Whilst the technology for the disabled is vital it is not so for the able bodied who are able to get out and about and it would be wrong for them to be sitting in house with an iPad becoming isolated, as many elderly people are.

This comment reflects suspicion about the notion that for older people and people with disabilities, modern technologies are only seen as being potentially useful when people are not able to the same tasks as more able bodied members of society. The focus of using technology can then be seen to be more on loss, rather than on something that can facilitate and empower older people. The second part of this quotation highlights further existing concerns that technology can be used as a substitute for face-to-face interactions, and that it may isolate rather than connect people. While the older learners we worked with were keen to use new technologies to keep connected to family and friends who were geographically remote, or to support the practical activities of daily life, none of them wanted technology to replace their more everyday social activities and connections. These mixed feelings are consistent with more general ambiguities about the legitimacy (or not) of using of particular technologies in particular circumstances. For example, individuals often struggle with decisions to start using a walking stick or a wheelchair – this might enable mobility, but it can also be seen as stigmatizing in representing frailty. Moreover, it may also be thought that accepting the use of something like a mobility aid might further degrade physical ability. People also express concern that using a GPS or SatNav diminishes the ability of people to read a map or navigate the public highway (Speake and Axon 2012). In addition, newly introduced technologies can prompt a range of emotional responses, from excitement and desire to fear and suspicion (Eisma et al. 2004) that may to some extent be ironed out by the passage of time and increasing recognition of utility. The introduction of domestic electricity and the spread of mobile phones are cases in point. However, the risk of the isolation, loss of skills and reduced physical function that may occur as technological applications in daily life and care services are developed may increase over time, and this must be acknowledged and considered on an on-going basis. In order to explore these issues the Opt-in project emphasized learning more than teaching: a broad aim of the project was to give the groups of older people involved the opportunity to handle and try out objects but also to talk about them with peers as well as professionals. As the mixed responses described above illustrate, this turned out to be just the beginning of some conversations of learning.

Discussion

This chapter has focused on European and in particular English older people's experiences of the spread of new technologies, yet in spite of local variations in access it remains the general case that globally older people are among those most likely to be technologically excluded. This is seen to be significant for several reasons, encompassing issues of individual well-being, social justice, and societal economic impact. It is claimed that technological solutions can help older people to live independently for longer; reduce costs of care; reduce social isolation; encourage active ageing and healthy living and hence contribute to 'successful ageing' (Blaschke et al. 2009). These concerns and expectations about the role of technologies in ageing societies are reflected in the policy, research and implementation investments that have been made in recent years to address them: see for example Digital Agenda for Europe[2] and worldwide e-governance initiatives (United Nations 2012). Messages emerging from such studies repeatedly reinforce the advantages of specific technologies, but also the need to ensure appropriate design, to overcome barriers to take-up, and to understand older people's attitudes.

Old age is just one aspect of an individual's experience, and as suggested in this chapter, it is the accumulation of past experiences alongside current circumstances that has an impact on both access and attitudes to new technologies. We suggest that this is fundamental to understanding how to introduce potentially beneficial technologies to older people. Further, there is a mismatch between efforts to introduce specific gadgets or services to cohorts of older people involved in research projects, and the barriers that face individual older people at the door of the technology store. Without a basic knowledge of what is on offer, the relative costs, including the costs of support, maintenance and upgrades, and the probable longevity of specific technologies, how is an older person to make informed judgements? Our experience suggests that there are benefits in producing an environment in which older people can – without the pressure to buy – handle and try out new technologies which they might not have considered but which, like the tablet in our study, come as a revelation.

As part of the process of involving people in the Opt-in project we asked the older learners to reflect upon their lifelong encounters with technologies as a prelude to thinking about these new technologies. Doing this reminded even those who considered themselves to be 'not technically minded' that they had met and mastered many innovations in technologies throughout their lives, sensitizing them to the reality of their previous experiences of everyday, collaborative, and often intergenerational or peer-group learning. Bringing this awareness to the use of peer learning and play has potential for creating situations in which older learners can learn about and use new technologies in non-threatening and low-risk environments, by which we mean places where it was easy and acceptable to fail and try again, to ask the same questions several times, and to share knowledge by helping someone else. We suggest that such environments could be about more than simply teaching specific devices, platforms or programmes, but rather about stimulating ideas on how technologies might be relevant to the older individuals' current and future lives, instilling the confidence to find out more about those that seem of most personal interest. The Opt-in workshops and social visits with adult learners using play and interaction were intended to provide an overall experiential learning environment to enable participants to make sense of the wider context and practical applications of technological innovations and gain more confidence in handling new technologies. Siedel (2011) argues that this is particularly important for mature learners who are more likely to use new learning experiences if they can see the practical purpose, the relevance and some connection to their own experiences. For example, in this study, using technology to enhance social interactions within social environments promoted a realization in some of the learners that social engagement physical exercise and mental stimulation could be combined in enjoyable ways that they could take on board. Achieving this combination of gains is important, and Simone and Haas (2009) suggests that bringing these stimuli together in the context of a leisure time activity can contribute to improved wellbeing in later life.

How could this approach be implemented more widely? We suggest that the themes that emerged from our project interviews, reflected in the wider literature, indicate some starting points. First, the approach that individual older people bring to even contemplating the use of technologies is informed by both previous experiences and current circumstances and for this reason a conversation about this 'positionality' is required: a generalized instruction approach is unlikely to convince the unconvinced or encourage the cautious. Second, more emphasis needs to be placed on the social and communication aspects of technologies, and the ways in which they can enhance rather than replace face-to-face interactions. Social interactions are fundamental to the wellbeing and self-esteem of older people, and in our view technologies for social interaction – provided they are demonstrated in the context of the person – are likely to interest older people. Attention to both these aspects would go some way to addressing barriers to engagement.

However, the big stumbling blocks remain cost and access to hands-on experimentation. These are not, of course, confined to older people and there is a more general sense in which most people must navigate their way through what is available and useful within their means. Hence there is a need for access to shared information as well as exposure to examples of specific technologies. During the course of the project Stephanie noted that this points to the need for spaces for sharing knowledge and experiences, good and bad, for example in sessions at existing social clubs or health centres. However, the recognition that social and peer-to-peer interactions can support and encourage the positive use of technology in daily life must also include recognition of the potential for technologies to stigmatize and isolate people as they age. Perhaps some of the resources currently used in general marketing and in trialling the use of technologies with groups of older people could be diverted to them to give the digitally disadvantaged access to demonstration devices so that they can more creatively comment on issues of use and design of technologies, and reflect on their potential to support and facilitate everyday life.

Conclusion

If technologies are seen as contributing solutions to some of the problems of modern life, it is clear that notwithstanding the minority who will always be keen to get involved, the lag in older people engaging with technologies has both economic and wellbeing consequences. Research has identified the kinds of barrier that confront older people, whether it be that individuals are deterred from even contemplating possibilities, that they have had unsatisfactory experiences with ill-designed products and services, and with inadequate technical support, or that they have been priced out of buying new equipment. Information is an absolutely essential tool for overcoming these barriers, and we suggest that one of the most effective ways of spreading information is by peer-to-peer and playful (hands-on) interaction in informal, sociable environments.

Acknowledgements

The Lifelong Learning programme has been funded with support from the European Commission. This publication reflects the views only of the authors, and the Commission cannot be held responsible for any use which may be made of the information contained therein. We gratefully acknowledge the support of Grundtvig, The Open University, AgeUK and Senior Voice, and of all the people who took part in and otherwise supported the Opt-in project.

Notes

1. http://www.grundtvig.org.uk.
2. http://ec.europa.eu/digital-agenda/.

References

Ancu, M. 2012. 'Older adults on Facebook: a survey examination of motives and use of social networking by people 50 and older', *The Florida Communication Journal* 40(2): 1–12.

Ballantyne, A., L. Trenwith, S. Zubrinich and M. Corlis. 2010. '"I feel less lonely": what older people say about participating in a social networking website', *Quality in Ageing and Older Adults* 11(3): 25–35.

Blaschke, C.M., P.P. Freddolino and E.E. Mullen. 2009. 'Ageing and technology: a review of the research literature', *British Journal of Social Work* 39(4): 641–56.

Broady, T., A. Chan and P. Caputi. 2010. 'Comparison of older and younger adults' attitudes towards and abilities with computers: implications for training and learning', *British Journal of Educational Technology* 41(3): 473–85.

Buse, C.E. 2010. 'E-scaping the ageing body? Computer technologies and embodiment in later life', *Ageing and Society* 30(6): 987–1009.

Charness, N. and W.R. Boot. 2009. 'Aging and Information Technology use potential and barriers', *Current Directions in Psychological Science* 18(5): 253–58.

Cody, M.J., D. Dunn, S. Hoppin and P. Wendt. 1999. 'Silver surfers: training and evaluating internet use among older adult learners', *Communication Education* 48(4): 269–87.

Commission of the European Communities. 2008. *Commission Staff Working Document. The use of ICT to support innovation and lifelong learning for all – A report on progress.* Brussels: European Commission.

Davis, F.D. 1989. 'Perceived usefulness, perceived ease of use, and user acceptance of information technology', *MIS Quarterly* 13: 319–39.

Druin, A., B.B. Bedersonn and A. Quinn. 2009. 'Designing intergenerational mobile storytelling', *Proceedings of the 8th International Conference on Interaction Design and Children.* New York: ACM New York, pp. 325–28.

Eisma, R., A. Dickinson, J. Goodman, A. Syme, L. Tiwari and A.F. Newell. 2004. 'Early user involvement in the development of Information Technology-related products for older people', *Universal Access in the Information Society* 3(2): 131–40.

Godfrey, M. and O.A. Johnson. 2009. 'Digital circles of support: meeting the information needs of older people', *Computers in Human Behavior* 25(3): 633–42.

Gorard, S. and N. Selwyn. 1999. 'Switching on the learning society? – questioning the role of technology in widening participation in lifelong learning', *Journal of Education Policy* 14(5): 523–34.

———. 2008. 'The myth of the silver surfer', Adults Learning 19(5): 28–30.

Hakkarainen, P. 2012. '"No good for shovelling snow and carrying firewood": social representations of computers and the internet by elderly Finnish non-users', *New Media and Society* 14(7): 1198–215.

Hamilton, M. 2011. 'I'm fascinated but I don't have the confidence', *Adults Learning* 22(6): 28–31.

Harris, P. and J. Daley. 2008. 'Exploring the contribution of play to social capital in institutional adult learning settings', *Australian Journal of Adult Learning* 48(1–2): 50–70.

Hill, R., P. Beynon-Davies and M.D. Williams. 2008. 'Older people and internet engagement: acknowledging social moderators of internet adoption, access and use', *Information Technology & People* 21(3): 244–66.

Holland, C. 2012. 'The role of technology in the everyday lives of older people', in J. Katz, S. Peace and S. Spurr (eds), *Adult lives: a life course perspective*. Bristol: Policy Press, pp. 151–60.

Housing LIN. 2012. *Older people and social networking*. View Point 29. London: Housing Learning & Improvement Network.

Kennewell, S. and A. Morgan. 2006. 'Factors influencing learning through play in ICT settings', Computers & Education 46(3): 265–79.

Khoo, E.T., A.D. Cheok, T.H.D. Nguyen and Z. Pan. 2008. 'Age invaders: social and physical inter-generational mixed reality family entertainment', *Virtual Reality* 12(1): 3–16.

McNair, S. 2012. *Older people's learning in 2012: a survey. Summary report*. Leicester: NIACE.

Maillot, P., A. Perrot and A. Hartley. 2012. 'Effects of interactive physical-activity video-game training on physical and cognitive function in older adults', *Psychology and Aging* 27(3): 589–600.

Millward, P. 2003. 'The "grey digital divide": perception, exclusion and barriers of access to the internet for older people', *First Monday* 8(7) July. Available at http://www.firstmonday.org/ojs/index.php/fm/article/view/1066/986 (accessed 25 January 2013).

Nehmer, J., U. Lindenberger and E. Steinhagen-Thiessen. 2010. 'Aging and technology – friends, not foes', *The Journal of Gerontopsychology and Geriatric Psychiatry* 23(2): 55–57.

Ofcom. 2012. 'Ofcom Communications Market Report 2012'. Available at http://stakeholders.ofcom.org.uk/binaries/research/cmr/cmr12/CMR_UK_2012.pdf (accessed 25 January 2013).

ONS. 2012. *Statistical bulletin: internet access – households and individuals, 2012*. London: Office for National Statistics.

Patomella, H.-A., A. Kottorp, C. Malinowsky and L. Nygård. 2011. 'Factors that impact the level of difficulty of everyday technology in a sample of older adults with and without cognitive impairment', *Technology and Disability* 23(4): 243–50.

Rainie, L., K. Zickuhr, K. Purcell, M. Madden and J. Brenner. 2012. 'The rise of e-reading Pew Research Center'. Pew Internet & American Life Project. Available at http://libraries.pewinternet.org/2012/04/04/the-rise-of-e-reading (accessed 4 February 2013).

Rosenberg, L., A. Kottorp, B. Winblad and L. Nygård. 2009. 'Perceived difficulty in everyday technology use among older adults with or without cognitive deficits', *Scandinavian Journal of Occupational Therapy* 16(4): 216–26.

Siedel, R. 2011. 'Principles and practices of mature-age education at U3As', *Australian Journal of Adult Learning* 51(3): 566–82.

Simone, P.M. and A.L. Haas. 2009. 'Cognition and leisure time activities of older adults', *LLI Review* 4: 22–28.

Speake, J. and S. Axon. 2012. 'I never use "maps" anymore: engaging with Sat Nav technologies and the implications for cartographic literacy and spatial awareness', *The Cartographic Journal* 49(4): 326–36.

United Nations. 2012. *E-Government Survey 2012: E-Government for the People*. New York: United Nations. Available at http://unpan1.un.org/intradoc/groups/public/documents/un/unpan048065.pdf (accessed 31 January 2013).

Watling, S. 2011. 'Digital exclusion: coming out from behind closed doors', *Disability and Society* 26(4): 491–95.

Woodward, A.T., P.P. Freddolino, C.M. Blaschke-Thompson, D.J. Wishart, L. Bakk, R. Kobayashi and C. Tupper. 2011. 'Technology and aging project: training outcomes and efficacy from a randomized field trial', *Ageing International* 36(1): 46–65.

3. OLDER PEOPLE AND CONSTANT CONTACT MEDIA

Rachel S. Singh

WHILE THERE IS A GROWING body of literature within the social sciences examining the ways in which new media are pervading the lives of teenagers and youth (Boyd 2010; Horst 2010; Ito 2008), very little has been written about the older adult's dexterity to live and learn with these forms of material culture. As a result of their own constant exposure and engagement with new media, older people[1] are also experiencing shifts in the structure of their social worlds, from changes in how they make friends to the ways in which they act as independent, participatory citizens.

In 2010, for a period of nine months, research was carried out in six counties of Ireland for a baseline study exploring the impact of new media on the sociality of the older adult. What became immediately apparent from the outset were the new dimensions of social awareness emerging from people's frequent engagement with various digital devices and platforms, such as forms of ambient awareness[2] and social proprioception.[3] As a result, the study quickly became couched within a narrower investigation of a group of twenty-two older people's notions of connectedness and presence resulting from their perpetual to regular contact with a mix of new personal communication technologies. This frequency of contact is referred to here as 'constant contact' and the media people are engaging with for this type of contact as 'constant contact media' (CCM).[4]

While the phenomenon of CCM has important implications for almost any age group, interest in the implications for the older adult is born out of the global need for healthcare solutions as a result of the impending 'demographic crisis' of increasingly ageing populations, diminishing resources and rising costs. At the same time it provides us with an opportunity to rethink our notions of older adults and their use of emerging technologies and recognize the far-reaching benefits that societies stand to gain from the continuing contributions of their older citizens.

The focus of this chapter, then, is to explore the impact of the older adult's use of CCM, and to investigate the ways in which they might contribute to their own health as they age. The discussion begins with an outline of the key concepts that guide the research, followed by a brief overview of the study's method to situate the reader. From there, a set of portraits are provided to illuminate some of the mediated social practices of older adults, and the way in which these practices are giving rise to new levels of social awareness and situations that support independent living and social inclusion. The chapter ends with a brief concluding discussion that includes suggested avenues for further exploration.

Key Concepts Guiding the Conversation

Constant Contact Media (CCM)

CCM Overview

CCM is introduced here as a term to describe the ecology of digital devices and platforms that people use to frequently exchange messages with people they know or find stimulating, which give rise to new kinds of social interactions as a result of the feelings of connectedness, presence and orientation that people experience from their constant contact with them. What is of particular interest to the study is the subset of CCM that is 'quick-ping', such as social networking sites, defined by Ito and colleagues as 'a term to describe a media ecology where more traditional media such as books, television, and radio are intersecting with digital media, specifically interactive media and media for social communication' (Ito et al. 2010: 10). The communicative ecologies of CCM are based on the individual and can include personal communication technologies such as mobile phones, tablets, laptop and desktop computer; ICTs like Twitter and Facebook; and computer-mediated communications like Skype and email accounts.

The main seeds for the idea of CCM are attributed to the research of communication scholars James E. Katz and Mark Aakhus (2002), in which Katz states that 'an age of perpetual contact, at least in terms of potential, is dawning' (Katz and Aakhus 2002: 2). That was more than ten years ago. At the time of writing, with the explosion of social networking, the move away from the traditional domain of connectivity powered via a fixed keyboard, mouse and screen, and the arrival of mobile 3-D technologies, implantable electronics and the 'Internet of Things', the age of perpetual contact has dawned.

The concept is also based on a small body of literature encompassing ethnographic research on people's regular to perpetual use of new information and communication technologies (ICTs) (Ito 2005; Ito et al. 2006; Baron 2008; Broadbent 2010a, 2010b). Finally, parallels are drawn from discussions of young people living and learning with new digital technologies (Ito et al. 2010), and media ethnographies of the role of the mobile phone and internet in developing countries and amongst diasporas (Miller and Slater 2000; Miller and Horst 2006).

The introduction of the term 'perpetual contact' in discussions of people's mobile phone use for private talk and public performance by Katz and Aakhus (2002), and concepts such as the notion of *keitai* culture in Japan[5] (Ito 2005; Ito et al. 2006; Ito et al. 2010), became particularly useful ways of conceptualizing CCM in terms of how they consider new media to be creating new dimensions of social awareness, like distributed copresence (Ito et al. 2006) where people share ambient awareness with people who are not physically copresent.

Finally, the research employs sociologist Shanyang Zhao's taxonomy of copresence,[6] in which he explicates the various meanings and subtypes of copresence, defining it as having two dimensions – as a (1) mode and as a (2) sense of being with others (Zhao 2003: 445). Alongside this is the concept of social presence which was pioneered by computer-mediated communication scholars as a way of analysing mediated communications (Ijsselsteijn 2003). This is one of the first theories of communication media, and has been translated and widely accepted in presence literature as 'the sense of being with another in a mediated environment' (Biocca et al. 2001).

CCM Characteristics

An analysis of the new media that people are in constant contact with demonstrates six defining features, or characteristics, as follows:

1. They are networked technologies, often feature-laden, used for personal communication;
2. They are distance-reducing technologies that are social, interactive and immediate;
3. They are used to constantly exchange messages;
4. They convey presence information (which includes varying degrees of haptic engagement), creating ambient awareness in everyday practice and place;
5. They allow for an 'always-on' connectivity/connection in real-time; and
6. They are paralinguistic, and as such not bound to any one sensory modality.

Beyond these, the key to considering a technology as a CCM is frequency of contact – contact being with device, platform or individual. In order to determine this, a rudimentary variable scale was created as a form of measure to determine what qualifies as 'constant contact'. To qualify as CCM, a device or platform has to display the six characteristics outlined above as well as register within the scale's definition of 'constant contact'. Constant contact is defined as a value of any type that is continually occurring and persistent, and then narrowed to a series of six frequencies, or varying degrees, of which five qualify a new media device or platform as a form of CCM as outlined in the table below (Table 3.1).

TABLE 3.1 Constant contact scale. A rudimentary, variable scale for determining the frequency of 'constant contact'.

CATEGORY	FREQUENCY	VALUE
Infrequent	<2/week	0
Semi-Regular	2-6/week	1
Regular	Daily	2
Frequent	>3 a day	3
Constant	>5/day	4
Perpetual	>10/day	5

For example, the mobile phone as a Personal Communication Technology (PCT) has all six characteristics but only becomes a form of CCM when its user is in constant contact with it – ping-ponging messages back and forth and conveying presence information in real-time.

'The Technosocial'

The second key idea guiding the research is the idea of the 'technosocial', a concept introduced several years ago by Ito et al. (2006) in one of their studies of *keitai*. The idea of technosocial incorporates 'the insights of theories of practice and social interaction into a framework that takes into account technology-mediated social orders' (Okabe and Ito 2006: 258–59). It does this by combining Erving Goffman's idea that social identity and practice are embedded in and contingent on particular social situations, with Joshua Meyrowitz's idea that the social situations mediated by digital technologies are structured by influences outside the boundaries of physically copresent and interpersonal encounters (Goffman 1959 and Meyrowitz 1985, cited in Okabe and Ito 2006: 258–59).

Alongside the concept of technosocial situations sit the frameworks of 'technosocial practices', or social practices mediated by digital technologies, and 'technosocial orders', or technologically-mediated social orders (Okabe and Ito 2006). For this study, the focus is mainly on the technosocial practices of communication and the technosocial situations and orders they create.

Taken together, concepts of 'the technosocial' are useful for understanding the new kinds of sociality experienced by the older adult as CCM user. The term is also employed to avoid a technically determinist assumption that electronic media erode social boundaries and the integrity of place while acknowledging that people's interactions with one another via new digital media differ from prior social settings such as 'workplace, restaurant, face-to-face interaction, or fixed-line telephony' (Okabe and Ito 2006: 258–59 passim).

Method

The study was carried out as a joint project for UCL and Intel Labs Europe. The core of the study is based on sixteen weeks of fieldwork with twenty-two participants, carried out across six counties in the Republic of Ireland (Meath, West Meath, Kildare, Dublin, Mayo and Wicklow). The initial site of participant recruitment was an active retirement group located in County Meath. The group is an organization run by older adults for older adults, involved in a broad range of eclectic initiatives that focus on changing perceptions of ageing. Because of the organization's national reach the recruitment for this study quickly expanded beyond its members and their wider communities in County Meath, to an additional five counties (as listed above) through a network of programmes and associations for older people that revolve around empowering active retirement and ICT use.

While recruitment grew organically, it is acknowledged that the sample was affected by the channels used to recruit. It is understood that the sample might look different if recruitment was pursued through other organizations or associations, such as a book or bridge club. Despite this, my on-going research and reported trends in ICT uptake by older Irish people demonstrates that the sample is representative of a larger group.[7]

Participants included ten males and twelve females,[8] aged between 56 and 83, the majority of whom are aged 60 to 68. Nationalities included Irish, British, South African and Filipino. At the time of the study all participants were retired, from careers spanning the fields of healthcare, business, IT, hospitality and childcare. Length of retirement varied from one to eight years. Socio-economic status was also varied and not necessarily reflective of their geographic location, which was often determined by where their children were living or by the areas they considered to be 'their roots'. The number of years spent using a variety of ICTs ranged from ten to thirty years, and CCM about three to ten years.

The fieldwork consisted of a mixture of methods for gathering information. Of these, this chapter draws primarily from three sets of data. The first set of data collected consists of observational records and ethnographic interviews conducted with the participants about their lives and use of technology over the course of sixteen weeks. The second data set used is a series of communication and technology diaries and logs of daily activities that participants were asked to complete over the course of several days. The third set of data used is a series of 'social maps', which illustrate people's social networks and were created with participants during the course of my participant observation.

New Dimensions of Social Awareness

The focus of this section is to highlight, through a set of portraits,[9] some of the new dimensions of social awareness and sociality experienced by older adults from their use of CCM. In particular I explore how from their ambient streams to their ambient senses,[10] they are inscribing new social situations and practices that are contributing to their health and wellbeing.

Portrait 1: Living Alone in Rural Ireland after a Life of Sex, Drugs and Rock 'n' Roll

Thomas (60) is retired and living alone in a small village in western Ireland after, as he describes it, having his 'mind blown by a life of sex, drugs, and rock 'n' roll'. Born in Dublin in 1950, at the age of 14 he went to boarding school in rural Ireland for three years before attending university to study architecture. Two years into his degree he went to New York on a student visa and did not return to Ireland until thirty-two years later. As he explains:

> It was 1969 New York, a very exciting place to be so I just didn't get the plane back. After that I got a job in advertising as a paste artist – you know the stuff you do with cut and paste on a computer now? Then I had this American girlfriend who gave me an expensive camera, so I got into photography and took a couple of years to busk around Europe. I met someone from Australia – who got pregnant, and I met someone from Norway – who nearly

got pregnant, and so I started having relationships with them. Eventually I moved to London with the woman who was pregnant to have the baby and raise a family. Long story short, I got left holding the baby.

As a result, Thomas trained as an electrician to provide for his daughter, a profession he was involved in for twenty years until he fell off a wall and shattered his arm, forcing him to retrain. He did so by completing an information technology course due to a love of computers. He explains:

> When I first came across computing I was not just interested by it, I was a bit electrified by it really. My friend down the street had a Sinclair ZX, so I went out and got one. That was followed quickly by a Commodore 64. I just remember sitting there and thinking, 'Oh My God, this is such a useful piece of kit'.

At the age of 50, Thomas decided to move back to Ireland, initially settling in Dublin to work as a network administrator for a large insurance company. Two years ago he was made redundant, an event that produced a move from the city to the village he is currently living in. He dreads to think of what life would be like for him now without his computer and mobile phone, as he explains:

> I had to move down here. I didn't want to do it. It is very isolated. But being made redundant, in my sector at my age, effectively means retired. I had a house here, so I came. And you know what? I found that the computer and mobile became my link to my past and everything outside of my village. I mean I lived OUT there, man. And now, I live alone here and am isolated ... they are *essential* for me. They connect me. I'd dread to think of life without them ... I'd go mental without them.

Thomas notes that he 'first started social networking online via email, a Hotmail account'. He was a very early subscriber to Skype, signing up for an account at its inception in 2003 – one of the first within his social circles. He also notes he was an early adopter of Facebook and tried MySpace but felt that 'it was for kiddies'. Now he uses 'Gmail, Facebook, online gaming, mobile and Skype on a daily basis'.

Thomas spends most of his day back and forth in front of the computer. As he notes, a typical day for him starts with 'rising, showering, booting up and checking mail, FB, international news and local weather forecast, while having breakfast'. This is followed by leaving his Gmail, Facebook and Skype accounts open whilst streaming BBC Radio 4 (through a hack) from the computer all day. He will check the accounts four or five times a day 'without fail', spending anywhere from two minutes to an hour each time posting things to his Facebook wall, writing emails, and instant messaging. He explains:

> Since I have my browser open all day I can see if any mail has come in, and FB will email me if someone has made a contribution, and even when I am passing by and I look over and I see the ink in dark bold, I know something has come in – and usually curiosity gets the better of me and I go check it out.

Thomas has about thirty to forty friends who he stays in regular contact with via Facebook and about fifteen close friends and family via Skype. He noted that he used 'to have a lot more, but then just got pissed off by constantly hearing what people were having for breakfast so blocked a huge number of people and if they had a problem with that, that was their problem'.

Through these 'always-on' (Baron 2008) connections he believes he is developing 'a sort of ESP', or what Ito (2005; 2006; 2010) refers to as the technosocial situation of 'ambient virtual copresence' in his social networks. He notes that as a result when he sees them in person it strengthens his connection with them, helping him start 'from a much richer and wider base of knowing, which is critical as you age. You've got to maintain social activity'. As he explains about his Skype use:

> I'll have Skype open in the background all day, usually set on 'orange' or 'busy', and the same with Gmail. But those that know me know that doesn't mean shit because, basically, if my computer is online I am there for them. Plus, I can see my people online, and it is just nice to know they are there. It gives a sense of comfort. It means there are people in your life that are out there, and you can see it by a little green icon, whereas if you didn't have that – well, out of sight, really is out of mind. I would imagine that people without internet connectivity living in a rural isolated community like mine, could end up feeling very lonely without that sense of presence... that's very important for my wellbeing. I mean, social interaction is important, you die without it, emotionally then physically – which is the worst death.

Thomas also stresses how essential CCM has been for him as he has aged, not only in maintaining long-distance friendships and social roles, but for creating new ones, using it to participate in the networked public culture[11] of his village then taking it offline for face-to-face interactions. He explains:

> It changes your life – you get to meet new people. So for instance we have a little Facebook account here. I posted a few photographs I took of the village, the flood and freeze, and suggested others do the same. From that we've arranged an exhibition, and to meet as a group with our photographs and

decide which ones should be hung. So I am going to be meeting a whole bunch of other people from this. And the thing that really does it for me is a shared common interest that we all liked to do – we're not talking about the weather or how Kilkenny is doing in the hurling – we're talking about something we are all interested enough in to get together and talk about. Brilliant. Wouldn't have happened without my constant use of FB. I'd probably be here staring at the wall.

Instead, I am aware of people all the time. It helps you feel nice about yourself, because at the end of the day you are the sum of your relationships and the sum of your memories. The most defining thing about anybody is their relationships, and certainly how you relate to yourself, but when you are geographically separated – and a lot of us are these days because we travel around, and we change jobs, and we change cities, and we change countries. You can't really stay in touch with everybody unless you do it with [CCM]. There is no other way, unless you're kind of completely free to travel and have no budget constraints – and that doesn't apply to a lot of people.

There is an interesting flip-side to Thomas' technosocial practices using CCM. He notes that while CCM help him maintain his relationships, they also help him maintain his distance from people in his local community. In this way it seems Thomas is using CCM as sign-vehicles to make and manage his social roles. He explains:

Well I go down to the pub twice a week at most. This is rural Irish culture and people who have pub relationships are the kind of people who go down every single night even if it is only for an hour. I don't do that because I am not a pub-centric person. So with [mediated] constant contact I do the lightweight messaging thing (SMS, FB, and so on) with them just to maintain connections and it makes them feel like we're in contact.

Thomas says he saw the potential of technology for constant contact 'right from day one', noting that he 'could kind of understand where [new networked technologies] were going to take people', explaining:

People aren't just using it, they are using it a lot. They are going to be using it a great deal more and should be educated and helped to do so, because it is keeping people, who might otherwise have shrivelled, alive emotionally. It's a lifesaver for some people, especially older folk like me. I've seen it first-hand. I taught some IT literacy courses for older people in Dublin in the evenings until I ran out of energy. These were people 65 and over who had never been on the Internet. And by God! did I see them light up. I mean really, like really light up – like suddenly you could have a private communication with your granddaughter without having to go through her mum. [...]

> In problem families for instance there was one woman who loved her granddaughter, but there was a problem with the parents splitting up and it was a nasty situation and so they kept in touch by the granddaughter Skyping from an Internet café and they had a private relationship outside the family that was breaking up. Yes! Wonderful. I think people should be born with a Dongle.

Thomas is representative of a set of people in the study who are 'tech-savvy' and have spent most of their life as part of large, often close-knit, social networks but due to a change in lifestyle (returning home from a life abroad, retirement, etc.) find themselves in situations that pose potential detrimental effects on their health and wellbeing. In the case of Thomas, a move to a rural village could have resulted in social exclusion[12] – a recipe for disaster for someone who use to being 'tuned in and always on'. Yet, through his engagement with CCM he is sometimes able to bypass feelings of loneliness and isolation through the sense of connectedness and presence to people near and far that his CCM use creates.

Similar examples can be found with South African expats, and husband and wife, Carla (62) and Ian (83). Carla and Ian were drawn to retire in County Meath by Ian's Irish roots, and are attempting to integrate into their community to live out their 'golden years'. They struggle to make friends in their rural Irish community and to find community support for financial and healthcare issues. Faced with this situation they have turned to a constant stream of emails, Skype chats and 'Facebook hangouts' to maintain a sense of connection and support. As Carla highlighted in one conversation:

> You don't really know what life is going to be like at any stage until you get there. It's been tough, but it's not a killer because we're in touch, we're supported (...) albeit from friends and family back home. Would I have thought that were possible when I were 20? No. But it is possible. They aren't here with us, but it *feels* like they're here with us. And that just feels good (...) At our age, feeling good is what can make all the difference.

Portrait 2: Finding Life at 68

Scrolling through Facebook on a MacBook Pro in a busy downtown Dublin café, Patsy (68) is completely absorbed by her task. She is walking me through the Facebook pages of her fellow volunteers – a group of four or five people with whom she travels to Africa every year to work in an orphanage in a small village in the Sahara desert, a seven-hour bus ride from Zambia. As she jumps from page to page, photo album to photo album, occasionally pausing to play a video of orphans receiving Christmas presents or new clothes, it is clear to see that Patsy's access to the daily goings on in Africa through Facebook gives her days a sense of purpose, and has become a viable unit of sociality (see Giddens 2001, cited in Kaspersen 2000) for her after being forced into retirement two years ago:

> This stage of my life came very fast, and I was dreading it because I didn't know what I was going to do. I was so used to being on my feet all day and talking and then suddenly you don't have to get up in the morning at 6:30 am and you think, 'I will have no one to talk to, I am going to miss the social interaction'. I could have worked another two years if the government wasn't so stupid. I said to them I can work, and they said Health and Social Care won't let you. [...]
>
> It is imposed, sure there are people that can't work – Grand, that's okay, but for the people that can do another few years, they should be able to. So, thank goodness for mobiles and computers – absolute lifelines.

CCM has facilitated Patsy's 'finding of life at 58'. When she left school at 17 her dream was to become a nurse. The day she graduated her bags were packed and she left for England to begin her training. Two years into it she realized that she did not want to be a nurse at all, and that what she really wanted to do was go on missions abroad. Despite this 'epiphany', she finished her training and for the following eight years worked in several hospices in various countries.

At the age of 27, Patsy's mother died and she had a nervous breakdown. She explains:

> My life as a nurse didn't work out for me. I stuck it for eight years and then my mother died, and I said to myself, 'That's it. I am leaving'. It was a big drama to leave, but in any case I did. I worked for nine years in restaurants in Dublin, but then one day I bumped into two former colleagues in town and we went off and had a cup of tea together. They asked me what I was doing and were very upset to learn I was not using my talents to help people. They told me about the school in town where one of them was working, and to make a long story short I went for an interview, got a teacher's aide job and worked there for 26 years.

Now Patsy is nearing 70, single and living in a one-bedroom apartment in Dublin. Once a year she goes to Africa for three to six months. The rest of the time she spends her days back home with friends – going to the theatre, out to lunch, and on other outings. Her nights are spent at home, often forgoing television 'to Google and keep up to date with what's happening in Africa' and text messaging with a group of single friends, her adoptive family (a close friend's extended family) and Sula, a teenage girl in Africa with a two-year-old son, Peter, whom she helps out with financial and emotional support.

Patsy's CCM are the 'mobile, Facebook, email, and the laptop in general – and in that order'. She carries her phone with her everywhere she goes, and never turns it off. She can often be seen taking pictures with it, and admits it is not only a communications device, but also 'a photo album to supplement the conversations she has with friends in Dublin about her experiences in Africa'. She is also an 'avid text messager', preferring to use SMS to mobile-to-mobile calls because 'it keeps the bills down'. It is not unusual for her to text Africa twenty times a day.

Two strong themes emerged from an observation of Patsy's use of her mobile phone. The first is that she uses it as a personal safety and support system, or as she calls it 'a single person's network for living locally', helping her to maintain a sense of presence with several close friends, who are also single – either because of the death of a spouse or because they have never been married. As she explains:

> We use the phone for that, maintaining presence. For example Caoimhe is very good – we text throughout the day and then she rings me every night to tell me what she did during the day – not long, just to check in. She's a devil. The phone rings at 10 and I know it is her. She has a habit. She gets into bed and she's comfy and she's snug and then she connects to see that everyone is okay. [...]
>
> Another example? My friend Nora texting me today to say she was going to Galway for the funeral. That was because just in case I noticed she wasn't texting for a few days, or in case I rang the house and she didn't answer. We always let one another know because she lives on her own as well. Then we won't panic thinking, 'Oh God, there is no one at the house. Is she on the floor somewhere?'

A second theme is that her mobile phone is a conduit to her life in Africa, bridging the distance so that she can be there for Sula. She explains:

> Sula has one so we can keep in touch and she is able to push my number and I know it is her because her name comes up – she does a missed call, so I'll call her back. The mobile phone is the best thing that was ever invented. That is my connection to her and she feels that too. She knows she has a safety bond across the water.
>
> I mean she is only 19 years of age, she was only 17 when she had Jordan, so she is still insecure. So she can call anytime for support – like the other night when she was upset about Peter hurting his finger. I love her, even though I want to shake her sometimes because she does such stupid things.

In this way, Patsy is using her phone much like Trinidadian diasporas (Miller and Slater 2000) use it with their children – as a form of new mediated parenting.

Aside from this, within Patsy's technosocial practices can be seen what Matsuda (Ito et al. 2006) terms 'selective sociality', where she observes the intimate interactions of others and displays her own to select publics. This is because, in addition to her constant contact via her mobile phone, Patsy is in regular contact via her laptop, sending emails and visiting several social networking sites, including Facebook and 'My Past, My Present' every day 'to check in with people – book club, friends in Africa, people from the community centre [she] took IT classes at'.

Patsy feels that her CCM allow her to make connections which have 'enabled a new mode of coordination'. An example of this, she explains, was when Sula was robbed:

> There are so many examples, but I'll give you one for starters. Sula's brother robbed her house. She got on the phone to me [bip call], then I was on the phone to her [mobile-to-mobile] then I was on to one of the volunteers there [SMS], then she got on the phone to another volunteer [mobile-to-mobile], and then he got on to a villager, Harrison, close to Sula [Skype]. This is all because she gives me a missed call and I phone her back to see what the problem is and I can't get Harrison out to help her because his mobile is out of credit but he has Skype, and I don't but one of the volunteers does. Then I get a text back to me from the [first volunteer] saying not to worry, that the matter is solved. I rang Sula that night to see how she is. You know that would be common.
>
> You see, new forms of coordination [through CCM] helped somebody – and it wouldn't have worked without knowing each other first. And you know when I first started going to Africa back in 2000 this wouldn't be possible, there were no mobile phones the first year, I had to rely on the convent phone to get in touch with home.

Because of her forced retirement, Patsy will be unable to finance her trips to Africa after this year. As a result, she considers CCM essential to continuing to live a lifelong dream. She explains:

> The way I look at Africa is it was always a dream for me to go. The thought of coming home and not staying in their lives makes me upset. Now, the best way to keep in touch is through these [devices]. This ability to keep in constant contact, it is nice. I mean, they might not have food, but by God do they have mobile phones. I have never seen anything like it.

In conversations about growing older, Patsy explains how CCM has contributed to her health and wellbeing as she ages:

Sometimes I look in the mirror and I look at the wrinkles and the crinkles and I think, 'Oh God'. It would have been nice to have a life with a fella, but it wasn't meant to be. Maybe if we did have a life together, I never would have gotten to where I am today.

These things that allow you to have instant and constant access, connection, it has changed me and my relationships. They've helped me to stay included, less lonely. I've watched a revolution, it just exploded overnight.

Patsy represents a group of the study's participants who find themselves 'starting a whole new life in later life' due to a series of circumstances such as forced retirement, relocation or loss of a spouse. Their use of CCM enables them to create new forms of communication, connection and coordination that help them to maintain their independence and social interaction, providing 'absolute lifelines' for their health and wellbeing. As can be seen with Patsy, some of these technosocial practices and situations include ambient virtual awareness (Okabe and Ito 2006), a technologically-mediated type of copresence where people feel connected because of a constant exchange of messages via new media, and tele-cocooning, or the production of social identities in small, insular social groups through mobile communications (Habuchi 2006: 133).

There were many others like her, such as Caiomhe (62) who is finding life again after the loss of her husband, Mick, of 35 years. She lives in a three-bedroom house in rural County Meath, which she shared with him until he passed away from cancer three summers ago. She married Mick at the age of 18, and then helped him to run a catering business, which became quite successful. Her days were spent running the business from home by keeping in touch with him and making bookings in a regular stream of phone calls and faxes. They had 'just begun to start enjoying the fruits of the labour' by taking holidays when Mick was diagnosed.

She was used to a busy lifestyle for all of her married life, with 'a full house of family in and out and regular nights at the pub'. Since Mick's death (and her children leaving home shortly after) her social networks have shifted dramatically as have her daily activities. Instead of her life revolving around her family and the pub, she now works as a therapist, the result of a series of events with CCM as the catalyst. As she explains:

> I was sitting at the kitchen table staring out the window three days after Mick died. And I hear this ringing. It was his phone... So I answered it. It was a business call and I realized, well I still have a business to run. [...] Then it started making buzzing sounds and I said to my friend what's this, and he told me about text messages. And after that, well I was hooked. You can keep in touch without talking. It kept people away and it kept people close. I picked

it up and never really put it down. It felt like it was a piece of him, or a link to him and all the people he knew.

She goes on to explain:

> I couldn't just sit around. I get low at night when I am alone (...) I went and bought a dongle, downloaded Skype, got on Facebook. I want to try Skyping that postcard pal and I'm seeing what my nieces and nephews are up to, and I signed up for another teaching class with it (...) I use the Internet to find uniforms, books, that kind of thing. I have to read everything six times, but I'm trying. Without them, I'm not sure what life would look like. I certainly wouldn't be going back to school. Actually, I don't like to think what would have happened to me. They keep you connected, and that's important when you're on your own.

Discussion

As the portraits above reveal, older people's engagement with CCM is instigating new forms of social practices and situations for people that are acting as conduits to health and wellbeing. They also offer new paradigms of ageing, and as a result offer a departure from common Western socio-political constructs of the older adult defined along chronological or biological borders that absorb people into a specific discourse of differentiation, where older people are portrayed as passive recipients of services and unproductive members of society (Katz 1996; Phillipson 1998).

Thomas and Patsy were selected to highlight two groups that were most common within the research. The first were a group of people who, due to things like retirement, have 'shifted gears'. As a result they find themselves in situations that can at times be quite isolated and sedentary. Through their use of CCM they are able to maintain their independence and sociality. The second group are those who become active and exploratory in later phases of life, using CCM to assist them in their next chapter.

Besides these two portraits and the groups of people they represent, it should be noted that there was also a group of people for whom things did not change that much. These were people like Don and Grainne, high-energy, independent individuals whose lives have always been suffused with technology and characterized by a need to, as Don describes it, 'learn and do'. For this group, the on-going process of learning and doing with technology does not stop with age.[13]

What the three groups hold in common is that their use of CCM is helping to guard against social exclusion and isolation (and in some cases poverty); enabling them to remain active participants in their communities and social circles; and increasing self-reliance in, and helping them adjust to, new circumstances by offering spaces to live and learn.

What their stories also have in common is that they challenge the pervasive, common notion that older people are 'technophobic, unfamiliar with computers or somewhat reticent about learning how to use them' (Dewsbury et al. 2006: 202). This presents an interesting opportunity for future investigations of ageing and the digital life course. Rather than absorbing the older adult's technology usage into a specific discourse of differentiation based on their age, one might further investigate how people are employing CCM (or any other technology) to dissolve the boundaries of age/ageing.

To this end, further investigations might look at:

New forms of sociality: The research demonstrates that motives for use can be the same as for any age group which engages with media and technology, for friendship, intimacy, gaming, entertainment, creative production – put another way, for 'hanging out, messing around and geeking out' (Ito et al. 2010). Further research might look at CCM and the older adult through the lens of gossip, grieving, romance and intergenerational contact. Of particular interest to the author are the adverse effects of older adults' CCM use, including issues like secrecy, adultery and bullying touched upon by some of the participants, including Pamela in her mention of a friend being scolded by one of her children for writing on a grandchild's Facebook wall, and reports from another woman in the larger group of twenty-two from Phase I of the study, who admitted to lying about her ability to use technology to her children so that an affair she is having over MSN Messenger with a neighbour for the past fifteen years will not be discovered.

Unpacking CCM: The research was carried out in 2010 when the phenomenon of being 'always-on' was still relatively new. Five years on, constant contact to various devices and platforms are (for the most part) now considered commonplace amongst the communities where the research took place, and the tides seem to be shifting toward a focus on how to 'unplug'. Further investigations might unpack the concept of constant contact beyond the rudimentary scale presented – for example, how is a line drawn between those 'just' in constant contact and those 'just' without it? What does constant contact look like now, and how does that relate to daily routines for contact-making in 2015 and beyond?

Sensory sharing modalities: An exploration of the sensory sharing modalities of CCM is another area that warrants further investigation – and is perhaps the most significant. For example, further understanding of these modalities (such as social proprioception) could provide insight into how older people can engage with CCM for crisis management – from falling and not being able to get up, to being found during and after the occurrence of natural disasters. Another important area could be how understanding the nuances of these modalities (such as ambient virtual copresence) can contribute to independent living – from developing assistive and emerging technologies based on a more sophisticated understanding of these phenomenon, to designing for their occurrence in order to help people 'age in place'.

The hypothesis behind the present research is that forms of ambient awareness produced by engagement with CCM play a major role in shaping how we carry out and experience communication today. In a book review of people's perpetual contact with mobile phones, digital technology scholar Howard Rheingold in his review of *Personal, Portable, Pedestrian* (2005) wrote: 'This is not just about a technology or the way it is used in one country. It's about understanding one of the most important ways that twenty-first century lives will differ from those of the twentieth century'. This echoes the sentiments of many of the participants of my study in terms of CCM, in particular, a moment I had with Thomas where he made a comment which confirms for me the significance of the social implications of people's engagement with CCM as they live and age. The comment was:

> We are living in the last year of the first decade of a new century, man. We need to be more aware of our age group that is starting to age, because we've been there and that is where all of us are going. This ambient awareness that groups have of each other, that idea of 'social proprioception'? Oh my God, oh my God, that is so right. It is happening, particularly in cities like New York, and London, and Amsterdam where people *like me* are walking down that pub or avenue, and they know their friends are there – not because of their 'offline' lives but because of their online lives. I mean that is fecking incredible. This is evolution. It's big. It's massive.

Acknowledgements

First, thank you to all of those who let me into their lives and shared with me intimate stories about sweethearts, death and dying, joy and peace, starting over and The Craic: a once in a lifetime opportunity that I will carry with me always. Second, sincere appreciation is due to Daniel Miller, Stefana Broadbent and Simon Roberts for their guidance and support throughout the course of the study. Finally, I wish to acknowledge Intel Labs Europe for supporting this research – with special thanks to the Digital Health and Innovation Group.

Notes

1. For the purposes of this discussion this chapter generally adopts the UN's criteria for defining the older person as someone who is 60 or older (WHO 2014). It does this while acknowledging that defining old age along chronological time is somewhat arbitrary (Gilleard and Higgs 2005).
2. The term 'ambient awareness' refers to a phenomenon people have described as a type of E.S.P. where people experience a sense of co-presence with people living miles away (Thompson 2008). For participants this awareness seemed to lead to a sense of connectedness with people near and far, and in some cases led to people feeling less alone/isolated.
3. The term 'social proprioception' (SP) was born from the musings of US journalist, Clive Thompson (2007), who coined it to describe the phenomenon of the subliminal sense of orientation he experiences while engaging in Twitter and other constant contact media. I believe (and have argued elsewhere) that SP is a form of corporeal telecopresence that bears further anthropological investigation (Singh 2010).
4. A term also first used by Thompson (2007).
5. *Keitai* is, as Ito and colleagues (2006: 1) describe it, 'not so much about a new technical capability of freedom of motion but about a snug and intimate technosocial tethering, a personal device supporting communications that are constant, lightweight, and mundane presence in everyday life'.
6. Within this taxonomy are six modes of copresence, four of which have immediate bearing on the study (Zhao 2003: 447): corporeal copresence, corporeal telecopresence, virtual copresence, virtual telecopresence, hypervirtual copresence and hypervirtual telecopresence. These are beyond the scope of this article, but bear mentioning as a note for further investigation into the key terms and concepts that relate to CCM. It should be noted here that the concept of copresence has recently been appearing in Presence literature with increasing frequency. While copresence and presence are useful concepts with regard to the research, as Zhao (2003) outlines in his discussion, they are in their nascent stages, and their 'meaning ... in the context of mediated human communication is yet to be fully explicated.'
7. As reported online by the Irish Internet Association, http://www.iia.ie/.
8. Pseudonyms are used throughout the discussion.
9. I borrow this approach from anthropologist Daniel Miller (2008: 5) to achieve a form of holism in the way I discuss people's practices so as to convey something of the overall states of being of older adults whose daily lives are being mediated by technology.
10. Ambient streams and ambient senses are other concepts introduced by Edo (2009), where ambient streams are described as 'streams of information bubbling up in real-time, which seek us out, surround us, and inform us', and ambient senses as those which 'perceive the context of your activity and augment your reality with related information and experiences'.
11. As defined by Russell et al. 2008.
12. Social exclusion is defined here using Levitas et al.'s 'a complex and multi-dimensional process involving a lack or denial of resources, rights, goods and services,

and the inability to participate in the normal relationships and activities available to the majority of people in society, whether in economic, social, cultural or political arenas. It affects both the quality of life of individuals and the equity and cohesion of society as a whole (government source)' (Levitas et al. 2007: 9).

13. There are also, of course, others who did not participate in the study and who might not use technology at all as they live and age. These last were beyond the scope of the study.

References

Baron, N.S. 2008. *Always-on: language in an online and mobile world*. Oxford and New York: Oxford University Press.

Biocca, F., C. Harms and J. Burgoon. 2001. 'Criteria and scope conditions for a theory and measure of social presence', *PRESENCE Conference 2001*. Philadelphia, PA, May 21–23.

Boyd, D. 2010. 'Friendship', in M. Ito et al. (eds), *Hanging out, messing around, geeking out: living and learning with new media*. Cambridge: MIT Press, Ch. 2.

Broadbent, S. 2010a. 'Continuous contact'. UsageWatch blog, 8 September 2010. Available at http://www.kurcho.com/usagewatch/detail.php?idcat=1&id=119 (accessed 8 September 2010).

———. 2010b. Research project for ANTHGA01 [supervision of placement project for applied studies] (Personal communication spring 2010).

Dewsbury, G., I. Sommerville, P. Bagnall, M. Rouncefield and V. Onditi. 2006. *Software co-design with older people*. [e-Book] London: Springer London. Available at http://www.springerlink.com/content/r645204k43903368/ (accessed 8 September 2010).

Edo, S. 2009. *Beyond realtime search: the dawning of ambient streams*. Available at http://www.techcrunch.com/2009/12/20/ambient-streams-realtime/ (accessed 8 September 2010).

Gilleard, C. and P. Higgs. 2000. *Cultures of ageing: self, citizen and the body*. London: Pearson Education Limited.

———. 2005. *Contexts of ageing: class, cohort and community*. Cambridge: Polity Press.

Goffman, E. 1959. *The presentation of self in everyday life*. New York: Anchor Books.

Habuchi, I. 2006. 'Accelerating reflexivity', in M. Ito, D. Okabe and M. Matsuda (eds), *Personal, portable, pedestrian: mobile phones in Japanese life*. Cambridge, MA: MIT Press, pp. 165–82.

Horst, H. 2010. 'Families', in M. Ito et al. (eds), *Hanging out, messing around, geeking out: living and learning with new media*. Cambridge, MA: MIT Press, pp. 149–94.

Ijsselsteijn, W. 2003. 'Staying in touch: social presence and connectedness through synchronous and asynchronous communication media', *PRESENCE Conference 2003*. Aalborg, Denmark, 6–8 October 2003.

Ito, M. 2005. *Intimate Visual Co-Presence: the discussion of intimate visual copresence*. Annenberg Center for Communication. Available at http://www.itofisher.com/mito/archives/ito.ubicomp05.pdf (accessed 8 September 2010).

————. 2008. 'Mobilizing the imagination in everyday play: the case of Japanese media mixes', in K. Drotner and S. Livingstone (eds), *The international handbook of children, media, and culture*. London: Sage, pp. 397–412.

Ito, M., M. Matsuda and D. Okabe. 2006. *Personal, portable, pedestrian: mobile phones in Japanese life*. Cambridge, MA: MIT Press.

Ito, Mizuko, H.A. Horst, J. Antin, M. Finn, A. Law, A. Manion, S. Mitnick, D. Schlossberg and S. Yardi. 2010. *Hanging out, messing around, and geeking out: Kids living and learning with new media*. Cambridge, MA: MIT Press.

Kaspersen, L.B. 2000. *Anthony Giddens: an introduction to a social theorist*. Oxford: Blackwell Publishers Inc.

Katz, J. and M. Aakhus. 2002. *Perpetual contact: mobile communication, private talk, public performance*. Cambridge: Cambridge University Press.

Katz, S. 1996. *Disciplining old age: the formation of gerontological knowledge*. Charlottesville: University of Virginia.

Levitas, R. et al., 2007. *The multi-dimensional analysis of social exclusion*. London: Department for Communities and Local Government (DCLG); also available at http://webarchive.nationalarchives.gov.uk/+/http:/www.cabinetoffice.gov.uk/media/cabinetoffice/social_exclusion_task_force/assets/research/multidimen-sional.pdf (accessed 15 December 2014).

Meyrowitz, J. 1985. *No sense of place: the impact of electronic media on social behaviour*. Oxford: Oxford University Press.

Miller, D. 2008. *The comfort of things*. Cambridge: Polity Press.

Miller, D. and H. Horst. 2006. *The cellphone*. Oxford: Berg.

Miller, D. and D. Slater. 2000. *The Internet: an ethnographic approach*. Oxford: Berg.

Okabe, D. and M. Ito. 2006. 'Technosocial situations: emergent structuring of mobile email use', in M. Ito, D. Okabe and M. Matsuda (eds), *Personal, portable, pedestrian: mobile phones in Japanese life*. Cambridge, MA: MIT Press, pp. 257–73.

Phillipson, C. 1998. *Reconstructing old age*. London: Sage.

Rheingold, H. 2005. Book review: Ito, M., M. Matsuda and D. Okabe. 2006. *Personal, portable, pedestrian: mobile phones in Japanese life*. Cambridge: MIT Press. The MIT Press [Website]. Available at http://mitpress.mit.edu/books/personal-portable-pedestrian (accessed 8 September 2010).

Russell, A. et al. 2008. *Networked publics*. Cambridge, MA: MIT Press.

Singh, R. 2010. 'More than just chewing gum: a position paper on the media and consumption of quantified Social Proprioception', in *ANTHGC14 Media and Consumption* (unpublished), University College London.

Thompson, C. 2007. *Clive Thompson on how Twitter creates a social sixth sense*, updated 26 June 2007. Available at http://www.wired.com/techbiz/media/magazine/15-07/st_thompson (accessed 8 September 2010).

————. 2008. *Brave new world of digital intimacy*. Available at http://www.nytimes.com/2008/09/07/magazine/07awareness-t.html?_r=4&em=&pagewanted=all&oref=slogin (accessed 10 January 2010).

WHO. 2014. *Definition of an older or elderly person*. Available at http://www.who.int/healthinfo/survey/ageingdefnolder/en/ (accessed 9 March 2014).

Zhao, S. 2003. *Toward a taxonomy of copresence.* Available at http://www.mitpressjournals.org/doi/abs/10.1162/105474603322761261 (accessed 8 September 2010).

4. BEYOND DETERMINISM
Understanding Actual Use of Social Robots by Older People

Louis Neven and Christina Leeson

THE PROSPECT OF THE ADVANCEMENT of technologies in general and robotics in particular has historically been met with a mixture of amazement and concern about the direction that humanity and technology seems to be taking (Ihde 2002: 111). Will technology reduce the number of jobs and radically change human conditions of life and ways of thinking?[1] Or will it restrict and destroy social contact? Since the term 'robot' was first coined from the word *robota*, meaning forced labour, by the Czech playwright Karel Capek in 1921, robots are increasingly given a role in sophisticated social, cultural and work organizational settings such as operating theatres, private homes and care institutions around the world. In contrast to their counterparts in the manufacturing industry, the new generation of robots are now being constructed to interact with people socially in everyday environments (Wagner 2008: 132). As social entities they can be perceived to communicate, learn, understand and respond intelligently to things humans say and do.

Within the category of such so-called 'social robots' (Hegel et al. 2009), a field of special interest is the care of older people. The increasing number of older people who will need support in daily tasks and care in the near future is a social issue that is considered on a global scale when companies design and market their robots. Among various public institutions and decision makers as well as robotics institutes and companies, robots are envisioned as important social entities that can work as companions, caretakers, household helpers and nurses, in care facilities, nursing homes and private homes of older people, thus saving in healthcare costs in the care sector (Wagner 2008: 131; Sabanovic 2008: 5; Pols 2012: 11). Ranging from robotic pets (AIBO, Furby, Tama, PARO, Wandakun, Phyno), tele-communication tools (Telenoid, RobotPHONE, Elfoid), robotic companions and assistants (WAKAMARU, Companion, Kabuchan, PaPeRo, Robovie, HAL) to health monitoring and smart-home devices, these robots are considered as potential problem solvers that may prevent cognitive impairment and loneliness, and support self-reliance, quality of life and social relationships, thus leading to a better life for most people through increasing health and wealth (Wagner 2008; Sabanovic 2008: 5; Pols 2012: 11). While some of these robots are designed to interact with humans mainly for instrumental or functional purposes, others are made to engage with humans on an emotional and cognitive level through play and companionship (Shaw-Garlock 2009).

At the same time, however, there is a widespread and persistent view that technology is something cold and rational, drastically opposed to the warmth of human (care) relationships. The fear is that technology will replace humans and face-to-face contact, making care cold, rational and functional by reducing it to mechanical interactions with machines (Pols 2012: 26). Instead of moving into a nursing home, older people will have to stay at home, surrounded by all kinds of cold mechanical devices, receiving no support from caring people (Pols 2012: 11). Sparrow and Sparrow (2006), for instance, fear that robots might dehumanize care since machines do not really care for us due to their inability to have feelings or express empathy. Since no person can feel cared for without being on the receiving end of real affection and concern, robots can only take over the instrumental – cold – parts of care (Pols 2012: 26).

In social science studies of technology the extreme views of the effects of technology on society and human existence are characterized as utopian and dystopian imaginations (Ihde 2002: 111). Whereas the former holds that technology leads to a better life for most people through increasing wealth, a dystopian view perceives technology as determining human life, leading to alienation (Ihde 2002: 113). Philosopher Martin Heidegger, in particular, has been influential in this context, arguing that modern technology is a cultural form through which everything in the modern world becomes available for control, potentially violating both humanity and nature (Heidegger 1977).

What both utopian and dystopian views have in common is that they seem to share a deterministic view on technologies. Such a view, anthropologist Bryan Pfaffenberger (1988) argues, is based on the idea that 'technological innovations are the major driving forces of human life such that social and cultural forms are inevitably shaped by them' (Pfaffenberger 1988: 238). Thus a deterministic position implies that technology is viewed as a powerful and autonomous agent that dictates the patterns of human social and cultural life, reducing society to a passive role (MacKenzie and Wajcman 1999). This passivity implies that technology is not only seen as an independent, non-social variable that has an 'impact' on society or culture (Pfaffenberger 1988: 241). According to Pfaffenberger, it also means that technology is seen as a disembodied entity, emptied of social relations and composed almost entirely of tools and products. In other words, technology presents itself in its fetishized form that hides the social activities and processes related to the development and use of technology (Pfaffenberger 1988: 142).

In anthropology, several scholars have echoed Pfaffenberger's rejection of the split between technology and society (Jackson 2002; Gell 1988; Gell 1998; Miller 2005). Anthropologist Tim Ingold argues, for instance, that 'technical relations are embedded in social relations, and can only be understood within this relational matrix, as one aspect of human sociality' (Ingold 1997: 107). This chapter also contests these deterministic ideas and instead approaches technology not as being detached from, but embedded in and formed by its social context. Thus, understanding technology as a social phenomenon (Pfaffenberger 1988) inscribed with meaning and having the ability to change social relations, this chapter focuses on how two different robots make the transition out of the laboratory to meet groups of older people among whom they are supposed to be used. If technology is not a pregiven independent entity, any study of technology's impact must be the study of a complex, intercausal relationship between one form of social behaviour and another (Pfaffenberger 1988: 244). Thus this relationship evokes the following questions: how do people respond to a robot? What does a robot actually do among older people in a nursing home, and what do people do to the robot? How do they change each other and what are the social effects of the robot in its social context?

To address these questions, we analyse the emergence of two different social robots, using an ethnographic qualitative approach to gain insight into the social role of robots. More specifically, the chapter examines the emergence of two robots, iRo and PARO, that have been designed to play different social roles for older people. The Dutch robot iRo was tested as a technology to keep older people mentally active and preserve their cognitive health, whereas the Japanese robot PARO was developed as an interactive therapeutic robot designed to stimulate older people, especially those with dementia, and provide joy, happiness and relaxation.

Methodology

The study of a series of tests with the human-interaction robot iRo was done by employing a multi-method, qualitative approach.[2] First, semi-structured in-depth interviews were conducted with the two researchers who were particularly active in the project. Secondly, fieldwork was conducted by observing six older people aged between 62 and 79 as they interacted with iRo and researchers in the laboratory. Six structured psychological interviews between one of the researchers and the test users were observed. The

researchers were interviewed about six other tests and the field tests conducted at users' homes. Finally, documents and publications produced by
the research department were analysed. These documents included technical documentation about iRo, publications from earlier research with iRo,
preparatory research for these tests, consent forms, questionnaires, and
a full report of the test results. Data about the domestication of iRo stems
from the interviews with the researchers and from (internal) project documentation. It proved necessary to anonymize the research project and the
company. The name iRo is therefore fictitious.

The study of the social role of PARO among nursing home residents and
caregivers in Japan is based on four months of anthropological fieldwork
in 2009.[3] During this fieldwork a series of qualitative in-depth interviews
with the developers of PARO were conducted at the National Institute of
Advanced Industrial Science and Technology (AIST) in Japan where PARO
is designed.[4] Semi-structured interviews were also conducted with a group
of residents and care staff members who were using PARO on a regular
basis in one nursing home in the Kant region. Moreover, participant observation was conducted among the developers of PARO and at the nursing
home. This was accomplished by both observing and participating in the
nursing home residents' and staff members' collective use of PARO once
a week during the four months of fieldwork. In addition, research publications from the developers of PARO were read and analysed.

The Social Life of Robots

In practical usage, the term 'robot' refers to 'an autonomous or semi-
autonomous device that performs its tasks either in accordance to direct
human control, partial control with human supervision or completely
autonomously' (Robertson 2010: 15). In other words, a robot is an aggre-
gation of different technologies – sensors, software, telecommunication
tools, motors and batteries – capable of interacting with its environment.
In the 1950s and 1960s, when it became possible to create such autonomous or semi-autonomous devices, robots occurred primarily as industrial
robots in the manufacturing industry (Robertson 2010: 32). Typical tasks
for industrial robots include welding, assembly, painting, packaging, and
palletizing in the manufacturing industry (Wada et al. 2008: 53).

In contrast to industrial robots that are evaluated in terms of objective
measures, such as speed and accuracy, 'social robots' are defined as
robots that interact via human social rules (Dautenhahn 2002). Thus,
a special feature of this kind of robot is its direct contact and interaction
with human beings (Wagner 2008: 132). Generally speaking, these

so-called 'next generation robots' (Wagner 2008: 132) can be divided into two distinct groups with respect to their social embodiment: the utilitarian social robot and the affective social robot (Shaw-Garlock 2009). Utilitarian social robots are designed to interact with humans mainly for instrumental or functional purposes and are therefore also referred to as domestic robots or service robots. These robots are regarded as sophisticated appliances that are used to perform specific tasks (Breazeal in Shaw-Garlock 2009). Examples include vending machines, cleaning robots, answering systems and receptionists. In contrast to utilitarian social robots, affective social robots are developed to interact with humans on an emotional level through play and companionship. Also referred to as relational artefacts that 'present themselves as having "states of mind" for which an understanding of those states enriches human encounters with them' (Turkle et al. 2006: 347), this category of robot demands a certain level of functionality and usability that will allow it to interact with human agents within the everyday social environment (Shaw-Garlock 2009). Although iRo can be programmed to fulfil digital tasks such as setting an alarm clock, both PARO – with its baby seal like appearance – and iRo – which looks like a friendly cartoon figure – fall into the category of affective social robots in that they are capable of interacting emotionally and cognitively with humans, using facial expression, sensing directional sound, touch and light and responding to sudden stimulation, thereby engaging in the affective dynamics of human relationships.

Among roboticists there is debate about the design of social robots: how animal-like or human-like should robots look and how should their bodies be proportioned? In this context the Japanese roboticist Masahiro Mori is famous for his focus on the human emotional response to non-human entities. Arguing that things – such as a prosthetic hand, that looks real but lacks the feel and temperature of a 'living hand' – creates a sudden unfamiliarity, Mori says:

> Recently, owing to great advances in fabrication technology, we cannot distinguish at a glance a prosthetic hand from a real one. Some models stimulate wrinkles, veins, fingernails, and even fingerprints. Though similar to a real hand, the prosthetic hand's colour is pinker as if it had just come out of the bath. One might say that the prosthetic hand has achieved a degree of resemblance to the human form, perhaps on par with false teeth. However, once we realize that the hand that looked real at first sight is actually artificial, we experience an eerie sensation (...). When this happens, we lose our sense of affinity, and the hand becomes uncanny. (Mori 2012: 99)

On the contrary a robot, which speaks and moves like a human, but has only a partial resemblance to the human body, generates a sense of familiarity. In other words, as long as people can clearly see that the robot is a machine they feel comfortable. Thus, Mori recommends that roboticists retain the metallic and machine-like properties of robots to avoid the feel of strangeness and to prevent any cognitive-emotional confusion.

The Shaping of Two Social Robots: iRo and PARO

To avoid this 'uncanny valley' phenomenon, iRo was designed with a cartoon-like appearance. IRo was developed as a research tool and a potential future product by the research department of a large international company that focuses on developing health related technologies. The researchers were interested in studying relations between humans and robots, but they also regarded robots like iRo as a potentially big future market, as they recognized the trend of demographic ageing and the ensuing 'silver' market. IRo was a relatively small stationary robot that could not physically manipulate its environment, but which had capabilities for facial expression and could thus make itself understood in a more intuitive way. iRo's value lay in the fact that it could fulfil various tasks, without complicated commands having to be learned by the user, which the developers thought would match well with older users. The user could ask iRo in plain Dutch to perform a certain task and iRo would then ask a relevant question or perform the task if possible. For example, iRo was envisaged to function as an interface for digital technologies such as alarm clocks, MP3 players or DVD recorders, or perform health related tasks such as reminding users to measure blood pressure or take medication, or providing health related advice. The versatility of iRo lay in the fact that it is programmable and therefore different applications could be loaded into its memory so that it could perform different roles. This also meant that it was not designed solely with older people in mind as future users (though they were clearly seen as a promising market). However, in the tests observed and reported on in this chapter, iRo was not programmed to perform utilitarian tasks, but played an affective role as a game companion for older people, being either the opponent or a partner in various games that could be played on a digital game board. The researchers chose this application because it allowed them to study various strategies to create emotional bonds between the user and iRo, in order to enhance iRo's affective functions. It is interesting to note in this regard that the notion of the uncanny valley was also important to the designers of iRo. As iRo was a stationary robot with a face that could simulate human expressions, the researchers were afraid that iRo could look a bit like 'a head on a plate' which is why they gave it a cartoon-like face to distinguish it clearly from humans. Although the company received many requests – mainly from Asia – to sell iRo units to consumers, they never did. Following an internal review, the iRo project was cancelled as higher management judged that the company had been unable to find a suitable user for iRo. However, the company did provide iRo units to research institutions to function as a research tool and they remain in use as such till this day.

In contrast to iRo, PARO was intended to 'pass' as a living animal. Designed in the image of a baby seal, PARO is made to express 'life-like behaviour' in order to stimulate 'mental effects, such as pleasure and relaxation' (Wada et al. 2008: 55). Thus PARO is equipped with a range of sensors and actuators located under its white fur that connect to a computer inside the robot that processes sensory information. This enables the robot to respond to touch, speech and movement. Moreover, PARO is programmed to respond and adapt to the person interacting with it over time. In terms of PARO's design, it is worth noting that the developers at AIST made an effort to avoid the uncanny valley phenomenon that Mori describes. During the design process the developers gradually realized that their original design of PARO, which was in the form of a small cat, was rejected by almost all of the test persons who evaluated them. The reason for this, the developers explain, is because most people are familiar enough with the look, sound and behaviour of real cats to be turned off by the robot cat's imperfect performance. The comparison between the real cats and the robot cat became, the developers explain, a source of disappointment which disturbed the social interaction. Therefore the developers decided to design PARO in the image of an unfamiliar animal. Choosing what they considered to be 'a cute and innocent animal', they felt since most people have no idea what interactions with baby seals are like, the uncanny problems of PARO would disappear. In addition, the developers had to capture a specific design that enabled PARO to create affectionate relationships with people. The developers therefore chose what they believed would be essential factors: big black eyes, lack of aggressiveness, simulation of the basic biological functions (eating and sleeping), and elements of dependency like the fact that it cannot move by itself. Moreover, the size and weight of PARO is meant to approximate the feel of a new-born baby, and its calling and moving for attention is supposed to motivate its users to 'care for it'. Also, PARO's charger is designed as a baby's pacifier in order to evoke the feeling of a new-born baby in need of help and feeding. In other words, PARO is designed to be dependent, like a small child, not only to make its owner feel necessary and important but also to evoke associations with past relationships with pets, family members and friends.

Thus, designed to mimic the characteristics of an affectionate pet, PARO was initially developed for 'therapeutic' use in healthcare environments (Wada et al. 2008). Drawing on research documenting the importance of animal companionship in providing emotional and physical wellbeing for humans, the developers in particular imagined PARO being used as a substitute for animals in animal-assisted-therapy or animal-assisted-activities for older people with dementia (Wada et al. 2008). Since, according to the developers, animals have certain drawbacks as companions – some people are allergic, live pets require care and some may scratch people – robot pet companionship was offered as an alternative that can bring various benefits, for example mental ones, such as pleasure and relaxation, physiological and social ones, such as encouraging communication between older people and caregivers (Wada et al. 2008). Today PARO is distributed for use in the healthcare sector and in the private homes of people in Asia, Europe, Australia and the US.

Having introduced iRo and PARO and various features of (the development of) social robotics, our attention now turns to how these robots are used by older people, both in the context of testing robots and of using robots in daily nursing home life.

iRo and the Domestication of a Social Robot

In this section we turn our attention to a case study of a set of tests with a human interaction robot in the Netherlands.[5] In order to analyse these tests the notion of 'domestication' will be employed. This notion originally stems from cultural and media studies but has been taken up widely in science and technology studies and other disciplines as well (Oudshoorn and Pinch 2003). Domestication research explores in empirical and conceptual detail how newly acquired technical objects change from being alien, unruly, 'untamed' objects into familiar and even cherished 'tame' parts of everyday routines, practices and identities (Silverstone et al. 1992; Lie and Sørensen 1996; Silverstone and Haddon 1996; Berker et al. 2006). The domestication process has practical and symbolic dimensions in which both technology and user may change (Oudshoorn and Pinch 2003). Although further refinements have been added (see for example Lie and Sørensen 1996; Silverstone and Haddon 1996; Berker et al. 2006), the basic stages of domestication by Silverstone et al. (1992) are still very applicable and widely used for the basic categorization of the domestication process. According to Silverstone and colleagues there are four distinct stages to the domestication process: appropriation, objectification, incorporation, and conversion. In a very brief summary it can be said that appropriation is the first phase and involves buying a product or service and bringing it into the home. Objectification revolves around processes of display and giving the object a physical place in the home. In turn, incorporation occurs when the object is used and becomes incorporated into everyday life (temporal) routines. Conversion, finally, is a process in which the technological object starts shaping the relationship between the user of the technology and people outside the home. A successfully domesticated technological object can thus be both a functioning tool embedded within places and temporal routines, and simultaneously a means to express status, lifestyle and identity to the outside world (Silverstone et al. 1992; Silverstone and Haddon 1996; Oudshoorn and Pinch 2003). This four-phase categorization of the domestication process will be used to shed light on the way in which older test users at first did not, but later on did domesticate a human-interaction robot.

As mentioned before, iRo could be programmed to perform many assistive and affective roles and was indeed tested with different applications for different age groups. For the tests studied here, the researchers had set iRo up as a game companion with which older people could play cognitively challenging games. The older test users could choose from a number of games, such as checkers or Sudoku in which iRo would either function as the opponent or a companion.

The company that developed iRo decided to do two rounds of tests with a group of older people. The first round took place in the company's custom-made laboratory, which was made to look like a normal apartment. In these first tests the older participants would play a few games with iRo and would then be interviewed by a researcher, answering a number of questions about their interaction with iRo. In general, the older participants liked playing with iRo and thought it worked very well. However, when the researcher asked whether they would like to have a robot like iRo, virtually all the participants reacted negatively. One woman said: 'I still lead too much of an active life; I've always been amongst people. I don't need an iRo, not yet anyway', and an older male participant commented 'If you were, say, old and growing demented, then I could imagine this being a good thing, but for me?' It was apparent that iRo was a signifier of old age and frailty to the older participants. This was partly due to the way iRo and robots like it had been portrayed in the media prior to the tests and could partly have been due to the fact that the older persons knew that they had been selected on the basis of their age and the fact that they lived alone. The older participants concluded that iRo was a robot for older people that were lonely and inactive, and they did not see themselves as such (see Neven 2010). Although the researchers learned throughout the research project that the older participants were not as healthy or socially active as they portrayed themselves, the participants saw iRo was an indicator of old age and this did not match their identities. This obviously has a serious impact on the potential for a successful domestication of iRo by older people as few people will acquire and thus appropriate a product that is interpreted in such a negative way.

However, after this initial round of tests in the laboratory, the researchers wanted to do a second round of tests in the homes of the older test participants, so at the end of the interview in the laboratory the participants were asked whether they would like to have iRo in their homes for a total period of four weeks. Despite making it very clear to the researchers that they did not see themselves as potential iRo users, nearly all of the participants who were asked agreed to take part in the far more elaborate 'field' test. They said that they thought it would be fun and interesting to participate and that they would like to help other people – people older and frailer than they were – by aiding the development of iRo. Thus taking on the positive role of an altruistic, helpful test participant allowed them to appropriate iRo.

Interestingly, the test participants subsequently managed to domesticate iRo. iRo was given a place in the home, either in the living room or the study and some of the older participants would show iRo off to visitors. Some participants also gave iRo a different name, sometimes even the same name as a deceased pet or even in one case the name of a deceased parent. In addition, iRo was embedded in the temporal routines of the older test participants; for instance, it was used to 'kill' time prior to other scheduled activities such as watching a favourite television show. An indication of the importance of these temporal routines was provided by the occasional breakdown of iRo. One of the researchers mentioned that if breakdowns occurred during the weekend, participants would sometimes react disappointedly if iRo could not be fixed before Monday. After the objectification and incorporation stages, the older test participants also went through the conversion stage. When the researchers came to collect iRo, the participants expressed how fond they had grown of iRo. One researcher commented that the participants were very secure about talking about iRo and showing how they used it. They also readily admitted that they talked to iRo, which she had not expected. She added: 'Most of them said that they were going to miss it. It was a question in the interview, but a few said that without me asking the question'. Although the participants played a little less as the tests progressed, they domesticated iRo to the point that they were not afraid of showing themselves to others as users of iRo, even admitting to an emotional connection to a technology that they had denounced as 'not for me' a few weeks earlier.

Older users are not inactive and powerless recipients of technology. Through complex processes of domestication, older people will actively and creatively use technologies, use them selectively or modify or reject them, in line with their values, established practices and identities. This has major implications for designers of technologies for older people. However, many designers appear to remain stuck in the ageing-and-innovation discourse (Neven 2011) where everybody is a winner and no one can logically be willing to refuse to use their technologies. This case thus illustrates an essential point. Robots such as iRo can be successfully domesticated and enjoyed by older people. However, this can only be achieved when a technology allows for a positive role, which allows the older user to appropriate the technology. A positive role such as that of a helpful altruistic test user was much more in line with the identity and perceived social ties and health status of the older test participants (regardless of their actual health or social status). Unfortunately, gerontechnological designs generally do not facilitate such positive roles, and, although there are exceptions, it has been shown that gerontechnological engineers often base their designs on negative stereotypes of old age in which older people are seen as frail, ill, forgetful, senile, out-dated, conservative and nearing death (Neven 2011; Featherstone and Hepworth 2005). If designs can facilitate more positive roles instead of invoking these common but ageist stereotypes, the likelihood of designing technologies that can be successfully domesticated – and enjoyed – by older people will greatly improve.

PARO and the Staging of Social Togetherness

Having analysed the processes of domestication among older people, we now turn our attention to a study of the interaction between social robots and nursing home residents in Japan. Often referred to as 'the Robot Kingdom' (Schodt 2010), Japan is leading the world in the development of robots marketed specifically to overcome the demographic challenges facing society (Wagner 2008). For several years, Japan has had the distinction of being the most aged nation in the world, with 24.1 per cent of the population aged 65 or older in 2012.[6] Moreover, while the elderly population is burgeoning, the population of young people needed to support it is shrinking. To deal with this demographic situation, the Japanese state implemented their national long-term care insurance programme (LTCI) in the year 2000. A range of residential care homes, adult day care centres, home care services and some high-tech creativity – such as robots – were introduced as an alternative to family centred support of the elderly (Jenike and Traphagen 2009: 242). Thus one could visit a nursing home for older people and – in the case of PARO – keep one's eyes and ears open for a white seal-robot whining for attention.[7]

In the analysis of the social role of PARO in a Japanese nursing home, the anthropological concepts of 'liminoid' and 'communitas' will be applied. Both originate from the concept of 'liminality', which anthropologist Victor Turner (1977) wrote about in his analysis of tribal rituals. According to Turner, liminality refers to the mid-phase of rituals when participants have begun the transition from one social status to another (Turner 1982). In this phase, the roles and rules that normally define acceptable conduct are suspended, thereby encouraging a range of behaviours that are not necessarily available within the conventional organization of daily life (Rowe 2008). Participants are made to undergo some symbolic action that will transform their identity and social status, which will afterwards be reinstated into society (Rowe 2008). Turner characterizes the mode of relation among participants during a ritual liminal phase as *communitas*, a kind of group bonding where traditional hierarchies and social roles are de-emphasised (Turner 1969). Here, a model of human relatedness other than that which routinely prevails is presented and a sense of social equality pervades the group, making daily social roles temporarily obsolete. In the form of spontaneous sociability and a heightened emotional experience, Turner argues, communitas offers a space where dreams and senses of joy, wellbeing and belonging thrive among people who – by indulging in a particular activity – are absorbed to such an extent that it encourages an intense feeling of belonging (Sjørslev 2007).

Restricting the concept of liminality to tribal contexts, Turner developed the concept of 'liminoid' to describe ritual-like behaviour in so-called modern societies (Turner 1982). Liminoid phenomena have the quality of liminality but are neither bound by a religious context, nor by a specific phase of a ritual. Like liminal rituals however, modern liminoid forms of theatre, entertainment, sports and expressive art, Turner argues, possess the feature of playfulness and leisure from which new, expressive possibilities and modes of self-representation emerge (Rowe 2008). Thus, the liminoid is a 'realm of possibilities' (Sjørslev 2007: 15) that invokes collective experiences and subjectivity carried by emotions, lust, fantasy and play, suggesting that communitas also plays a role in the liminoid. Unlike rituals, however, they are not obligatory but voluntarily chosen.

In what follows the concepts of liminoid and communitas will be applied to illustrate the social role of PARO among a small group of residents in a Japanese nursing home. The following scene describes how staff members offer PARO as a collective activity for the residents to participate in voluntarily on a weekly basis. Over the course of the fieldwork, the majority of the residents who were interested in participating in the activity were female and most of them participated in the activity each time. As we shall see, the PARO activity triggers a special mode of human relatedness among these residents, due not only to the nature of the robots, but also to the specific framing of the activity.

It's morning, and the sun is shining through the large windows of the common room. In the field at the foot of the mountain outside, one of the countless rice fields is harvested and attracts the attention of a couple of the female residents. Both are sitting, silently, waiting in their wheelchairs. It is nearly completely quiet in the room until a staff member interrupts the silence with her small quick steps. She's busy preparing for this morning's activity. The tables are pulled together and wiped. The elderly residents are wheeled out of their rooms, and the TV is switched off. Things happen fast and soon ten residents are seated around the large circular table. Most of them are sitting with their hands folded in their lap. Silently. It takes a couple of minutes before the staff member hurries to the table bringing the three robot-seals we are all waiting for. I look at one of the elderly women, Matsura-san, who lights up in a big smile when she sees 'Hana-chan', one of the robot-seals. She stretches her hands out towards Hana-chan, gives the robot-seal a kiss and laughs loudly as it turns its head towards her and makes a shriek. Matsura-san turns towards another female resident and receives immediate confirmation that Hana-chan is *kawaii* (cute) before the robot-seal is pushed on to the next person at the table. There is much activity whilst the robots are circulating among the residents. Several residents actively engage with the robots, speaking to them, touching them and kissing them. Whereas some residents place the robot-seal in their lap, reacting promptly by stroking and kissing it when it closes its eyes and rests its head against the person's body or when it lifts its head, winks its eyes and calls for attention, others are sharing the robots and talking about them. Some residents call out for the robot-seals while they clap their hands in a regular rhythm. The hour passes quickly, and soon the staff members start preparing for closing the session. They ask the residents to say goodbye to the robot-seals and soon they bring the room back to what it looked like before the session started. With the seal-robots back in the closet, the TV switched on and tea served, the day carries on as usual.

Based on anthropological observations at the nursing home, this scene offers an insight into the typical use of PARO in this specific setting. While the robot is originally designed for both individual and shared use, PARO was used only as a shared object in groups of approximately ten residents at this nursing home. Primarily due to limited resources that prevented the staff members from using the robots on a daily basis as therapeutic tools to calm, motivate or stimulate residents, but also due to a wish to protect the robots from being damaged, staff members explained, residents were thus gathered to use PARO only for one hour twice a week corresponding to additional activities provided by the nursing home. In the meantime the robots were stored and kept safe in the staff room, out of the residents' sight.

While the framing of the PARO activity was not a calculated and articulated strategy by staff members to control ownership of the robots, this practice had specific unforeseen social consequences. Following Turner (1982), staff members seemed to create a space separated from ordinary daily life which shared with liminoid phenomena the feature of playfulness. In contrast to the hours spent in bed or watching television, the activity offered a space where residents could meet and interact around their common interest: PARO. As the scene above indicates, this space was in particular driven by emotions and desire, as the robots became shared objects for the residents to engage with. The residents communicated directly to and about the robots and emotional reactions, such as enthusiasm, laughter, collective joy, calling and clapping of hands, were often prompted by the responses of the robots. These emotional reactions from the residents created a situation that – according to the residents themselves – was a stark contrast to the normality of everyday life, where they rarely experienced a common basis for conversation.

According to Turner, the conditions for establishing such a communitas are particularly good when the attention is focused on a limited area or object, as for instance when on a stage (Turner 1977). Among the residents participating in the PARO activity, the robots often became the subject of such attention. By calling and moving, the robots continuously invited the residents not only to interact with them emotionally by stroking, embracing and kissing them, but also to personalize the robots with their own name, gender and personality. Several of the residents participating in the activity indicated that they believed the robots had emotions, the capacity to feel pain and pleasure, and the ability to answer questions. As one resident explained, 'Maru-chan is so cute. She likes when we pet her and play with her'. Then again, by providing feedback in the form of whining, opening their eyes and moving their bodies, the PAROs did offer the possibility to engage with them in ways that encouraged anthropomorphism, by which non-human and inanimate objects are attributed life and human characteristics (Ellen 1996). In this context, the robots demonstrated their emotional and social performance, becoming a 'magnetic pole of the sociality' in a similar way to the poet who recites poems or the singer who performs on stage (Sjørslev 2007: 21). Both receive attention from the audience, thus forming a specific sense of community among the participants. In the PARO activity, this is a community based on emotional engagement and caring. During the course of the activity, however, some residents left the social community often due to exhaustion or loss of interest. Some expressed the opinion that they had 'had enough' whereas others explained that they found playing with such a robot inappropriate behaviour for an adult. These residents would be encouraged by the staff members to leave the activity. As a consequence the PARO activity was formed as a social event for people who were continuously attentive and attracted to the robots.

Whereas the liminoid space and the nature of the robots have their own effects on the residents and their social community, the concept of circulation that structures the activity at the nursing home seems to fashion the social role of the robots. As already described, rather than being easy accessible objects, the presence of the robots is strictly limited, due to their continuously spatial and social circulation, facilitated by staff members. While the spatial circulation refers to the movement of the robots from the staff room to the common room twice a week, the social circulation takes place during the hour of activity. Thus, when the robots are used they continuously circulate among the residents who have the chance to interact with them for about five minutes before they are passed on to the next person. If the residents do not comply with the rules associated with receiving a robot – that is to send it on to the next person – the staff members will do this for them. That is, staff members explained, to be sure that each person has had an equal opportunity to interact with the robots. This context of circulation functions as a specific activity that seems to create what sociologist Georg Simmel calls 'objects of desire' (Simmel 1997). According to Simmel, objects possess value in proportion to how much they resist our desire to obtain them, thus becoming increasingly valuable and desirable when they are impossible to own. In this context it is thus the object's resistance to being owned which is the source of its desirability. Returning to the rules at the nursing home, which are set for the residents' use of the robot, they can therefore be said to constitute the mechanisms that make the robots become a source of admiration and desire. Even though these restrictions are made for reasons related to limited resources, protection of the robots and a wish to provide the residents with equal opportunities, the staff members thereby create the possibility of the robots becoming desired objects that capture the interest and attention of the residents by restricting their access to the robot seals.

To sum up, it is not only the nature of the pet-like robots but also the staging of the use of such robots via a restricted circulation system that provides the robots with the potential of becoming desirable objects that form a certain community among the residents participating in the activity at the nursing home. For example, when the robots are introduced, an emotional engagement often occurs and social relations among the residents are being constituted, illuminating the manner in which the social setting of the activity and the robots actively generate a sociality characterized by feelings of presence and community.

Conclusion

This chapter has provided an insight into several key issues around the development of social robotics in general and the use of such robots by older people in particular. Robots for older people often invoke very strong – and strongly opposing – reactions. On the one hand, robots are seen as a solution to the problems posed by demographic ageing. Robots can serve as carers and companions in situations where there are no longer sufficient financial means and human hands to perform the necessary care work. On the other hand, robots are seen as cold, rational, mechanical machines, which dehumanize care. Robotic care becomes instrumental, devoid of empathy, feeling and communication. Underlying both of these views is a technologically deterministic view of the effect of robots on the lives of older people. In such a view technological development follows its own logic and humans are relegated to finding the best way to adapt to these technological changes.

However, disciplines like Science and Technology Studies (STS) have long taken issue with technological determinism, showing time and again that there are complex and subtle processes of co-construction or mutual shaping at work, meaning that humans shape technologies, and technologies shape humans. We have shown in this chapter that the reality of the domestication and use of social robots by older people is far too complex to be captured in a simple dichotomy of deterministic viewpoints. The iRo case showed that many older people will reject a technology if they feel it positions them as old and frail. But if a suitable role, such as that of a helpful altruistic test user, can be created, they can fully domesticate a robot up to the point that they establish an emotional bond with it. Moreover, instead of robotic pets having a dissocializing effect, the PARO case showed that PARO had the potential to become an object capable of facilitating a certain social togetherness among a group of nursing home residents. These findings do not fit easily into deterministic dichotomies, but are more complex instances of what the use of robots by older people might entail.

All in all, the relations that emerged between iRo and the older Dutch test participants, or between PARO and the group of Japanese nursing home residents, are just a small sample of the potential relations that can be formed between robots and older people. It is important to realize that there is a great diversity of social robots and this diversity of designs of robots is more than matched by the diversity of older people. This makes it impossible for 'robots' to have one clear and unequivocal effect on 'older people' as both categories are grossly oversimplified in such reasoning. There is also no need to stick with such simplifications as the tools to investigate the mutual shaping between specific robots and specific older people are amply available in disciplines such as sociology, geography, anthropology, and science and technology studies. If we are truly interested in understanding relations between older people and robotics and are truly interested in shaping both policy and design regarding robotics and elder care, we would do well to trade in simple deterministic views for a more complex understanding of the way in which older people and social robots shape and give meaning to each other.

Notes

1. This clearly has roots in Marxist's analysis of nineteenth-century capitalism.
2. A more elaborate description and discussion of the methods used in this research project can be found in Neven (2010; 2011).
3. This research project is described in more detail in Leeson 2010.
4. For more information about PARO and AIST visit http://www.parorobots.com and http://paro.jp/english/index.html.
5. In the context of this chapter only a relatively brief exposé of this case study can be provided. More detailed information can be found in Neven (2010), Neven (2011) and Peine and Neven (2011).
6. By October 2012, according to the Ministry of Internal Affairs and Communications, Statistics Bureau, Japan: http://www.stat.go.jp/english/data/jinsui/2012np/index.htm.
7. It should be noted, however, that despite governmental visions of robots overcoming the challenges of aging societies in Japan, market-ready robots for older consumers are still considered to be rare (Wagner 2008: 141).

References

Berker, T., M. Hartmann, Y. Punie and K. Ward (eds). 2006. *Domestication of media and technology*. Maidenhead: Open University Press.

Dautenhahn, K. 2002. 'Design spaces and niche spaces of believable social robots', *IEEE Int. Workshop on Robot and Human Interactive Communication ROMAN 2002*, 192–97.

Ellen, R. 1996. 'The cognitive geometry of nature', in P. Descola and G. Pálsson (eds), *Nature and society, anthropological perspectives*. New York: Routledge, pp. 103–24.

Featherstone, M. and M. Hepworth. 2005. 'Images of ageing', in M. Johnson, et al. (eds), *The Cambridge handbook of age and ageing*. Cambridge: Cambridge University Press, pp. 354–62.

Gell, A. 1988. 'Technology and magic', *Anthropology Today* 4(2): 6–9.

———. 1998. *Art and agency: an anthropological theory*. Oxford: Oxford University Press.

Hegel, F. et al. 2009. 'Understanding social robots', *Advances in Computer-Human Interactions*, 169–74.

Heidegger, M. 1977. *The question concerning technology*. New York: Harper and Row.

Ihde, D. 2002. *Bodies in technology*. Minneapolis: University of Minnesota Press.

Ingold, T. 1997. 'Eight themes in the anthropology of technology', *Social Analysis* 41(1): 106–38.

Jackson, M. 2002. 'Familiar and foreign bodies: a phenomenological exploration of the human-technology interface', *The Journal of the Royal Anthropological Institute* 8(2): 333–46.

Jenike, B. and J. Traphagen. 2009. 'Transforming the cultural scripts for aging and elder care in Japan', in Jay Sokolovsky (ed.), *The cultural context of aging: worldwide perspectives*. Santa Barbara: Greenwood Publishing Group, pp. 240–58.

Leeson, C. 2010. *Mennesker Mellem Robotter. Robotter Mellem Mennesker. Om Materialitet og Socialitet i det japanske Samfund*. Copenhagen: Faculty of Social Sciences Reprocentre.

Lie, M. and K. Sørensen (eds). 1996. *Making technology our own? Domesticating technology into everyday life*. Oslo: Scandinavian University Press.

Mackenzie, D. and J. Wajcman. 1999. 'Introductory essay: the social shaping of technology', in, D. Mackenzie and J. Wajcman (eds), *The Social Shaping of Technology*. 2nd edn. Buckingham: Open University Press.

Miller, D. 2005. *Materiality*. Durham and London: Duke University Press.

Mori, M. 2012. 'The uncanny valley', trans. K. MacDorman and N. Kageki, *IEEE Robotics and Automation* 19(2): 98–100.

Neven, L. 2010. '"But obviously not for me": robots, laboratories and the defiant identity of elder test users', *Sociology of Health and Illness* 32(2): 335–47.

———. 2011. 'Representations of the old and ageing in the design of the new and emerging'. PhD dissertation. Enschede: University of Twente.

Oudshoorn, N. and T. Pinch. 2003. 'Introduction: how users and non-users matter', in N. Oudshoorn and T. Pinch (eds), *How users matter: the coconstruction of users and technologies*. Cambridge, MA: MIT Press, pp. 4–22.

Peine, A. and L. Neven. 2011. 'Social-structural lag revisited', *Gerontechnology* 10(3): 125–35.

Pfaffenberger, B. 1988. 'Fetishised objects and humanized nature: towards an anthropology of technology', *Man* 23(2): 236–52.

Pols, J. 2012. Care at a distance. *On the closeness of technology*. Amsterdam: Amsterdam University Press.

Robertson, J. 2010. 'Gendering humanoid robots: robo-sexism in Japan', *Body & Society* 16(2): 1–36.

Rowe, S. 2008. 'Modern sports: liminal ritual or liminoid leisure?', in Graham St John (ed.), *Victor Turner and contemporary cultural performance*. New York: Berghahn Books, pp. 127–48.

Sabanovic, S. 2008. *Automatic for the people: engineering cultures and imagining communities through social robotics in US and Japan*. Paper presented at AAA, San Francisco, CA.

Schodt, F.L. 2010. *Inside the robot kingdom: Japan, mechatronics, and the coming robotopia.* San Francisco: JAI2.

Shaw-Garlock, G. 2009. 'Looking forward to sociable robots', *International Journal of Social Robotics* 1(3): 249–60.

Silverstone, R., E. Hirsch and D. Morley. 1992. 'Information and communication technologies and the moral economy of the household', in R. Silverstone and E. Hirsch (eds), *Consuming technologies – media and information in domestic spaces.* London: Routledge, pp. 15–31.

Silverstone, R. and L. Haddon. 1996. 'Design and the domestication of information and communication technologies: technical change and everyday live', in R. Mansell and R. Silverstone (eds), *Communication by design – the politics of information and communication technologies.* Oxford: Oxford University Press, pp. 44–74.

Simmel, G. 1997. 'On the psychology of money', in D. Frisby and M. Featherstone (eds), *Simmel on culture. Selected writings.* London: Sage, pp. 233–43.

Sjørslev, I. 2007. 'Ritual, Performance og Socialitet. En Introduktion', in S. Sjørslev (ed.), *Scener for Samvær. Ritualer, Performance og Socialitet.* Aarhus: Aarhus Universitetsforlag, pp. 9–33.

Sparrow, R. and L. Sparrow. 2006. 'In the hands of machines? The future of aged care', *Mind Match* 16: 141–61.

Turkle, S. et al. 2006. 'Relational artifacts with children and elders: the complexities of cybercompanionship', *Connection Science* 18(4): 347–61.

Turner, V. 1969. 'Liminality and communitas', in V. Turner. *The ritual process: structure and anti-structure.* Chicago: Andine Pub. Co, pp. 94–130.

———. 1977. 'Variations on a theme of liminality', in S. Moore and B. Myerhoff (eds), *Secular ritual.* Amsterdam: Van Gorcum, pp. 36–52.

———. 1982. 'Liminal to liminoid, in play, flow, ritual: an essay in comparative symbology', in V. Turner. *From ritual to theatre: the human seriousness of play.* New York: Performing Arts Journal Publications, pp. 123–64.

Wada, K. et al. 2008. 'Robot therapy for elders affected by dementia. Using personal robots for pleasure and relaxation', *Medicine and Biology Magazine* 27(4): 53–60.

Wagner, C. 2008. '"Silver robots" and "robotic nurses"? Japan's robot culture and elderly care', in A. Schad-Seifert and S. Shimada (eds), *Demographic change in Japan and the EU: comparative perspectives.* Düsseldorf: Düsseldorf University Press, pp. 131–54.

PART TWO
Health and Wellbeing

IN THE SECOND SECTION OF this volume, the focus switches towards technologies for healthy living and wellbeing. Even though it is our aim to avoid the pitfalls of deterministic and dependency based models of ageing, equally we do not wish to depict an idyllic picture of ageing that fails to acknowledge many of the serious challenges of the later life course. Growing old, for many, is often associated with trajectories of diminished mobility, health related problems, sensory and cognitive degradation, and social contraction as people relocate and friends pass away. Technology is, most certainly, not the answer to all problems and cannot always be the solution. But it can help at times, especially if carefully designed and implemented. This is what we want to explore with the chapters in this section.

The first selection by Joseph Wherton and colleagues discusses ways in which technology can support people living through loneliness and isolation and the difficulties of maintaining social connectedness in older age. It provides us with an overview of several projects in this area and with a section on co-design methods. In fact, social media are mostly designed for younger people, and although we discussed in the previous section the fact that many older people are active users of these systems, the chapter highlights some of the cultural, physical (e.g. sensory impairment) and practical barriers (e.g. hospitalization) that need to be taken into account when thinking of how best to design these technologies for this user group.

The following two chapters continue along the same theme, the first by exploring challenges in designing technology enabled programmes to support behavioural change in chronic diseases management, and the other by discussing one of the most important and yet challenging user group for whom to design technology: people with dementia.

John Dinsmore introduces us to the complex world of behavioural change research and some of its challenges when mixing with developing technologies. He proposes a model based on two principles: firstly, technologies have to be developed by keeping the patient at the centre, and, secondly, devices have to be designed so that they enhance social interaction and can be incorporated into daily life. The chapter focuses on the role of education and information provision for self-management through video and multimedia. It does so by providing us with an overview on a project where numerous short films for the self-management of Chronic Obstructive Pulmonary Disease (COPD) were developed following the principles above.

But what happens when the population being catered for are living with cognitive impairment? Arlene Astell takes us through the difficult and much needed topic of designing and implementing technologies for people with dementia and for their caregivers. She does so by providing a brief overview of the different types of dementia and the range of impairments that have to be taken into account when designing for this population. The chapter includes the discussion of a project that looked at the everyday priorities of people with dementia and aimed at creating a new technology specifically for them (CIRCA). It also includes a case study of one person trying to learn using new technologies (Brian's blog) in recognition of the fact that technology is not a panacea for all problems of people with dementia, but that it could help in certain aspects if designed in appropriate ways.

The last two chapters of this section discuss some well-established technologies in this field: telemedicine and telecare. The first by Delaney and Somerville is an overview discussion of some of the reasons behind the difficulties that telehealth has encountered (and still encounters) in implementation. The authors discuss the problem of the gap between existing technology pilot projects and wide application from the perspective of three key stakeholders: the industry (providers of technologies), clinical community (gatekeepers of technologies, and providers of care) and health systems (implementing technologies, and providers of service). The first focuses on care model barriers, whereby a disconnection is identified between different suppliers of care to older people which are not coordinated centrally. The second one focuses on evidence based barriers and the lack of proof that these technologies enable better care and use of resources. When discussing the third, the authors suggest the Normalization Process Theory (NPT) as a possible way out of this gridlock for the benefit of patients.

In the final chapter of this section, López and Sánchez-Criado take us on a journey into the homes of older adults during the installation of telecare devices. Ethnographically and empirically informed, they do so by exploring the complex negotiations between the person installing and the person receiving this technology-based service. The chapter raises important questions such as: What counts as care? Who is the user of the service? Who wants the service? What are the identity compromises that people have to make when installing a 'frailty' device in a 'public' place in their home? What counts as a care contact and how to establish it? The authors highlight the ambiguity of these issues by rendering visible the 'invisible work to make technology work'. They conclude by suggesting that, considering all the above, we should probably move away from designing technologies based on 'plug-and-play' models and instead embrace one that acknowledges these 'frictions' and supports hands-on-tech care.

5. DESIGNING TECHNOLOGIES FOR SOCIAL CONNECTION WITH OLDER PEOPLE

Joseph Wherton, Paul Sugarhood, Rob Procter and Trisha Greenhalgh

SOCIAL PARTICIPATION AND INTEGRATION IS important for mental and physical wellbeing. However, for many older people, declining health, reduced mobility, and separation from family members and friends can make it difficult to maintain an active social life. A large number of technological interventions have been developed to prevent social isolation and alleviate loneliness. Information and communication technologies (ICTs) have the potential to maintain social inclusion by supporting social interaction. However, these are generally designed for younger users, and may not always meet the needs and wishes of older people with regard to social connection.

This chapter focuses on the development of ICTs to help older people remain socially connected. Our starting point is that the design of such interventions must be grounded in an understanding of how older people manage their social relationships and deal with loneliness to ensure that any technologies developed are easy to use and fit for purpose. In turn, this can only be achieved if older people are involved in the design process. 'Co-design' refers to a range of methods and tools to enable users to engage fully in the design process and so assist IT professionals and other stakeholders to understand users' everyday practices, needs and experiences (Hartswood et al. 2008).

The first section looks at the range of interventions to prevent and alleviate loneliness in older adults. The second section focuses on the involvement of older people in the design of ICTs to support social connection. The final section explores the deployment of technology prototypes in real social contexts and calls for providers of technologies and services for older people to pay more attention to 'co-deployment', supporting users in exploring, learning and adapting technologies and services 'in-use'.

Preventing and Alleviating Loneliness through ICTs

Loneliness and health

The terms 'social isolation' and 'loneliness' have often been used inter-changeably but are actually distinct concepts. Social isolation is a term related to social network size, frequency of contact and level of support. Loneliness, on the other hand, refers to the negative subjective experience related to a perceived lack of social contact or companionship than that desired, and is therefore a subjective state. Some people may be isolated but not feel lonely, some may feel isolated and lonely, and some may have frequent social contact but still feel lonely.

The concept of loneliness has also been divided further. Weiss (1973) made a distinction between 'social loneliness' related to a lack of social contacts or integration (e.g. friends, neighbours) and 'emotional loneli-ness' resulting from the absence of a close emotional attachment (e.g. spouse, close friend). Social loneliness may occur, for example, following relocation or restricted mobility due to illness, whereas emotional loneli-ness could arise from loss of a partner relationship through divorce or widowhood. Distinctions have also been made on the basis of duration, frequency and severity of loneliness. Young (1982) distinguished between 'transient' (brief and occasional), 'situational' (resulting from a specific change or event) and 'chronic' (stable, long-term) loneliness.

Research suggests that between 5 and 16 per cent of older people often or always experience loneliness (Pinquart and Sorensen 2001; Victor et al. 2002). However, these figures may be an under-estimate because of under-reporting (due to the negative connotations of being lonely). A number of self-report scales to measure the type and severity of loneliness have avoided explicit reference to loneliness. The UCLA Loneliness Scale, for example, consists of twenty items (e.g. 'How often do you feel you lack companionship?', 'How often do you feel there is no one you can turn to?'). In a revised version of the scale, ten of the items were reversed to reduce the negative wording (Russell et al. 1980). Similarly, the De Jong Gierveld Loneliness Scale includes positive and negative items related to the 'social' loneliness dimension (e.g. 'There are plenty of people I can rely on when I have problems') and 'emotional' loneliness dimension (e.g. 'I sense a gen-eral feeling of emptiness') (De Jong Gieveld et al. 2006).

Aside from age, other risk factors for loneliness include living alone, widowhood, poor physical and mental health, cognitive impairment, income and education (Victor, Bowling and Bond 2002; Victor et al. 2005). Loneliness may also be exacerbated by social or environmental factors, such as design of urban areas, changes to service infrastructure (e.g.

transport, closure of post offices), crime and population change (Phillipson 2007; Scharf and De Jong Gierveld 2008).

Links between loneliness and health are well documented. Loneliness is closely related to mental health problems including depression (Golden et al. 2009; Cacioppo et al. 2006), anxiety (Fees et al. 1999) and cognitive decline (Tilvis et al. 2004; Wilson et al. 2007); and with physical health conditions such as lung disease (Penninx et al. 1999), high blood pressure (Hawkley et al. 2006; Steptoe et al. 2004), poor sleep (Cacioppo et al. 2002; McHugh and Lawlor 2012), obesity (Lauder et al. 2006) and arthritis (Penninx et al. 1999).

Although associations are well documented, the chain of causation between loneliness and health remains speculative. Decline in mental and physical health has often been considered as a cause as well as a consequence of loneliness. For example, restricted physical mobility could reduce engagement in social activities, which could further increase depression, alter sleep or disrupt appetite, leading to further decline in health and subsequent increase in isolation (Tijhuis et al. 1999). Various mediating factors might also come into play, such as personality, stress and social support networks (Hawkley and Cacioppo 2003; Schnittger et al. 2012; McHugh and Lawlor 2012).

Reducing loneliness through ICTs

A number of interventions have been developed to help older people establish and maintain satisfying interpersonal relationships, including group meetings or activities (e.g. bereavement support, carer support, exercise and gardening projects) and befriending schemes, in which a volunteer would routinely visit those who are isolated or homebound. A systematic literature review of intervention studies conducted between 1970 and 2002 concluded that their effectiveness remained unclear (Cattan et al. 2005). In that review, group interventions with an educational component, such as training workshops on health, exercise and caregiving, showed most potential for alleviating social isolation and loneliness in older people. They found that the involvement of the target groups in planning and developing these activities facilitated the effectiveness of the interventions. A review by Dickens et al. (2011) also indicated that social and support activities in a group format appeared more effective than one-to-one interventions, particularly when they involved active input from participants (e.g. peer support, sharing experiences), rather than simply being recipients of the training and education.

ICTs have long been considered as potential tools for alleviating loneliness. Telephone befriending services, in which the older person receives one-to-one or teleconference calls at scheduled times for a chat, have been widely used (Hartke et al. 2003; Cattan et al. 2011). Older users have reported positive outcomes from these services, which provide them with a 'sense of belonging', a feeling that somebody cared about them, and self-confidence to become more physically and socially active (Cattan et al. 2011). One reason for the success of these schemes is that the telephone is a familiar technology. It is immersed in cultural understanding and routine and does not require time to learn how to use it (Monk and Reed 2007). However, there are some possible limitations, most notably the need to be available to receive the call, and the absence of face-to-face and non-verbal communication (Heller et al. 1991; Cattan et al. 2011; McHugh et al. 2012).

Internet and mobile devices could provide further scope and flexibility in communication. However, there are a number of barriers to their use by older people. Recent reports show that most people over 65 are not regular computer users. In the UK, the Oxford Internet Survey for 2011 found that only 25–35 per cent of people over 65 used the internet (Dutton and Blank 2011). The UK Office for National Statistics also reported that only 30 per cent of adults aged 75 years and over had ever used the internet (Office for National Statistics 2012). Although mobile phone ownership has grown rapidly among older adults, from 47 per cent in 2005 to 68 per cent in 2012, use of smart phones still remains low. In 2012, only 3 per cent of people over 65 used a smart phone, compared to 66 per cent of those aged 16 to 24, and 60 per cent of those aged 25 to 34 (Ofcom 2012).

With this in mind, a number of studies have evaluated the effect of providing older people with computer training and internet access (Cody et al. 1999; Fokemma and Knipscheer 2007; Mellor et al. 2008; Shapira et al. 2007; Slegers et al. 2008; White et al. 1999; White et al. 2002; Woodward et al. 2011). These projects have typically used a randomized controlled trial design with pre- and post-measures of loneliness, and findings have been mixed. Shapira et al. (2007) provided twenty-two nursing home and day care centre attendees with computers and training (e.g. in email and online forums). Between the group training sessions, participants were encouraged to use a communal computer room in their own time. After fifteen weeks, participants showed a significant decrease in scores on the UCLA Loneliness Scale, compared to controls. Fokemma and Knipscheer (2007) provided fifteen home-bound elders with one-to-one tuition and a computer with internet connection for three years. They observed a significant reduction in 'emotional' loneliness measured using the De Jong-Gierveld Loneliness Scale. The intervention enabled participants to stay in touch with social contacts despite poor health, and increased self-confidence in general, leading to more social activities outside the home.

These studies, however, are open to confounding. In particular, improvements in loneliness may be due to one-to-one and group training sessions rather than the ICT intervention itself. White et al. (1999) found that immediately following a computer training period, the intervention group showed a significant decrease in loneliness, but after five months this significant effect had disappeared. Slegers et al. (2008) isolated this effect by providing a comparison group with training, but no computer or internet access. They found no significant difference with regard to mood, quality of life or loneliness between the intervention or comparison groups.

Many trials of ICTs in loneliness had high withdrawal rates (13 per cent to 60 per cent). Reasons included illness, hospitalization, limited time, unwillingness to learn, difficulty using the technology and lack of perceived need for the technology (Cody et al. 1999; Fokemma and Knipscheer 2007; Mellor et al. 2008; Shapira et al. 2007; Slegers et al. 2008; White et al. 1999). Many potential participants were excluded from the studies for practical reasons, such as sensory, physical and cognitive impairment, as well as insufficient space in the home for the technology.

The inconclusive evidence emerging from these studies, and the barriers to taking part, suggest a need for new ICT solutions. One study conducted twenty years ago sought to modify existing technology. Czaja et al (1993) redesigned a 'POMS' (Plain Old Message System) specifically to encourage social interaction among older people with no experience with computers. The technology consisted of a 'simplified' communication system with a text editor, display, keyboard, modem and printer. The design was specialized for message communication. It was always 'on', and there were no log-on procedures, disk operations or file access. To begin, the user pressed any key. The screen would then display a single line of text with the word 'To?' The user typed the name of another participant, and the system dialled automatically. The user then pressed a key boldly labelled 'Return' on the keyboard. They could then write the message. When the message was completed, the user would press a boldly labelled 'Send' key. When the message arrived it was printed automatically. The system was placed in the homes of thirty-six women aged 55 to 95 who had minimal or no prior experience with computers. It was reported that they used the system with little difficulty, enjoyed using it and felt that it facilitated social interaction and a chance to meet new people. However, use fell significantly over the course of the trial, signifying that the early positive findings were partly due to novelty effect. Other reasons for disengagement included being too busy, limited functionality and boredom.

In 2009, the EU Ambient Assisted Living (AAL) Joint Programme invested 60.9 million euros into twenty-three different projects that focused specifically on developing 'ICT based solutions for advancement of social interaction of elderly'. Various approaches were taken, including virtual community networks accessible through computers or televisions (e.g. 'Co-LIVING' and 'ELDER-SPACES'), 3-D virtual environments where the older user's 'avatar' can meet with other users' avatars (e.g. '3rD-Life'), computer games (e.g. 'SILVERGAME') and robotic devices that support webcam communication though mounted screens (e.g. 'ExCITE') (www. aal-europe.eu/call-2/).

Notwithstanding these and other rapid technological advancements in internet-based, mobile and robotic systems, it is important that design is driven by an understanding of older users' daily lives and needs. As was demonstrated in the early work by Czaja et al. (1993), design must go beyond generic usability features and initial attitudes towards the technology. For prolonged use, it must fit around users' daily lives and meet their social needs. The cultural gap between young designers and older adults is particularly wide when developing ICTs intended to facilitate social interaction. Gerontology literature has shown various changes in social behaviours, roles and relationships over the life course (Rook 1987; Carstensen et al. 2003; Schwarz et al. 2005). This highlights the need to include older people in the design process to ensure that the technology meets their needs and wishes.

Designing with Older Users

'Co-design' is a participatory design approach that brings designers and users together to develop new technologies and services. It aims to ensure that design is grounded in the lived experience of users and that users are fully engaged in the design process (Hartswood et al. 2008). This section looks at some of the methods used to understand the lived experience of older users, and methods of engaging them in the design of ICT to enhance social interaction.

Exploring Social Connection 'in the Wild'

Ethnographic research techniques (e.g. visiting people in their homes, semi-structured and narrative interviews, observations and field notes) can be employed to learn how older people approach their relationships and how they deal with loneliness and isolation. However, pursuing ethnographic research within domestic and private settings raises practical and ethical challenges. 'Cultural probe' methods offer a relatively unobtrusive way of exploring social and domestic routines (Wherton et al. 2012). Cultural probes are open-ended and evocative activities for participants to pursue in their own time to help narrate and depict their lives to researchers and technology designers. They employ everyday artefacts, such as digital cameras, audio-recorders, diaries and notebooks to allow participants to record and capture everyday activities to help gain insight into how technology might be embedded within people's lives.

The cultural probe method supports ethnographic data collection by promoting dialogue between researcher and participant, allowing participants to reflect on their lives and relationships, and recall events and subjective experiences (Boehner et al. 2007; Graham et al. 2007; Graham and Rouncefield 2008; Wherton et al. 2012). Visual materials also offer a means for 'cognitive offloading', helping to communicate complex aspects of daily living, such as social network structures and relevant places, objects and routines that promote positive social and mental wellbeing. This helps researchers to gain insight into the lived experience of older people, their social relationships and how they deal with loneliness, and to consider how ICTs should be designed to address real needs.

Cultural probes were initially developed by Gaver et al. (1999), who used a range of materials for participants to record their daily lives in order to inspire creative responses among a design team. The cultural probe packages included local and world maps, postcards, a disposable camera, a photo album and a diary. These were given to participants to use and return after a period of time. For example, cameras included suggestions for photographs written on the back (e.g. 'what you will wear today', 'something desirable' and 'something boring'). The materials were left with the older participants to return fragmentary data over time. Responses were used in an open-ended way to inspire design ideas.

This approach has subsequently been used in different ways with different affordances in order to gather information about people's social relationships and routines. The probe tools were used in combination with other ethnographic methods (e.g. interviews, observations and 'home tours') to help establish dialogue between researcher and participant and facilitate qualitative data collection. Riche and Mackay (2010) used cultural probes to understand the supportive role of social networks and the way in which technology could help the elderly stay in touch with family, friends and neighbours. Findings revealed themes to be considered in the design of ICT, including 'PeerCare', in which the role of reciprocal support behaviour (e.g. check-up calls and exchanging house keys for emergencies) played an important part in their social relationships; 'Awareness, rhythms and routines', in which daily routines and behaviour patterns played an important part of helping elders remain aware of each other (e.g. if neighbours had not left the house, if curtains were drawn), as well as knowing each other's routines (e.g. knowing when to contact each other and when to expect a call or visit); and privacy, in which there was a trade-off between a desire to maintain their privacy but also the need to disclose, such as providing sensitive information (e.g. about their health) in exchange for peace of mind.

Similarly, Pedell et al. (2010) focused on the role of domestic technologies in addressing social isolation. Participants were asked to take at least one photograph per day and write what it meant to them with regard to social interaction. The diary included cued phrases (e.g. 'Today I feel lonely because...' or 'Every day I...') to prompt entries. These probes helped to capture personal and subjective events in situ and foreground these for the interview. For example, a widow with no family relations commented that other members 'can bore you silly with their tales about children and grandchildren'. Photos and diary entries also highlighted how the use of artefacts within the home supported reminiscence and triggered memories of meaningful past relationships.

The cultural probe method was used as part of the ATHENE (Assistive Technologies for Health Living in Elders: Needs Assessment by Ethnography) project, which explored the healthcare and social care needs of older people with different health conditions, ethnic backgrounds and family settings (Greenhalgh et al. 2013). A range of materials, including a digital camera, diary, lists (e.g. likes, dislikes, concerns), body outline (to draw/write areas of pain, discomfort or decline), and 'relationship maps' (to indicate important people, places and objects) were given to participants for one week between home visit interviews. The visual representations helped the researchers follow discussions regarding social support networks and how they related to participants' health and social wellbeing. One participant, for example, recorded various locations for face-to-face interaction. This included visits to the local shop, even if she did not need to buy anything. She also included the 'front door' as an important place to greet and chat with people passing by. A major fear she had was moving into sheltered accommodation, where she would not have her own front door or access to local shops as places for opportunistic social interaction (Wherton et al. 2012).

Collectively, these studies highlight the fact that older users may not be as 'homebound' as designers typically assume, and that even those with multiple impairments value opportunistic and flexible interactions outside the home. Relationships often involve a degree of reciprocity (e.g. checking-in on each other), common ground (shared knowledge or experience) and insight into each other's routine behaviours (e.g. knowing when to call, when to expect a call). However, they also raise concerns around privacy and intrusion (not wanting to intrude, but also not being disrupted by others). Understanding the social routine and relationships of older people can inform the design of ICTs to support social interaction, so that they meet users' needs and fit within existing settings and behaviours.

Including Older People in Design

Focus groups and workshops are an effective way of directly engaging older people in the design of ICT, but they pose practical challenges such as fatigue and boredom, as well challenges for researchers to keep a focus on the design topic (Lindsay et al. 2012). Users may also lack the technical knowledge or confidence to offer design input or express their opinions (Eisma et al. 2004).

A number of techniques have been developed to support involvement of older people in the co-design process. Visual materials and hands-on activities may help trigger ideas and focus attention on essential parts of the design. Scenarios and storyboards can help to communicate how a novel technology might be used and cue general discussion about the idea. Storyboards can depict (in cartoon-strip format) a narrative of the technology being used. The story is presented in a series of frames to include the character(s)/setting, their problem, the solution, and the consequences of using it. Once the facilitator has presented the storyboard, participants are invited to comment on the scenario. This approach is not intended for detailed evaluation of technical features and user interface designs, but can promote a general discussion about how the technology might fit (or not) within daily lives, and raise important issues or concerns related to social connection, such as privacy and security, social obligation, fitting social interactions into daily routines and need for common ground between users (Wherton and Prendergast 2009). Newell et al. (2006) suggested the use of live 'interactive theatre' with professional actors as a means of communicating user scenarios. Short five-minute plays were scripted to enact ways in which users might behave in the context of novel applications. The use of humour and dramatic tensions were found to be enjoyable and engaging for older adults and designers, facilitating creative discussions about the technology.

Sketching and cards prompts may elicit discussion and talk through design ideas with other members of the group (Beck et al. 2008; Rice and Carmichael 2011; Rice et al. 2012). For example, Rice and Carmichael (2011) sought to elicit ideas of what would be required to design a 'social TV' (social interactive applications through digital television) for older people. Participants were first presented with prompt cards representing each interactive step to initiate a call through the TV, and asked to write or sketch design ideas for each step. This helped participants externalize design ideas and share them with the group. For example, they raised concerns about privacy and intrusiveness, particularly with regard to video calls. They proposed familiar metaphors for icons that represent availability to talk, and options to hold a video call so that they could prepare themselves before talking to the other person. Following this activity, participants were then given cardboard cut-outs of graphical components that could be included on the user interface of the call applications. They were asked to select and re-assemble the interface components themselves. This triggered ideas about how to simplify the interface design, organize tools (e.g. address book), eliminate redundancies in the design and include more meaningful icons. The versatility of the cardboard cut-outs also meant that individuals could revert back to change or swap them over at any stage during discussions.

When preparing workshop structure and materials, it is important to consider a wide range of age-related impairments and health problems, including loss of vision, hearing, memory and physical mobility. Furthermore, the need to create a friendly atmosphere, in which participants feel free to mutually inspire each other through collaboration, should not be overlooked (Lindley 2012).

User involvement is required throughout the design of a technology prototype. At successive design iterations, users can request more specific and detailed modification. This helps to achieve a balance between maintaining simplicity and adding functionality (Dewsbury et al. 2007).

Pilot Studies in the Home

Garattini et al. (2012) explored the use of 'Building Bridges', a prototype communication device designed to encourage social interaction among older people at risk of loneliness. The device was inspired by the wide use of telephone befriending schemes and primarily intended to support interaction between strangers. With the involvement of potential users, the design aimed to help overcome intrusion, privacy and need for common ground (Wherton and Prendergast 2009; Prendergast, Somerville and Wherton 2012). The device consisted of a 12-inch touch screen with phone handset and speakers. The software used VoIP (Voice over Internet Protocol) with a user interface to allow older users to access four features. The main feature was 'Broadcast and Chat', in which users could listen/watch regular audio/video broadcasts (e.g. news, documentaries, health lectures and music) at scheduled times throughout the day and join a 'group chat' afterwards by lifting the phone handset. During the group chat, the screen displayed icons and first names to indicate who had entered/left the conference call. Hence, the broadcast was designed to create opportunities to meet new people and offer some common ground (topic of the broadcast) to facilitate the conversations. Additionally, participants could initiate one-to-one or group calls, send one-to-one or group messages, and enter an audio chat room that could be entered at any time during the day or night.

The device was deployed in the home of nineteen older adults for ten weeks. Participants could talk during post-broadcasts chats, or communicate at any point using the call, messaging and chat room features. If they did not wish to be contacted, they could switch their device off, and their icon status would indicate that they were unavailable.

Home visit interviews and logging of usage (feature, time, frequency and duration) provided insight into how the device was used over the course of the pilot. Although frequency of calls dropped over time, the duration of conversations increased. The logs also revealed aspects of the solution that were most effective in facilitating interaction. For example, educational broadcasts, particularly those about managing health (e.g. 'helping your memory' and 'coping with falls'), led to more frequent and longer post-broadcast chats than other broadcast genres, such as news programmes, documentaries (e.g. history) and entertainment (e.g. music and comedy). However, participants varied in their use of the system. In particular, those who scored high for 'social' loneliness, according to the De Jong Loneliness Scale, became lead users and advocates of the platform, attempting to focus social interaction and encourage usage among other members. However, those who scored high for 'emotional' loneliness were generally more ambivalent.

The opportunistic nature of the broadcasts and post-broadcast chats helped to overcome some of the concerns of intrusion and a need for common ground. One woman commented that she was 'too shy to make a call and so would talk to people after the broadcasts'. One man likened it to the 'lamp post on the corner of the street and three of four [people] chatting'.

Over time, the pilot revealed changes to system requirements. Concerns about intrusion and privacy led to requests to remove video call functionality within the device. However, as users became familiar with each other, they wanted to share information (e.g. interests, where they lived) as well as the ability to see each other via a webcam. Many felt that they had reached a limit, that they could develop a friendship through the device and wanted to meet each other face-to-face. Some perceived this to be a limitation, while others adapted their use of the device to meet this need, using the messaging feature to set up meetings with those they found things in common with (e.g. went to the same school or similar profession) and sent out group messages to arrange scheduled events (e.g. walk in the park). It therefore became a tool to prompt social interaction outdoors, as opposed to merely communicating from home.

Lindley (2012) deployed a novel communication device across three households within a family network. The case study was part of a wider field trial with a prototype device, 'Wayve'. The prototype consisted of a touch screen display that allowed sending and receiving of written messages. Messages could be created through handwriting or drawing with coloured pen-strokes, entering text using an onscreen keyboard, or by taking photos using a camera in the top right corner. The device was designed to allow messages to be quickly scribbled and sent from home. The case study focused on an extended family of a couple, their two sons and two grandchildren. Home visit interviews and remote logging of system usage was carried out for a period of eighty-nine days.

The authors found that the grandparents spent more time and energy in sending messages to other family members. The flexibility of the device allowed them to invest effort into their communication to achieve the degree of personalization that they desired (e.g. digital photos of meal ingredients and cooking, trips out during the day). At the same time, the asynchronous nature of the communication made it easier for the grandparents to work around the busy schedule of one son and the unusual working patterns of the other. Sharing photos and allowing people to comment upon mundane aspects of daily life created a sense of closeness, which could not be achieved through telephone or mobile phone communication. The grandparents valued the device for a number of other reasons beyond sharing everyday activities. They used 'social touch' messages (e.g. 'night all') as a way of creating a sense of social presence or awareness across households. The flexibility of the device allowed them to engage with teenage grandchildren quite differently. Sending 'silly pictures' and playing word games (e.g. hangman) appeared to be the most effective way to establish direct contact with them. Importantly, the Wayve device did not replace other communication practices, such as telephone or face-to-face contact. In fact, it prompted and helped to co-ordinate these forms of communication. The grandfather took ownership of the device, and became responsible for creating and sending messages. The grandmother had a supportive and coordinating role, viewing the images and using the device to establish when the sons were available to talk on the phone.

These pilot studies illustrate the need to observe how technologies are used in real contexts to inform the design. In both cases, the device became as much of a prompt or facilitator to other forms of contact (e.g. telephone, face-to-face, events) as a mode of social interaction. This highlights the fact that technologies cannot be viewed in isolation, but must be considered within the broader context of existing social routines and practices and the way in which technologies can support them. These devices, for example, could be embedded within the volunteer befriending schemes previously discussed, rather than presented as an alternative solution to loneliness.

Observing variations in levels of engagement and the use of specific design features highlights areas for further development. For example, with the 'Building Bridges' device, educational broadcasts appeared most effective in facilitating conversation between strangers. This suggests that informative or educational content, which is perceived as beneficial in itself, acts as an effective channel for encouraging social interaction.

These pilots revealed different needs and expectations among users with regard to social interaction, reflecting individual differences in needs, expectations, social roles and communication styles. This presents a challenge for designing ICTs for social connection, as the system is made up of the user, the technology and numerous other users whose profiles are unknown at the time of design or installation. Insights into how older people adapt their use of technologies in real social contexts, to better suit their needs, is an important part of the design process.

Conclusion

The ageing of the population in many countries is fuelling interest in ICTs to support independence and delivery of health and social services to the home. With advances in internet and mobile technologies, there has also been growing interest in supporting social connectivity and alleviating loneliness. Older people experience loneliness in diverse and complex ways, which are, in turn, the product of a range of factors. If ICT-based interventions are to address loneliness, then their design must be informed by an understanding of older users' roles and relationships across different social contexts. In order to achieve this, older people need to be directly involved in their design and development.

There is a growing research literature showing how older people can be involved in co-design. Different elicitation methods can provide insight into older people's social routines and relationships, and engage them in design. The literature highlights a diverse set of requirements, including reciprocity (being able to offer help as well as receive it), education, reminiscence, common ground, opportunistic interaction, concerns of disrupting others or becoming a burden, maintaining a sense of privacy and fitting social activities around daily routines. The social importance of mundane, everyday tasks (e.g. trip to local shop) must also be considered when developing ICT-based interventions as this could impact on existing social encounters. Understanding how users feel constrained by technologies, or exploit flexibility within them, provides valuable insights into how solutions can be improved to better support social interaction. Through co-design workshops, older people can directly inform how these issues are addressed and, for example, help maintain a balance between simplicity and building in sufficient functionality for meaningful social interactions.

However, we must be careful not to assume that co-design workshops alone hold the key to understanding older people's needs and that engagement can be concluded at this point. Studies emphasize how people continue to adapt – and adapt to – technological innovations over time (Williams et al. 2005). Users respond differently to new technologies and utilize them in different ways that may not have been considered at the design stage. The challenge, then, is to devise ways to progress from co-design with older people to co-deployment: the mutual shaping of technologies 'in-use'. Particularly for technological interventions intended to enhance social interaction, it should not be too difficult for providers of technology and services to older people to use these same technologies to put in place mechanisms to continue supporting older people as they seek to explore what they are capable of, learn how to use them effectively and adapt them to meet their specific needs. The ATHENE project has revealed how older people and their formal and informal carers (e.g. family, friends, neighbours) take the initiative in customizing technologies and adapting routines to fill the gap between the limitations of a priori design and the lived realities of ageing in place (Procter et al. 2014). These findings highlight the fact that older people, their carers, service providers and technology designers must be able to work together to shape technologies and services over time. Therefore, in order to develop social connection technologies that fit the lives of older users, and address the complex problem of loneliness, it is important that designers have the capacity to track the use of such technologies and feed these insights back into the design.

References

Beck, E., M. Obrist, R. Bernhaupt and M. Tscheligi. 2008. 'Instant card technique: how and why to apply in user-centered design', in J. Simonson, T. Robertson and D. Hakken (eds), *Proceedings of the Participatory Design Conference 2008*. New York: Association for Computing Machinery, pp. 162–65.

Boehner K., J. Vertesi, P. Sengers and P. Dourish. 2007. 'How HCI interprets the probes', in *Proceedings of CHI'07: 28 April – 3 May 2007*. San Jose, CA, pp. 1077–86.

Cacioppo, J.T., L.C. Hawkley, E. Crawford, J.M. Ernst, M.H. Burleson, R.B. Kowalewski and G.G. Berntson. 2002. 'Loneliness and health: potential mechanisms', *Psychosomatic Medicine* 64: 407–17.

Cacioppo, J.T., M.E. Hughes, L.J. Waite, L.C. Hawkley and T. Thisted. 2006. 'Loneliness as a specific risk factor for depressive symptoms in older adults: cross-sectional and longitudinal analyses', *Psychology and Aging* 21: 140–51.

Carstensen, L.L., H.H. Fung and S.T. Charles. 2003. 'Socioemotional selectivity theory and the regulation of emotion in the second half of life', *Motivation and Emotion* 27(2): 103–23.

Cattan, M., M. White, J. Bond and A. Learmouth. 2005. 'Preventing social isolation and loneliness among older people: a systematic review of health promotion interventions', *Ageing and Society* 25: 41–67.

Cattan M., N. Kime, A.M. Bagnall. 2011. 'The use of telephone befriending in low level support for socially isolated older people – an evaluation', *Health and Social Care in the Community* 19(2): 198–206.

Cody, M., D. Dunn, S. Hoppin and P. Wendt. 1999. 'Silver surfers: training and evaluating internet use among older adult learners', *Communication Education* 48(4): 269–86.

Czaja, S.J., J.H. Guerrier, S.N. Nair and T.K. Landauer. 1993. 'Computer communication as an aid to independence for older adults', *Behaviour and Information Technology* 12(4): 197–207.

De Jong Gierveld, J. and T. Van Tilburg. 2006. 'A 6-item scale for overall, emotional and social loneliness: confirmatory tests on survey data', *Research on Aging* 28(5): 582–98.

Dewsbury, G., M. Rouncefield, I. Sommerville, O. Victor and P. Bagnall. 2007. 'Designing technology with older people', *Universal Access in the Information Society* 6: 207–17.

Dickens, A.P., S.H. Richards, C.J. Greaves and J.L. Campbell. 2011. 'Interventions targetting social isolation in older people: a systematic review', *BMC Public Health* 11: 647.

Dutton, W.H. and G. Blank. 2011. *Next generation users: the internet in Britain.* Oxford Internet Survey. Oxford: Oxford Internet Institute, University of Oxford.

Eisma R., A. Dickinson, J. Goodman, A. Syme, L. Tiwari and A. Newell. 2004. 'Early user involvement in the development of information technology-related products for older people', *Universal Access in the Information Society* 3(2): 131–40.

Fees, B.S., P. Martin and L.W. Poon. 1999. 'A model of loneliness in older adults', *Journal of Gerontology: Psychological Sciences* 54(B): 231–39.

Fokkema, T. and K. Knipscheer. 2007. 'Escape loneliness by going digital: a quantitative and qualitative evaluation of a Dutch experiment in using ECT to overcome loneliness among older adults', *Aging & Mental Health* 11(5): 496–504.

Garattini, C., J. Wherton and D. Prendergast. 2012. 'Linking the lonely: an exploration of a communication technology designed to support social interaction among older adults', *Universal Access in the Information Society* 11(2): 211–22.

Gaver, W., A. Dunne and E. Pacenti. 1999. 'Design: cultural probes', *Interactions* 6: 21–29.

Golden, J., R.M. Conroy, I. Bruce, A. Denihan, E. Greene, M. Kirby and B.A. Lawlor. 2009. 'Loneliness, social support networks, mood and wellbeing in community-dwelling elderly', *International Journal of Geriatric Psychiatry* 24: 694–700.

Graham, C., M. Roucefield, M. Gibbs, F. Vetere and C. Cheverst. 2007. 'How probes work', in *Proceedings of OZCHI 2007*, Adelaide, Australia, pp. 29–37.

Graham, C. and M. Rouncefield. 2008. 'Probes and participation', in *Proceedings of Participatory Design Conference*, Bloomington, IN.

Greenhalgh, T., J. Wherton, P. Sugarhood, S. Hinder, R. Procter and R. Stones. 2013. 'What matters to older people with assisted living needs? A phenomenological analysis of the use and non-use of telehealth and telecare', *Social Science and Medicine* 93: 84–94.

Hartke, R.J. and R.B. King. 2003. 'Telephone group intervention for older stroke caregivers', *Topics in Stroke Rehabilitation* 9(4): 65–81.

Hartswood, M., R. Procter, M. Rouncefield, R. Slack and A. Voss. 2008. 'Co-realisation: evolving IT artefacts by design', in M. Ackerman, T. Erickson, C. Halverson and W. Kellogg (eds), *Resources, co-evolution and artefacts*. Berlin: Springer, pp. 59–94.

Hawkley, L.C. and J.T. Cacioppo. 2003. 'Loneliness and pathways to disease', *Brain, Behaviour and Immunity* 17: 98–105.

Hawkley, L.C., C.M. Masi, J.D. Berry and J.T. Cacioppo. 2006. 'Loneliness is a unique predictor of age-related differences in systolic blood pressure', *Psychology and Aging* 21: 52–164.

Heller, K., M.G. Thompson, P.E. Trueba, J.R. Hogg and I. Vlachos-Weber. 1991. 'Peer support telephone dyads for elderly women: was this the wrong intervention?', *American Journal of Community Psychology* 19(1): 53–74.

Lauder, W., K. Mummery, M. Jones and C. Caperchione. 2006. 'A comparison of health behaviours in lonely and non-lonely populations', *Psychology, Health & Medicine* 11: 233–45.

Lindley, S. 2012. 'Shades of lightweight supporting cross-generational communication through home messaging', *Universal Access in the Information Society* 11(1): 31–43.

Lindsay, S., D. Jackson, G. Schofield and P. Olivier. 2012. *Engaging older people using participatory design*. Austin, Texas: CHI.

McHugh, J. and B. Lawlor. 2012. 'Perceived stress mediates the relationship between emotional loneliness and sleep quality over time in older adults', *British Journal of Health Psychology*, 18(3): 546–55.

McHugh, J. Wherton, D. Prendergast and B. Lawlor. 2012. 'Teleconferencing as a source of social support for older spousal caregivers' initial explorations and recommendations for future research', *American Journal of Alzheimer's Disease and Other Dementias* 27(6): 381–87.

Mellor, D., L. Firth and K. Moore. 2008. 'Can the internet improve the well-being of the elderly?', *Ageing International* 32: 25–42.

Monk, A.F. and D.J. Reed. 2007. *Telephone conferences for fun: experimentation in people's homes*. Chennai, India: HOIT, Springer.

Newell, A.F., A. Carmichael, M. Morgan and A. Dickinson. 2006. 'The use of theatre in requirements gathering and usability studies', *Interacting with Computers* 18: 996–1011.

Ofcom. 2012. Communications Market Report, Ofcom London, http://stakeholders.ofcom.org.uk/binaries/research/cmr/cmr12/CMR_UK_2012.pdf.

Office for National Statistics. 2012. Internet Access Quarterly Update, Q3 2012, http://www.ons.gov.uk/ons/dcp171778_286665.pdf.

Pedell S., F. Vetere, L. Kulik, E. Ozanne and A. Gruner. 2010. 'Social isolation of older people: the role of domestic technologies', in *Proceedings of OZCHI*. Brisbane, Australia: ACM Press, pp. 164–67.

Penninx, B.W., T. van Tilburg, D.M. Kriegsman, A.J. Boeke, D.J. Deeg and J.T. van Eijk. 1999. 'Social network, social support, and loneliness in older persons with different chronic diseases', *Journal of Aging and Health* 11: 151–68.

Phillipson, C. 2007. 'The "elected" and the "excluded": sociological perspectives on the experience of place and community in old age', *Ageing and Society* 27: 321–42.

Pinquart, M. and S. Sorensen. 2001. 'Influences on loneliness in older adults: a meta-analysis', *Basic and Applied Social Psychology* 23(4): 245–66.

Prendergast, D., C. Somerville and J. Wherton. 2012. 'Connecting communities: the role of design ethnography in developing social care technologies for isolated older adults', in J.C. Augusto, M. Huch, A. Kameas, J. Maitland, P. McCullagh, J. Roberts, A. Sixsmith and R. Wichert (eds), *Handbook of ambient assisted living: technology for healthcare, rehabilitation and well-being*. Amsterdam: IOS Press, pp. 791–804.

Procter, R., T. Greenhalgh, J. Wherton, P. Sugarhood, M. Rouncefield and S. Hinder. 2014. 'The day-to-day co-production of ageing in place', *Journal of Computer Supported Cooperative Work*, 23: 245–67.

Rice, M. and A. Carmichael. 2011. 'Factors facilitating or impeding older adults' creative contributions in the collaborative design of a novel DTV-based application', *Universal Access in the Information Society* doi 10.1007/s10209-011-0262-8.

Rice, M., Y.L. Cheong, J. Ng, P.H. Chua and Y. Theng. 2012. 'Co-creating games through intergenerational design workshops', *Proceedings of the Designing Interactive Systems Conference 2012*. New York: ACM Press, pp. 368–77.

Riche Y. and W. Mackay 2010. 'Peer care: supporting awareness of rhythms and routines for better aging in place', *Journal of Computer Supported Cooperative Work* 19: 73–104.

Rook, K.S. 1987. 'Reciprocity of social exchange and social satisfaction among older women', *Journal of Personality and Social Psychology* 52(1): 145–54.

Russell, D., L.A. Peplau and C.E. Cutrona. 1980. 'The revised UCLA Loneliness Scale: concurrent and discriminate validity evidence', *Journal of Personality and Social Psychology* 39: 472–80.

Scharf, T. and J. De Jong Gierveld. 2008. 'Loneliness in urban neighbourhoods: an Anglo-Dutch comparison', *European Journal of Ageing* 5: 103–15.

Schnittger, R., J. Wherton, D. Prendergast and B.A. Lawlor. 2012. 'Risk factors and mediating pathways of loneliness and social support in community dwelling older adults', *Aging and Mental Health* 16(3): 335–46.

Schwarz, B., G. Trommsdorff, I. Albert and B. Mayer. 2005. 'Adult parent-child relationships: relationship quality, support, and reciprocity', *Applied Psychology: An International Review* 54(3): 396–417.

Shapira, N., A. Barak and I. Gal. 2007. 'Promoting older adults' well-being through internet training and use', *Aging & Mental Health* 11(5): 477–84.

Slegers, K., M.P.J. van Boxtel and J. Jolles. 2008. 'Effects of computer training and internet usage on the well-being and quality of life of older adults: a randomized, controlled study', *Journal of Gerontology, Psychological Sciences* 63B(3): 176–84.

Steptoe, A., N. Owen, S.R. Kunz-Ebrecht and L. Brydon. 2004. 'Loneliness and neuro-endocrine, cardiovascular, and inflammatory stress responses in middle-aged men and women', *Psychoneuroendocrinology* 29: 593–611.

Tijhuis, M.A.R., J. De Jong-Gierveld, E.J.M. Feskens and D. Kromhout. 1999 'Changes in and factors related to loneliness in older men: the Zutphen Elderly Study', *Age and Ageing* 28(5): 491–95.

Tilvis, R.S., M.H. Kahonen-Vare, J. Jolkkonen, J. Valvanne, K.H. Pitkala and T.E. Strandberg. 2004. 'Predictors of cognitive decline and mortality of aged people over a 10-year period', *Journals of Gerontology Series A: Biological Sciences and Medical Sciences* 59: 268–74.

Victor, C.R., C.R. Bowling and J. Bond. 2002. *Loneliness, social isolation and living alone in later life*. ESRC Report.

Victor, C., S. Scambler, A. Bowling and J. Bond. 2005. 'The prevalence of, and risk factors for, loneliness in later life: a survey of older people in Great Britain', *Ageing & Society* 25(3): 357–75.

Weiss, R.S. 1973. *Loneliness: the experience of emotional and social isolation*. Cambridge, MA: MIT Press.

Wherton, J.P. and D.K. Prendergast. 2009. 'Building bridges: involving older adults in the design of communication technology to support peer-to-peer social engagement', in A. Holzinger and K. Miesenberger (eds), *HCI and usability for e-inclusion*. Berlin: Springer-Verlag, pp. 111–34.

Wherton, J.P., P. Sugarhood, R. Procter, M. Rouncefield, G. Dewsbury, S. Hinder and T. Greenhalgh. 2012. 'Designing assisted living technologies "in the wild": preliminary experiences with cultural probe methodology', *BMC Medical Research Methodology* 12: 188.

White, H., E. McConnell, E. Clipp, L. Bynum, C. Teague, L. Navas, S. Craven and H. Halbrecht. 1999. 'Surfing the net in later life: a review of the literature and pilot study of computer use and quality of life', *Journal of Applied Gerontology* 18: 358–78.

White, H., E. McConnell, E. Clipp, L.G. Branch, R. Sloane, C. Pieper and T.L. Box. 2002. 'A randomized controlled trial of the psychosocial impact of providing internet training and access to older adults', *Aging & Mental Health* 6(3): 213–21.

Williams, R., J. Stewart and R. Slack. 2005. *Social learning in technological innovation: experimenting with information and communication technologies*. Cheltenham: Edward Elgar.

Wilson, R.S., K.R. Krueger, S.E. Arnold, J.A. Schneider, J.F. Kelly, L.L. Barnes and D.A. Bennett. 2007. 'Loneliness and risk of Alzheimer disease', *Archives of General Psychiatry* 64: 234–40.

Woodward, A.T., P.P. Freddolino, C.M. Blaschke-Thompson, D. Wishart, L. Bakk, R. Kobayashi and C. Tupper. 2011. 'Technology and aging project: training outcomes and efficacy from a randomized field trial', *Ageing International* 36: 46–65.

Young, J.E. 1982. 'Loneliness, depression and cognitive therapy: theory and application', in L.A. Peplau and D. Perlman (eds), *Loneliness: a sourcebook of current theory, research and therapy*. New York: John Wiley, pp. 379–406.

6. AVOIDING THE 'ICEBERG EFFECT'
Incorporating a Behavioural Change Approach to Technology Design in Chronic Illness
John Dinsmore

RISING POPULATION NUMBERS, INCREASED AGE demographics, stretched healthcare services and limited government finances are common introductions to publications analysing the societal impact of chronic health conditions such as heart disease, cancer, stroke, chronic respiratory diseases, dementia and diabetes. Normally following this worrying introduction is the suggestion that it is now imperative for chronically ill individuals to increase their ability to self-manage at home. This will require each individual to adopt new practices and change existing behaviours to those best suited to living with a debilitating chronic condition. This process is termed 'behavioural change'.

Self-management is a systematic multi-faceted educational approach to patient care that aims at teaching skills necessary for patients to carry out disease specific routines via healthy behaviour change in order to control and improve their health and wellbeing. As an umbrella concept self-management is comprised of multiple sections, which include: improving psychological and physical health; adhering to treatment plans; monitoring one's condition; implementing relevant changes based on health fluctuations; improving quality of life and maintaining social function.

Constructing a viable self-management, behavioural change programme in chronic illness is a challenge. Models regularly used in the behavioural health modification field include the Transtheoretical Model (TTM) (Prochaska and DiClemente 1984; Prochaska et al. 2002); the Theory of Planned Behaviour; the Theory of Reasoned Action (TRA); Health Belief Model; and the Attitude, Social Influence and Self Efficacy model (ASE model) (Fishbein and Ajzen 1975; Ajzen and Fishbein 1980; Ajzen et al. 1991; Rosenstock 1966; De Vries et al. 1988; De Vries et al. 1995). These models focus on building patient confidence to carry out a behaviour (e.g. an activity as part of an exercise programme) that is necessary to reach a desired goal. Key to achieving this confidence is the shaping of patient beliefs and perceptions around their condition and potential recovery. Factors highlighted by these models that are important in the construction of behavioural change materials for chronic illness are personal control, weighing pros and cons and finally social attitudes (Brug and Van Assema 2001; Armitage and Connor 2000).[1]

The TTM is the most commonly used behavioural change model, concentrating on the processes of change (stages, decisions, self-efficacy) and support required to adopt a healthier lifestyle. However, it has been criticized by some scholars for containing too few categories to explain human functional changes (e.g. Bandura 1997).

The academic interpretation of behaviour change in health identifies that action, thoughts, feelings and physiology are tightly interlinked and therefore affect the way in which a patient manages his or her illness. Behavioural change techniques influence change by using motivating techniques, improving education, constructing a problem definition, collaborative goal setting, collaborative problem-solving and contract for change, continuing support and evaluation (Peyrot and Rubin 2007). The use of these techniques within specific targeted technologies and associated materials may raise patients' awareness of the processes of change, assist in the adoption of appropriate self-care behaviours, and help patients and their families to cope better with their chronic illness. If we seek to incorporate these techniques into healthcare technologies we face two daunting questions:

1. How do we change behaviours via the introduction of technology to improve the quality of life of chronically ill individuals?
2. How do we develop adequate resources, materials and services for these technologies to sustain behavioural changes and improve both healthcare, and self-management practices?

The overall challenge for healthcare in the chronic illness field is to develop a framework with recommendations in each respective health system to support an effective self-management and behavioural change paradigm. In this chapter we will seek to address the complexities of the chronic illness, self-management paradigm. We will discuss how behavioural change can potentially help to improve the quality of life and wellbeing of chronically ill individuals as well as reduce pressure on healthcare services if incorporated efficiently into self-management based assistive technologies. The chapter will then focus on a case study that utilized behavioural change design and development recommendations to construct peer-learning videos for older individuals living with chronic obstructive pulmonary disease (COPD).

Behavioural Change Design with Assistive Technologies in Healthcare

The aim of introducing technology to healthcare is to help patients maintain independence, improve quality of life, support carers and reduce admissions to hospital (Bayer et al. 2005). As discussed in other chapters in the volume, over the last decade technologies have primarily been used as remote monitoring devices (e.g. Telehealth). Feedback and reports to these devices have been mixed, mainly due to the lack of alignment between technology and health professionals' proficiency in using it, with not one study to date holistically adopting principles of behavioural change to the development of user centric device construction, software architecture and user interface (UI) design. A recent systematic review of mHealth (mobile health) trials (Free et al. 2013) showed that only 7 of 26,221 reviewed studies used behavioural change theories as part of the construction of their mHealth intervention (e.g. Free et al. 2009; Free et al. 2011).

The objective of introducing behavioural change techniques to technology construction is to help chronically ill individuals maximize their ability to act on personal and health professional feedback to their self-management routine. In light of this the healthcare industry is increasingly exploring the relationship that defines each new technology's user experience (UX) and how this can be used to improve the healthcare self-management practice. The relationship between an individual and their personal self-management routine is complex, particularly in chronic health, and can generally incorporate many factors. Acknowledging this complexity is paramount to the design and development process in healthcare technology, as we build systems for mass appeal that also provide a personalized and intuitive user experience to support a behavioural change model.

Currently, however, there is no commonly agreed framework for approaching the convergence of health and technology to induce behavioural change in chronic conditions. This is not surprising as the development of an adequate technology design into a holistic treatment model which accommodates efficient service re-design, and which is easily understood by patients, carers and health professionals, has been difficult to deliver.

This chapter will explore possible steps that may help to facilitate a potential model. As a first step the 'theory of innovation diffusion' (Rogers 2003) states that individuals are more likely to consider technology use when it is relevant to them. Therefore an important 'first foundation principle' is to ensure the design of new self-management technologies (including content) is from a patient centric point of view, both with reference to the health condition and cultural context of the end user. This is crucial to the development of a strong behavioural change framework.

Incorporating behavioural change into healthcare technology design is in its infancy and behavioural change studies in chronic conditions are scarce. Those available show significant positive effects for self-efficacy and behavioural change on administration of a programme (e.g. Scherer and Schmieder 1997). However, only a few studies have occurred in recent years, which have adopted the use of modern mainstream technologies such as mobile devices in chronic illness self-management (e.g. Cole-Lewis and Kershaw 2010; Fjeldsoe et al. 2009). The primary focus for assistive healthcare technology to date has been on remote monitoring and measurement of vital signs such as temperature, blood pressure, pulse and breathing rate with little attention paid to the motivational and psychological drives that maintain patient engagement with the device or programme content, delivered by the technology (Davey 2007; Rice and Doughty 2004). Collecting physiological data regarding patients' progress, while an important element of the self-management process, should be developed in parallel to improving psychological and social factors that assist in the adoption of new lifestyle routines. Failure to effectively implement this dual approach may produce a potential 'Iceberg Effect' to technology design and development in chronic illness. This occurs when a research, design and/or development team focuses too heavily on the hardware and visual usability of the technology (the tip of the iceberg), thereby failing to fully address complex underlying social and psychological factors crucial to developing an efficient and effective relationship between user and technology.

This leads us to the 'second foundation principle' to the design and development process for healthcare technologies used to promote behavioural change. People often long for social interaction through personal connection, thus better preliminary psychological and social engagement with technologies may occur if we design them as perceived 'companions' to our daily routine rather than as clinical devices. Lessons can be learned from everyday consumer products that induce the 'companion' feel. For example within the 'iPhone' applications such as 'Facetime', 'iTunes' and 'Photo Galleries' all help to not only personalize the device but give it the feel of a companion. What is important here is the synchronous engagement in activity between the individual and the phone. Studies have shown that synchronous behaviour promotes social attachment or bonding (Wiltermuth and Health 2009; Haidt and Kesebir 2008). Therefore assistive health technologies should aspire to become one of our daily living accessories similar to the mobile/smart phone, the success of which has been due in part to our perception of its use within a societal behaviour framework as a key daily living accessory.

Developing Structured Educational Programmes

Behavioural change with patients is primarily used to aid formulation of 'structured educational programmes' for self-management and rehabilitation. Structural education programmes are defined as 'comprehensive in scope, flexible in content, responsive to an individual's clinical and psychological needs and adaptable to his or her educational and cultural background' (NICE 2003: 14). Studies using educational programmes suggest that modifying behaviour in self-management occurs by improving internal control (Worth and Dhein 2004) and thus empowerment. Constructs affecting patient empowerment include motivation, health professional involvement and knowledge (Casey et al. 2011). These well-acknowledged psychological constructs were also found to be important within the COPD case study explored in this chapter (McCabe et al. 2011). Of particular note is the construct of knowledge acquisition, as many studies have shown that 'knowledge' of disease specific self-management (embedded in a structural education programme) increases the skills needed for people to treat their own illness, particularly in COPD (e.g. Emery et al. 1998; Dang-Tan 2001; Nault et al. 2000).

Kheirabadi and colleagues (2009) investigated the impact of combining self-management and behavioural modification termed 'psycho-educational plans', which are personalised forms of psychologically based therapeutic intervention designed to teach patients about their condition and assist them in learning how to manage the related symptoms, consequences and associated behaviours. Results indicate that psycho-educational plans were associated with significant decreases in symptom severity and improved function and mental state. Another notable education based pulmonary rehabilitation programme developed in the National University of Ireland Galway adopted the TTM to deliver content based on patient empowerment. The programme, known as PRINCE (Pulmonary Rehabilitation In Nurse-Led Community Environment), includes areas such as managing symptoms, breathlessness and exercise (Casey et al. 2011). A potential problem with programmes constructed from these models is that few of them examine which specific behavioural changes contribute to improved health effects. Even scarcer in the wider literature is evidence regarding which exact educational interventions or combination of interventions effectively induces behavioural change. Much more research is needed across conditions to refine the approach and best practice models for implementation. Overall no conclusive evidence exists to support the theory that behavioural change programmes improve health by improving knowledge; rather, people memorize information well but are not necessarily able to act upon it (Mazzuca 1982). However, it must be remembered this is a field in its infancy.

Role of Video and Multi-Media in Behavioural Change and Self-Management

Teaching self-management skills to chronically ill patients is, however, not enough to induce lifestyle modification. Providing structured educational approaches which incorporate theories of behavioural change offers a better learning environment but these approaches need to be multi-faceted and need to supplement teaching with implementation strategies. Central to using structured educational approaches is the inclusion of a plethora of tailored content aimed at providing clinical knowledge, rehabilitation programmes, guides to medical device use, and personal peer-perspectives to coping with varying conditions. The use of varied video and multi-media materials, particularly in tablet and smart devices, lends itself particularly well to the development of structured education models and may provide a potentially effective medium to help guide and increase user (patient, carer and/or health professional) knowledge and improve the self-efficacy process.

As we move forward, one-to-one self-management coaching of patients is unlikely to be feasible or cost effective for health service providers. The use of home-based video education and rehabilitation will be of increasing importance to enhance patient outcomes. Video material can provide a medium for increased information and access to peer support; however, no clear research exists as to the full effectiveness of a home-based video programme service for self-management and rehabilitation. If such a programme was correctly administered, research does indicate a distinct correlation between improved health benefits, motivation and behavioural change with video interventions that provide a potential medium to disseminate knowledge and allow individuals to receive some benefits as part of a self-management and rehabilitation plan (e.g. Rose Bio-Medical 2004). Early quasi-experimental studies evaluating the ability of remote video technology in home-based healthcare settings (Johnston et al. 2000), such as the 1996–1997 Kaiser Permanente Tele-Home trials, also show the potential for video to be effective as a well-received platform for patients to maintain quality of care in line with reducing care costs.

However, on the flip-side randomized controlled trials (RCT's) using video forms of tele-healthcare have also shown that even though those that use the technology report high levels of satisfaction, up to 80 per cent declined use for fear that it may replace nurse visitations (Mair et al. 2006). Annadale and Lewis (2011) also reported that 15 per cent of patients have refused to use video based technology for fear of not being able to use it properly. Overall patients appear unlikely to use equipment if it is not user friendly or does not easily guide them on how to conduct a specific activity

(Janna et al. 2009). It must also be remembered that a balance should be provided between cognitive, visual and motor loads when using multi-media materials to induce learning especially with older adults and people with sensory or cognitive impairments. Technological advances over the last decade suggest that more can be achieved with video to disseminate and educate patients outside of face-to-face remote monitoring; therefore, assessing the impact of video and multi-media learning in 'real time' is an important issue facing developers.

Case Study: Developing Behavioural Change Design for COPD

Chronic Obstructive Pulmonary Disease (COPD) is presently the fourth leading cause of death worldwide (GOLD 2008). In the UK alone 835,000 individuals were diagnosed between 2008/9 and an estimated two million were undiagnosed (NICE 2010). The prevalence of diagnosis by age for the UK goes from less than 1% for the 45–54 age bracket up to nearly 8% in the over 75 (NICE 2010: 10). The cost to the NHS for COPD treatment currently stands at an unsustainable annual figure (when indirect costs are included) of £982,000,000 (Osman et al. 2002). COPD is anticipated to be a major challenge to health services worldwide, with increased patient caseloads, competing patient demands and increased time constraints, limiting the ability of health professionals to provide effective self-management support (Ostbye et al. 2005). Research in the last decade to off-set health professional workloads and rising health service costs for COPD has focused on innovative methods to develop enabling and assistive technologies towards patient self-management, orientated around a home-based paradigm of lifestyle modification and behavioural change.

COPD is a chronic illness that requires considerable self-care effort from patients. In many cases, patients have to follow complex treatment regimes, from different medications to diet to exercise, and make significant life-style changes to accommodate their condition. Smoking cessation is perceived by healthcare providers as a crucial part of managing COPD. As a result of the complexity involved in self-managing COPD, non-compliance with recommended lifestyle changes is a common problem. This results, especially amongst older patients, in frequent hospitalization when symptoms worsen (Grady 2006). The pattern of care for patients often involves lengthy hospital admissions, followed by a return home with limited follow-up support for the management of symptoms. This inevitably leads to the readmission of patients to hospital with acute symptom onset. Such a pattern of care is both financially unsustainable for increasingly stretched health services and undesirable for sufferers, given the diminishing quality of life which accompanies such erratic and inadequate symptom control.

In 2011 a collaborative venture between Intel (Ireland), the Technology Research and Independent Living (TRIL) centre and Trinity College Dublin (TCD) School of Nursing and Midwifery sought to address behavioural change and self-management of patients with chronic illnesses, focusing in particular on COPD (McCabe et al. 2011). Building on the first foundational principle outlined above, the team focused attention on the needs of the individual self-managing with COPD to develop a supportive model for video adoption to self-management learning. This approach, commonly referred to as 'user centred design' (UCD), focuses on the development of technologies and associated software that pay specific attention to the core needs and experiences of an individual with a disease specific condition to ensure maximum efficiency and ease of use in the technology adopted by the individual. UCD is a complex process, which at a basic level involves a detailed iteration process conducted by designers, developers and usability specialists (including for example psychologists and ethnographers) to make sure a product is easy to use and learn. In essence the UCD process may be viewed as creating a strong conceptual model of learning and/ or feedback to the product design from the mental model of what the patient expects to learn and achieve from engaging in a particular healthcare regime. If, however, the aim of a new technology is to create a new mental model or learning experience, the design process should also include a significant training element for the end user to ease adoption of the model and build a new cognitive learning framework (Weinschenk 2011).

Core to introducing a new learning based technology paradigm in healthcare is the ability to merge strong UCD and technology into a framework that provides easy dissemination of materials specific to the patient's condition. It is important that all parties involved in developing new technologies understand first of all the intricacies of the condition they are developing for and the impact of the condition on the patient. Therefore, choosing the correct skill sets from designers, developers, clinical staff experts in the condition and social scientists who can determine key components in the design process for integration to a particular cultural and societal context is an important first step.

In order to achieve a unique insight into patients' perspectives of living with COPD, quantitative and qualitative methodologies using semi-structured interviews and focus groups were employed in this project in an action research capacity with 60 participants from support groups in counties Wicklow and Sligo (Ireland) over two development phases (n=32 at phase 1 and n= 28 at phase 2). Action research is a process by which behavioural science knowledge is integrated with scientific knowledge and applied to solve real organizational problems (Shani and Passmore 1985). The strength of this process of inquiry lies in its capability to generate solutions to practical problems that involve participant contributions throughout the project. In this study it was proposed that an initial reflective process would enable user/carer support needs to be better identified (phase 1). To complete the action research cycle, participants of the patient/carer group were invited to evaluate the developed material (phase 2). This resulted in 25 behavioural recommendations constructed around the key themes of knowledge, symptoms, self-management, rehabilitation and support related to COPD. These results were further used to develop 18 design principles (e.g. keep content short, use high-quality sound, provide key points summaries) to video based support technologies in COPD. This chapter will focus on the recommendations for behavioural change. Overall 28 patient-peer-perspective educational, motivational and health-promoting videos to support self-management in patients with COPD were constructed based on these recommendations and techniques. The aim of these videos was to supplement current self-management multi-media materials constructed in the Irish context and provide novel, culturally relevant patient-perspective commentaries to living with COPD.

Themes and Behavioural Change Recommendations Extracted

Initial mapping of the core user needs revealed that the concept of self-management had to be supported by four other areas. As discussed above, these were knowledge, symptoms, rehabilitation and support. Indeed, in the model constructed, self-management related primarily to patient management practices and strategies of implementation in conjunction with learning from the five associated areas (as listed in Table 6.1).

An in-depth analysis of the self-management theme produced a potential inter-logically related model (e.g. where one domain in the model is positively affected, then all other areas replicate a positive outcome) on areas that need to be simultaneous addressed to improve patient practice. It was important that these strategies should address in a holistic way the personal needs of the individual on breathing related, functional, psychological and social levels. In total 28 videos constructed in this project sought to cover all aspects of peer learning associated with the outputs discussed in Table 6.1.

TABLE 6.1 Core learning themes for COPD self-management.

THEME	SUB-THEMES	DESCRIPTION
Knowledge	Knowledge of the condition, diagnosis and cause; awareness of COPD; stigma due to lack of knowledge	This theme relates to the positive aspects of increased knowledge in COPD as well as the problems caused by a lack of knowledge.
Symptoms	Psychological; breathing related; infections; associated comorbidities and symptom triggers	This theme relates to the symptoms, both functional and psychological, experienced by participants with associate comorbidities that affect their condition. This also covers COPD triggers (e.g. weather, smoke, sprays) that exacerbate the condition.
Rehabilitation	Exercise; diet; smoking cessation; medical rehabilitation (including pulmonary)	This theme outlines the main rehabilitation processes relevant to individuals with COPD, both in hospital and in the community.
Self-Management (Practice and Strategies)	Covers 4 areas: breathing related; functional management; psychological; social management	This theme covers a 4-piece inter-logical model of patient COPD self-management practices and strategies.
Support	Health professional; peer support; friends and family; community and social support	This theme covers the sources of hospital, home and community based support.

Once the themes for video development had been established, it was important to understand potential recommendations specific to this cohort that would be needed to improve potential adoption and sustained use of the videos as part of a behavioural change process. The results revealed 25 behavioural change based recommendations (summarized below) to be employed in the design and development of video output as well as any assistive technology development in COPD self-management.

Tailoring information to the level of severity and to cultural context was the first recommendation extracted. Indeed, individuals in milder stages did not engage with materials intended for more severe stages. It was also important to ensure that individuals are confident in their knowledge of COPD at the early stages of diagnosis. This knowledge was critical to informing a realistic outlook and associated coping responses best employed to deal with adverse events associated with the condition. The level of social and peer support was seen as key to reducing negative psychological symptoms such as depression. While videos were created from a peer perspective it was seen as important to any future application development that structures should be designed to also understand and improve the already existing social and peer support in place for a particular individual. This may be done via links to COPD related social networking or contact mediums such as Skype. In relation to negative psychological symptoms, depression might be a 'silent phenomena', with individuals failing to report this and other negative symptoms (both physical and psychological) related to their condition due to personal guilt felt for causing COPD through a previous history of smoking. Indeed 'guilt' was seen as a fundamental barrier that individuals must overcome in order to seek and accept support as part of a behavioural change model. In dealing with symptoms, however, participants reported that developing strong peer sharing and learning networks is important to a behavioural change framework, particularly as peers have experience and can relate to issues such as symptom onset and how best to avoid and deal with 'symptom onset triggers' when they arise. Finally in relation to symptoms, it is also important to address knowledge of comorbidities associated with COPD.

We have already discussed the need to break self-management practice into four separate areas (Table 6.1). Within these areas, the discussion of 'symbolism' involved with one's management was an interesting output. This was primarily related to more severe COPD cases and the use of assistive technologies such as oxygen to support activities of daily living, which was seen as linked to a loss of independence. It is therefore important that learning materials address the negativity around such symbolic issues and provide coping strategies to overcoming the psychological barrier to using potential assistive technologies, particularly in public. Indeed for individuals on oxygen it was also stressed that as part of any physical rehabilitation or exercise self-management programme, tools to monitor oxygen use are incorporated into the design of these programmes. This is because increased exercise is associated with higher levels of oxygen use as the lungs work harder to perform the exercise. This reinforces the need to tailor approaches to behavioural change programmes to provide information on resources linked to content within the programmes.

One area often overlooked is the need for home modification to support changes in behaviour. Patients in this study felt that modifying the home (e.g. hand rails in the bathroom, lowering of toilet set, stair-lift installation, etc.) is important for conserving energy and maximizing daily self-management practice. Outside the home it was seen as important to provide information to individuals on how to sustain existing social connections and also build new ones. Key to supporting the development of social connections was providing information on how best to travel with COPD. Questions participants felt necessary to address include: How does one fit their car for oxygen use when driving? Can smaller oxygen cylinders be bought for travel? Where do you buy portable equipment for travelling with oxygen? Participants in this study felt that information concerning long haul travel was particularly limited; this not only restricted an individual's social network but also their quality of life. One's ability to be mobile was seen as an incentive for behavioural change; indeed, this was viewed as extremely important in building an individual's confidence and level of independence.

It was clear that the psychology of self-management is fundamental to behavioural change. Results mirrored Baltes model (Baltes and Baltes 1990) of 'Selection, Optimisation and Compensation' (SOC). In this model individuals diagnosed with a particular condition that limits their physical, psychological or social capacity select and optimize their current abilities in line with developing compensatory coping strategies to maximize these abilities to address these domains. Areas that were suggested as being important to develop as part of this framework, outside of maximizing functional capacity/ability, were financial management and support, improving breathing strategies and relaxation techniques, promoting better engagement in exercise programmes that include peer and family interaction, developing subjectively tailored diet plans and communication pathways with key health professionals. Indeed maximizing the ability to facilitate these strategies, beginning from the home environment, was seen as crucial.

The final recommendation from patients centred on their ability to monitor and understand the progression of their condition. Feedback was seen as crucial to tailoring responses as part of a potential SOC model. This included the ability to access key health, peer, community and professional resources with ease when needed, although it was suggested that individuals in this study had little confidence in their general practitioners' level of understanding and ability to provide tailored self-management solutions to COPD. It was recommended that this be addressed as part of an assistive technology learning framework, to develop better training and learning tools not only for patients but also for health professionals and family members as part of a holistic ecosystem approach to learning. Building a framework that encompasses all COPD ecosystem stakeholders is therefore important and while this study clearly outlines the user experience and relevant areas to be addressed, there are several additional key factors that need to be acknowledged in a potential framework to facilitate change.

Key Factors to Facilitating Change

Time

Modifying individual behaviour is a complex, gradual process. The literature is currently inconclusive on both the timescale and regularity of programme delivery needed to induce potential behavioural change. Several studies claim that a minimum of three months should be allowed before the effects of a supported behavioural change programme are assessed (e.g. Wempe and Wijkstra 2004; Griffiths et al. 2000), thus suggesting that long-term initiatives are necessary for individuals to form healthy lifestyle habits that improve quality of life (QoL).

Lally and colleagues (2010) suggest it takes an individual an average of 66 days to form a new habit. However, this is subjective to the individual, with a reported range from 18 to 254 days to make the behaviour automatic. This reinforces the idea that a long-term approach should be taken to the design of patient learning systems. Developing platforms that house content for short durations only may limit the effectiveness of a behavioural change programme. It can be argued that technologies that focus attention over a short duration do so to concentrate energy on quickly practising certain core tasks to automate behaviour. The aim of this is to decrease the time it takes to develop a new skill by repetitively practising it in quick succession, to the point that it can be deployed with minimum conscious attention (thus becoming automatic). In some tasks short-duration repetitive models may focus attention but a trade off occurs, if individuals are not stimulated enough over the learning period, making errors in learning due to reduced attention from lack of new stimuli. Behaviours follow an asymptote curve, therefore it is important to be ready for the individual to learn new associated behaviours when a habit is finally formed in order to sustain and build upon initial changes, thus it is important to change content in short learning models if deployed over long periods.

Improving Self-Efficacy

The next challenge to facilitating behavioural change through the video medium is the development of a platform by which patients can monitor the impact of their learning over time and improve their confidence in self-managing. This finding also came through in the results of the case study discussed above. Improving self-efficacy is strongly linked with patient empowerment in the literature as a central component in how individuals view their illness and adopt self-management learning practices. Unfortunately chronic illness literature on the relationship between self-management, self-efficacy and behavioural change is scarce; and even more limited is research into the role of behavioural change in facilitating technology adoption for self-management practices in chronic conditions. However, available studies have shown that increased engagement with particular tasks provided by a well-structured and supportive behavioural change educational programme improved self-efficacy with patient groups (Kasikci 2011; Scherer and Schmieder 1997; Atkins et al. 1984).

Increasing self-efficacy via the user experience is important in determining which tasks an individual will perform or avoid based on knowledge they receive as to what will hinder or facilitate positive lifestyle modification. Providing condition specific information to individuals with chronic illness allows for the recognition of problems and the development of subjective solutions. Self-efficacy therefore appears to play a major role in explaining health related behaviours (Kaplan et al. 1994) and thus it is essential that it is factored into any knowledge and learning based technology design, in particular the delivery of educational material using colours, animations, videos and sound to draw people's attention to particular pieces of learning and help to avoid filtering of information that is important. For example, if an individual needs to pay attention to a specific piece of information, that information must stand out ten times more than all other pieces accompanying it (Weinschenk 2011). Overall, the delivery platform for information should aim to ensure that outcomes are geared towards increasing patient confidence not only in understanding and managing their condition but also in guiding their use of technology.

Sustaining Change

Unfortunately research into face-to-face behavioural change programmes does not stipulate a best practice methodology for patients maintaining effective self-management practices after exiting. Evidence based technology self-management innovations in chronic conditions housed under the umbrella term of telehealthcare have centred on sustaining patient practices in areas that include smoking cessation, maintenance pharmacology, rehabilitation, education and equipment use (see for example Cooper and O'Hara 2010; McLean et al. 2011).

Current studies show a lack of patient adherence to learned practices following the end of a healthy lifestyle modification programme. This suggests the need to develop programmes which are constantly available for patient participation and not just given to individuals for a short duration on a one-off basis or intermittently post-diagnosis. Building a 'real time' interactive on-going service component to any new healthcare technology to increase an individual's engagement, particularly in a peer-learning related context, may be beneficial when designing a programme for chronic illness self-management.

One issue which is detrimental to sustaining change is the lack of knowledge and skill that individuals may have when it comes to technology use. It must also be recognized that prior to technology use the recipient must be sufficiently motivated to make changes and possess specific competencies to engage in any lifestyle modification processes aside from any technology developments. Novel technologies must show various capabilities before they receive user/client endorsement. This includes being user friendly, safe to use, time efficient and cost effective. Potentially, incorporating models of 'real time' health monitoring as part of behavioural change practice is also important in increasing patient motivation to use technology as part of their daily routine. Hibbert and colleagues (2004) further suggest that when introducing a new technology, risks have to be minimized in order to ensure a user friendly and intuitive interface and all care must be taken to acknowledge the relationship with existing health professional services in areas that go beyond mere simple training issues.

The challenge for technology solutions in healthcare is to have the ability to engage and motivate patients to use tools over time without becoming frustrated. Detailed evaluation is needed to determine those factors perceived by patients as important to facilitating or hindering lifestyle modification. Studies need to evaluate any new technology to learn how best to facilitate for societal adoption. Overall, more large design and development studies are needed to confirm the most reliable and valid content and furthermore structure of self-management, educational and behavioural change programmes tailored to specific chronic conditions, as well as help understand the best assistive technologies required to best facilitate such programmes.

Innovating and Embracing New Technologies

It is also important to see trends developing in new self-management technologies that may make viable components of a behavioural change framework. Creativity and intuition are important in the process of innovation, which is integral to pre-empting technology changes in society. While innovations in chronic illness related technology have increased over the last decade in line with a recognition for the need to produce sustainable management outside acute treatments (Fromer et al. 2010), the truth is that we are still only at the exploratory phase of developments in this field of expertise. Using new technologies as part of a long-term telehealthcare service has been identified as a means to reduce health professional home visits, improve patients' knowledge of illness, motivate changes in behaviours to help manage illness and allow better use of limited health professional time to address patient care (Annadale and Lewis 2011). Thus it is important to constantly innovate and improve the means of information dissemination and learning through technology.

To date, however, the majority of studies investigating self-management education programmes in chronic conditions have not adopted the use of modern technologies and are primarily facilitated by community based nursing health professionals. One reason for this may be the failure to engage health professionals fully in the design and development process, thereby resulting in products that do not reflect the needs and requirements of the person living at home with a chronic illness or the practicing health professional.

Evidence to date for technology adoption in tele-healthcare studies, has been primarily criticized for using 'non-user friendly' and bulky equipment, low participant numbers, elements of sampling bias and lack of knowledge by nursing and allied health professional staff administering new technology (Horton 2008). Spotting technology trends that support behavioural change should, however, also be balanced by affordability, which could also be a predictor for the best ecosystem to house technologies that may effectively find societal adoption. For example, the touch screen, which ten years ago was seen as slow with mixed responsiveness, is now viewed as a fast and intuitive part of the mobile user experience, and shows not only how best we can maximize innovation but also how spotting trends in user devices is important.

Bespoke Devices or Consumer Technologies?

A key issue for employing new innovation trends in technology is whether we develop self-management platforms for use on bespoke healthcare devices or for current, existing, mass market, consumer technologies such as the iPad. Companies designing bespoke technologies tend to have price evaluations that some individuals may find too costly, particularly those with chronic health conditions living on a pension or assistive living benefits. Bespoke technologies in most cases only provide several core services and, due to design patents held by many non-healthcare multi-national consumer device companies, are limited in their hardware design, leading to possibly less user-friendly products.

Mass-market technologies, such as the smart phone or tablet, are generally more affordable, highly sophisticated with well-designed, user-friendly interfaces and associated ecosystems. In leading mass-market technologies (e.g. iPhone, Samsung Galaxy Tablet), increased bandwidth together with a better user interface (UI) design means rich interactions can become a major part of the self-management educational experience. The benefit of this is that individuals are becoming increasingly accustomed to these consumer devices and therefore need little additional training to operate. Also, in most cases a relative or carer may have a similar device to help facilitate use, which was also seen in our case study. Embracing devices that are becoming common place in home and community environments may be the best option to facilitate the adoption of technology. However, it must be recognized that there are still limitations when repurposing market products for healthcare. Areas of concern that need better development on this front include data security, hardware that can sustain aggressive cleaning, and ensuring feedback to patients is personalised and within best clinical guidelines.

Technology Adoption and Healthcare Service Re-design

The final key factor to facilitating change is the need for health services to re-design current practice to incorporate new technology adoption. A need exists to educate patients and health professionals in how best to use technology as part of a campaign to provide greater access to online and/ or mobile self-management knowledge and treatment. In the US insurance companies are increasingly adopting technology and tele-monitoring into their current services to reduce face-to-face nurse visits, without any supporting evidence that it improves better health outcomes (Blue Cross and Blue Shield Minnesota 2008); therefore, it is essential that strong research studies develop in parallel with increased technology use to ensure that patients achieve the highest standards of remote support in behavioural change programmes, especially if the introduction of these technologies increases patient premiums.

Mair and colleagues (2005) suggest that patients feel positive towards the introduction of new technologies that aid self-management despite limited evidence for clinical effectiveness. However, for those using technology as part of their daily self-management, no research has yet established the emotional and functional impact on these patients when the technology is withdrawn or becomes inaccessible (Smith et al. 2009).

Focusing on the grass-roots level, technologies associated with patient self-management need to be orientated to the cultural context and health system norms of the end user. Constructing user-friendly hardware and software with parallel training methods including patients, carers and health professionals is also recommended to facilitate the adoption of technology. However, there is presently no clear-cut pathway for how best to achieve a balance between these groups to produce best practices in home-based technology-facilitated self-management.

It is insufficient to just re-design technologies around behavioural change. Health systems incorporating new technologies also need to strategically re-design services to facilitate the rise of mobile and mainstream technologies in modern life as part of new models of treatment and care. Strength lies in the ability of a strong model to facilitate societal adoption of self-management healthcare technologies with ease. Governments also need to improve the communication infrastructure particularly in rural areas, anticipating the rise of 4G. The formulation of a health consortium with mass-market technology providers such as Samsung, Google, Intel and Apple to introduce technologies to the home and community environment may see costs for delivery to the healthcare system massively reduced as individuals seek highly attractive market products sold by these companies outside of healthcare use.

A key part to any on-going long-term service solution is the development of online resource materials that patients can access at any time to create an effective educational framework for self-management and behavioural change. In 2011 there were 491.4 million smart phone units sold worldwide (IDC 2012) and with tablet sales estimated at 118.9 million units at the end of 2012 (Gartner 2012), it is inevitable that mobile platforms (capable of accessing 4G from 2013) will be a primary focus for sustainable engagement to new potential behavioural change services.

Integration of assistive technology will only be fully effective if the structural framework exists in each respective healthcare system to deliver and sustain the technology. Government and healthcare bodies must seek to ensure that patients have home-based access to internet facilities and that hardware costs are subsidized via a means tested system in line with personal circumstances. Finally health authorities need to consider a re-design of services to incorporate technology use particularly in community care. Training should be made available where needed to patients, carers and health professionals in the use and delivery of technology programmes geared towards improving patient self-management practices.

The Future for an Assistive Healthcare Technology Behavioural Change Framework

The design of a mobile assistive healthcare framework which uses primarily smart technologies and is flexible in terms of achieving a range of patient centric self-management goals is particularly important as we progress into the future. However, building a relevant support system, integrated effectively into the home environment in line with approved clinical guidelines, recommendations and treatments, is a major challenge for developers aiming to deliver validated, subjective, secure and accessible technologies (Bayliss et al. 2007). Central to a 'mobile' delivery framework is the inclusion of constantly updated multi-media content aimed at providing clinical knowledge, rehabilitation programmes, guides to medical device use and personal perspectives to cope with each respective chronic condition. Building such a framework presents multiple challenges, which Bayliss and colleagues (2007) eloquently summarize as follows: firstly, patients have unique self-management support needs, personal barriers and subjective resources for developing an individualized self-management strategy; and secondly, developing technology based self-management support material must be done in the healthcare context in which the individual is based. Currently the Western model is centred on a single disease model of care, rather than integrated care.

Mobile healthcare applications will play an increasingly important role in patient self-management practices. With this growth will come tighter regulations for validating stand-alone software and applications that influence healthcare practice. This is important as the majority of health based 'apps' available in applications stores claiming to be intended for self-management in chronic conditions not only have poor content but also lack a strong user centric design to target the condition they are developed for. As we move forward, one-to-one self-management coaching of patients is unlikely to be feasible or cost effective for health service providers, therefore the use of mobile, home-based video education and rehabilitation will be of increasing importance in enhancing patient outcomes. Mobile video material can provide a medium for instant personal access to information and peer support, no matter the location. However, no clear research exists as to the full effectiveness of a mobile-based video programme service for self-management and rehabilitation.

Conclusion

The role of behavioural change in the design and dissemination of self-management materials via technology is in its infancy. Preliminary research suggests that the introduction of technology can play an important role in improving patient quality of life, wellbeing and functional recovery, while simultaneously reducing the hospitalization and burden on currently stretched health systems. Further research is required, however, to validate the processes necessary to develop effective, condition specific self-management and behavioural change platforms. Meeting the diverse needs of individual patients on a daily basis within their respective illness populations is a central design challenge. Improving knowledge, while important, also needs to be translated to effective self-management practice.

Building a framework to motivate and sustain the use of technology as part of chronic illness self-management in homes and in the community is the mammoth task that faces healthcare providers and academics. Any developed framework needs to robustly investigate the potential of technology and associated content delivery used to facilitate self-management practices as part of a new home-based chronic condition management paradigm. The aim must be to design patient centric programmes tailored to cultural and health system context. Time needs to be invested into the development of user interfaces and user experiences which are relevant to the specific condition treated in line with associated behavioural recommendations that influence change, such as those discussed in our case study above. While research in chronic illness is beginning to realize the importance of social, cognitive and behavioural change theory in technology design, few studies actually incorporate this holistically into the design and development process. Finally, improving communication between users, stakeholders and interdisciplinary teams within a behavioural change framework is an important step to facilitating societal adoption of new assistive (and particularly mobile) healthcare technologies.

Note

1. Control is perceived as being either internal or external: internal is when the patient perceives that they can control their own condition; and external is when the sense of control comes from external sources such as the health professional. 'Pros and cons' refers to the approaches an individual will have to a particular behaviour, which will be shaped by key social attitudes and influences, including the support and opinions of family and friends. 'Weighing pros and cons' is when an individual comes to a decision on a behaviour based on the perceived outcomes.

References

Ajzen, I. 1991. 'The theory of planned behavior', *Organizational Behavior and Human Decision Processes* 50: 179–211.

Ajzen, I. and M. Fishbein. 1980. *Understanding attitudes and predicting social behavior.* Englewood Cliffs: Prentice Hall.

Annadale, J. and K.E. Lewis. 2011. 'Can telehealth help patients with COPD?', *Nursing Times* 107(15–16): 12–14.

Armitage, C.J. and M. Connor. 2000. 'Social cognition models and health behaviour: a structured review', *Psychological Health* 15: 173–89.

Atkins, C.J., R.M. Kaplan, R.M. Timms, S. Reinsch and K. Lofback. 1984. 'Behavioural exercise programs in the management of Chronic Obstructive Pulmonary Disease', *Journal of Consulting and Clinical Psychology* 52: 591–603.

Baltes, P.B. and M.M. Baltes (eds). 1990. *Psychological perspectives on successful aging: the model of selective optimization with compensation.* New York: Cambridge University Press.

Bandura. 1997. 'The anatomy of stages of change [editorial]', *American Journal of Health Promotion* 12(1): 8–10.

Bayer, S., J. Barlow and R. Curry. 2005. 'Assessing the impact of a care innovation telecare', *Tanaka Business School Discussion Papers*: TBS/DP05/38. Tanaka Business School, Imperial College London.

Bayliss, E., H.B. Bosworth, P.H. Noel, J.L. Wolff, T.M. Damush and L. Mciver. 2007. 'Supporting self-management for patients with complex medical needs: recommendations of a working group', *Chronic Illness* 3: 167–75.

Blue Cross and Blue Shield Minnesota. 2008. *CHF/COPD Telemonitoring Services for CareBlue and SecureBlue Provider Bulletin.* Minnesota 2008.

Brug, J. and P. Van Assema. 2001. 'Beliefs about fat', in L.J. Frewer, E. Risvik and H. Schifferstein (eds), *Food, people and society.* Berlin: Springer, pp. 39–54.

Burnard P. 1991. 'A method of analysing interview transcripts in qualitative research'. *Nursing Education Today* 11(6): 461–66.

Casey, D., K. Murphy, A. Cooney, L. Mee and M. Dowling. 2011. 'Developing a structured education programme for clients with COPD', *British Journal of Community Nursing* 16(5): 231–37.

Cole-Lewis, H. and T. Kershaw. 2010. 'Text messaging as a tool for behavior change in disease prevention and management', *Epidemiologic Reviews* 32(1): 56–69.

Cooper, R. and R. O'Hara. 2010. 'Patient's experiences of an automated telephone weather forecasting service', *Journal of Health Services Research and Policy* 15(2): 41–46.

Dang-Tan, T. 2001. *Efficacy of a pulmonary rehabilitation program on knowledge and self-efficacy for elderly Chronic Obstructive Pulmonary Disease patients.* Thesis. Department of Epidemiology and Biostatistics, McGill University, Montreal.

Davey, J. 2007. 'How collaborative care is becoming a reality in COPD management', *Primary Health Care* 17(9): 36–39.

De Vries, H., M. Dijkstra and P. Kuhlman. 1988. 'Self-efficacy: the third factor besides attitude and subjective norm as a predictor of behavioral intentions', *Health Education Research* 3: 273–82.

De Vries, H., E. Blackbier, G. Kok and M. Dijkstra. 1995. 'The impact of social influences in the context of attitude, self-efficacy, intention and previous behavior as predictors of smoking onset', *Journal of Applied Social Psychology* 25: 237–57.

Eisner, N., C. West, S. Evans and A. Jeffers. 1997. 'Effects of psychotherapy in moderately severe COPD: a pilot study', *European Respiratory Journal* 10: 1581–84.

Emery, C.F., R.L. Schein, E.R. Hauck and N.R. MacIntyre. 1998. 'Psychological and cognitive outcomes of a randomized trial of exercise among patients with Chronic Obstructive Pulmonary Disease', *Health Psychology* 17: 232–40.

Fishbein, M. and J. Ajzen. 1975. *Belief, attitude, intention and behavior: an introduction to theory and research.* Reading, MA: Addison-Wesley.

Fjeldsoe, B.S., A.L. Marshall and Y.D. Miller. 2009. 'Behaviour change interventions delivered by mobile telephone short-message service', *American Journal of Preventative Medicine* 165–73.

Free C., R. Whittaker, R. Knight, T. Abramsky and A. Rodgers. 2009. 'Txt2stop: a pilot randomised controlled trial of mobile phone-based smoking cessation support', *Tob Control* 18: 88–91.

Free, C., R. Knight, S. Robertson, R. Whittaker, P. Edwards et al. 2011. 'Smoking cessation support delivered via mobile phone text messaging (txt2stop): a singleblind, randomised trial', *Lancet* 378: 49–55.

Free, C., G. Phillips, L. Galli, L. Watson, L. Felix, P. Edward, V. Patel and A. Haines. 2013. 'The effectiveness of mobile-health technology-based health behavior change or disease management interventions for health care consumers: a systematic review', *PLOS Medicine* 10(1): e1001362. doi:10.1371/journal.pmed.1001362.

Fromer, L., T. Barnes, C. Garvey, G. Ortiz, D.F. Saver and B. Yawn. 2010. 'Innovations to achieve excellence in COPD diagnosis and treatment in primary care', *Postgraduate Medicine* 122(5): 150–64.

Gartner Inc. 2012. 'Gartner says worldwide media tablets sales to reach 119 million units in 2012', Garner Website Newsroom. Available at http://www.gartner.com/it/page.jsp?id=1980115 (accessed 16 November 2012).

Global Initiative for Chronic Obstructive Lung Disease (GOLD). 2008. 'Global strategy for the diagnosis, management, and prevention of Chronic Obstructive Pulmonary Disease. Available at http://www.goldcopd.org (accessed 7 March 2012).

Grady, K. 2006. 'Management of heart failure in older adults', *Journal of Cardiovascular Nursing* 21(5suppl 1): S10–S14.

Griffiths, T.L., M.L. Burr, I.A. Campbell, V. Lewis-Jenkins, J. Mullins, K. Shiels, P.J. Turner-Lawlor, N. Payne, R.G. Newcombe, A.A. Ionescu, J. Thomas and J. Turnbridge. 2000. 'Results at one year of outpatient multidisciplinary pulmonary rehabilitation: a randomised controlled trial', *Lancet* 355: 362–68.

Haidt, J., P. Seder and S. Kesebir. 2008. 'Hive psychology, happiness and public policy', *Journal of Legal Studies* 37(2): S133–S156.

Hibbert, D., F.S. Mair, C.R. May, A. Boland, J. O'Connor, S. Capewell and R.M. Angus. 2004. 'Health professionals' responses to the introduction of a home telehealth service', *Journal of Telemedicine and Telecare* 10(4): 226–30.

Horton, K. 2008. 'The use of telecare for people with Chronic Obstructive Pulmonary Disease: implications for management', *Journal of Nursing Management* 16: 173–80.

International Data Corporation (IDC). 2012. 'Smartphone market hits all-time quarterly high due to seasonal strength and wider variety of offerings, according to IDC'. Available at http://www.businesswire.com/news/home/20120206005252/en/Smartphone-Market-Hits-All-Time-Quarterly-High-Due#.VIsekYseZ9s (accessed 16 November 2012).

Janna, M., G. Pare and C. Sicotte. 2009. 'Home telemonitoring for respiratory conditions: a systematic review', *American Journal of Managed Care* 15(5): 313–20.

Johnston, B., L. Wheeler, J. Deuserand and K.H. Sousa. 2000. 'Outcomes of the Kaiser Permanente Tele-Home Health Research Project', *Archives of Family Medicine* 9: 40–45.

Kaplan, R.M., A.L. Ries, L.M Prewitt and E. Eakin. 1994. 'Self-efficacy expectations predict survival for patients with Chronic Obstructive Pulmonary Disease', *Health Psychology* 13: 366–38.

Kasikci, M.K. 2011. 'Using self-efficacy theory to educate a patient with Chronic Obstructive Pulmonary Disease: a case study of 1 year follow up', International *Journal of Nursing Practice* 17: 1–8.

Kheirabadi, G.R., M. Keypour, N. Attaran, R. Bagherian and M.R. Maracy. 2009. 'Effect of add-on "self management and behaviour modification" education on severity of Chronic Pulmonary Obstructive Disease', *European Psychiatry* 24(Suppl 1): S1252.

Lally, P., H. Van Jaarsveld , H. Potts and J. Wardle. 2010. 'How are habits formed: modelling habit formation in the real world', *European Journal of Social Psychology* 40(6): 998–1009.

Lincoln, Y.S. and E.G. Guba. 1985. *Naturalistic enquiry.* Newbury Park, CA: Sage.

Mair, F.S., P. Goldstein, C. May, R. Angus, C. Shiels, D. Hibbert, J. O'Connor, A. Boland, C. Roberts, A. Haycox and S. Capewell. 2005. 'Patient and provider perspectives on home telecare: preliminary results from a randomised controlled trial', *Journal of Telemedicine and Telecare* 11(Suppl. 1): S95–97.

Mair, F.S., P. Goldstein, C. Shiels, C. Roberts, R. Angus, J. O'Connor, A. Haycox and S. Capewell. 2006. 'Recruitment difficulties in a home telecare trial', *Journal of Telemedicine and Telecare* 12(Suppl. 1): S26–28.

Mazzuca, S.A. 1982. 'Does patient education in chronic disease have therapeutic value?', *Journal of Chronic Disorders* 35: 521–29.

McCabe, C., A. Brady, G. McKee, S. O'Donnell, D. Prendergast, S. Allen, P. Thompson, and J. Dinsmore. 2011. 'COPD behavioural change, self-management and peer perspectives report'. *Internal Project Report – TRIL Research Programme.*

McLean, S., U. Nurmatov, J. LY Liu, C. Pagliari, J. Car and A. Sheikh. 2011. 'Telehealthcare for Chronic Obstructive Pulmonary Disease', *Cochrane Database of Systematic Reviews 2011* 7: Art. No: CD007718. DOI: 10.1002/14651858.CD007718.pub2.

National Institute for Health and Clinical Excellence (NICE). 2003. *Guidance on the use of patient-education models for diabetes.* NICE Technology Appraisal Guidance 60. Available at: http://www.nice.org.uk/guidance/ta60/resources/guidance-guidance-on-the-use-of-patienteducation-models-for-diabetes-pdf (accessed 12 December 2014).

National Institute for Health and Clinical Excellence. 2010. *Chronic Obstructive Pulmonary Disease: management of Chronic Obstructive Pulmonary Disease in adults in primary and secondary care.* London: National Clinical Guideline Centre. Available at http://guidance.nice.org.uk/CG101/Guidance/pdf/English (accessed 7 March 2014).

Nault, D., J. Dagenais, V. Perreault, J. Pepin, S. Labrecque, M. Seguin et al. 2000. 'Qualitative evaluation of a disease specific self-management program "Living Well with COPD"', *European Respiratory Journal* 16: 317S.

Osman, L.M., C. Calder, D.J. Godden et al. 2002. 'A randomised trial of self-management planning for adult patients admitted to hospital with acute asthma', *Thorax.* 57: 869–74.

Ostbye, T., K.S.H. Yarnall, K.M. Krause, K.L. Pollak, M. Grandison and J.L. Michener. 2005. 'Is there time for management of patients with chronic diseases in primary care?', *Annals of Family Medicine* 3: 209–14.

Peyrot, M. and R. Rubin. 2007. 'Behavioural and psychosocial interventions in diabetes – a conceptual review', *Diabetes Care* 30: 2433–40.

Prochaska, J. and C. Di Clemente. 1984. *The transtheoretical approach: crossing traditional boundaries for therapy.* Homewood, IL: Dow-Jones-Irwin.

Prochaska, J.O., C.A. Reeding and K.E. Evers. 2002. 'The transtheorectical model and stages of change', in K. Glanz and B.K. Rimer (eds), *Health behaviour and health education: theory, research and practice*, 3rd edn. San Francisco: Jossey-Bass, pp. 99–120.

Rice, T. and K. Doughty. 2004. 'Tackling the COPD burden with technology', *Primary Health Care* 14(2): 16–18.

Rogers, E.M. 2003. *Diffusion of innovations.* 5th edn. New York: The Free Press.

Rose Biomedical, 'Chronic obstructive pulmonary disease; NIH funded study identifies new tool to help individuals with COPD', Obesity, Fitness & Wellness Week, NewsRX, Atlanta, GA, 2004.

Rosenstock, I.M. 1966. 'Why people use health services', *Milbank Memorial Fund Quarterly* 83(4): 1–32.

Scherer, Y.K. and L.E. Shmieder. 1997. 'The effect of a pulmonary rehabilitation program on self-efficacy, perception of dyspnea, and physical endurance', *Heart Lung* 26: 15–22.

Shani, A. and W. Pasmore. 1985. 'Organizational inquiry towards a new model of the action research process', in D. Warrick (ed.), *Contemporary organisation development: current thinking and applications.* Glenview, IL: Scott, Foresman and Co.Wrench. p. 439.

Smith, S.M., S.L. Elkin and M.R. Partridge. 2009. 'Technology and its role in respiratory care', *Primary Care Respiratory Journal* 18(3): 159–64.

Wempe, J.B. and P.J. Wijkstra. 2004. 'The influence of rehabilitation on behaviour modification in COPD', *Patient Education and Counselling* 52: 237–41.

Weinschenk, S.M. 2011. *100 things every designer needs to know about people.* Berkeley, CA: New Riders, Pearson Education.

Wiltermuth, S. and C. Health. 2009. 'Synchrony and cooperation', *Psychological Science* 20(1): 1–5.

Worth, H. and Y. Dhein. 2004'. Does patient education modify behaviour in the management of COPD?', *Patient Education and Counselling* 52: 267–70.

7. SUPPORTING A GOOD LIFE WITH DEMENTIA

Arlene J. Astell

FOR PEOPLE WHO DEVELOP DEMENTIA the proactive and prospective use of technology could assist them in daily life and support them in maintaining their independence and autonomy. To achieve this requires recognition and understanding that the major problems faced by people with dementia are due to impaired cognitive function, that this differs in different types of dementia, and that this changes over time. A major shift in attitude towards people with dementia and how we can best enable them to live with this condition is also overdue.

This chapter considers three lines of evidence for how technology could help people to live well with dementia. First is bespoke technology designed to respond to the cognitive profiles of people with dementia. This is illustrated through CIRCA, a touchscreen system to support conversation between people with dementia and caregivers by maximizing the unaffected aspects of behaviour and cognition and minimizing the impact of impaired ones. Secondly, we need to look at how an understanding of the cognitive processes that underlie everyday activities, such as cooking, shopping, etc., could support development of technology-enabled interventions for people with dementia. This is illustrated by a project examining the priorities and needs of people with dementia in everyday life. The third point discussed is the use of mainstream technology by people with dementia to support and maintain their everyday lives. This is illustrated through a selection of blog posts by a person with dementia who describes his efforts to re-learn previously used technology and learn a new one as part of a project looking at barriers to technology adoption. Together, these three lines of evidence illustrate the challenges and possibilities of developing technology to support people to live well with dementia.

Dementia

Dementia is not one condition but many. There are several different causes of dementia, each of which has a different profile of cognitive impairment but all are characterized by irreversible brain damage and progressive worsening over time. Age is the greatest risk factor for developing dementia and as longevity increases the number of people with dementia is predicted to rise. Current estimates put the number of people in the UK with some form of dementia at approximately 820,000 (Luengo-Fernandez et al. 2010) with this number expected to reach almost 1 million by 2021 (Alzheimer's Society 2013). However, the number of people affected by dementia is at least triple this when the family members and caregivers of people with a diagnosis are taken into account.

Due to the progressive erosion of cognitive function over the course of the illness, people with dementia gradually lose the skills that allow them to look after themselves, leaving them dependent on others to meet all of their needs. This places major demands on health and social care services and has a massive impact on families, as the majority of people live at home and are cared for by their relatives. The costs of this unpaid care in the UK is currently estimated to be approximately £12.4bn per annum with a further £29m loss of productivity from family members giving up work to care for a relative, contributing to the total estimated cost of dementia care of £23bn (Luengo-Fernandez et al. 2010).

Early intervention targeted at maintaining the independence and functioning of people with a dementia diagnosis to keep them well for longer and their relatives at work for longer would undoubtedly have economic benefits. Early intervention would also benefit the wellbeing and quality of life of people with dementia by enabling them to keep active and participating in everyday life for as long as possible. This would have a positive impact on people they come into contact with and go some way to tackling the stigma and negative perceptions that currently exist towards dementia. The challenge is to develop interventions that can maximize the spared abilities of people with dementia, whilst minimizing the impact of impairment to those aspects of cognitive and behavioural functioning that are affected early.

Cognitive Function in Dementia

To develop technological solutions for dementia it is important to recognize that there are different causes of dementia with different profiles of impairment. The main ones are: Alzheimer's disease (AD), which accounts for approximately 42 per cent of cases (Brunnström et al. 2009), is characterized by slow progressive decline, primarily interferes with laying down new memories, but also impacts executive functions, including planning and monitoring activities and later all aspects of cognition; Vascular Dementia (VaD), approximately 24 per cent (Brunnström et al. 2009), which typically starts abruptly, and includes slower thinking, poor concentration and impaired communication (Bayer and Iliffe 2011) – a further 22 per cent of cases of dementia are thought to exhibit a combination of AD and vascular brain changes (Brunnström et al. 2009) and the related changes in cognition and behaviour that occur in both conditions; Dementia with Lewy Bodies (DLB; percentage unconfirmed), which involves problems with attention, alertness, navigating the environment and executive functions, shares symptoms with both AD and VaD, and may be under-diagnosed (McKeith 2010); and Fronto-temporal Dementia (FTD), which includes Pick's disease, frontal lobe degeneration, and dementia associated with motor neuron disease, and is the second or third most common cause of dementia among people under 65, with primary symptoms that include lacking insight, losing inhibitions and being easily distracted (Fox 2012). Rarer forms of dementia, which together account for approximately 5 per cent of cases, include Creutzfeldt-Jacob disease, Parkinson's disease, progressive supranuclear palsy, and multiple sclerosis (Bayer and Metzler-Baddeley 2012). These affect cognitive function and concomitant behaviour in different ways but due to their infrequency there are fewer specific interventions and services for people diagnosed with these conditions.

Recognizing that there are a range of different causes and profiles of impairment highlights the challenge of developing interventions to support people to live well with dementia. Given that the different types of dementia can disrupt cognitive functioning in different ways, one approach is to focus not on the dementia as the starting point but on the activities people carry out and de-construct them into their component parts. Linking these components to the specific cognitive processes needed to carry them out should facilitate the development of interventions appropriate to different types of dementia that maximize unimpaired abilities while minimizing impaired ones. This is particularly important for ensuring that engineering and ICT solutions take full account of cognitive function when developing novel solutions. It is hoped that the following examples will provide a starting point for understanding how cognition operates in daily activities and how it can be taken into account.

The patterns of impairment do not just differ across disorders, they also change over time, with some aspects of function affected early and others preserved far into the disease process. For example, executive functions, that is, the cognitive processes that allow us to plan and initiate activities, and successfully carry them out, are affected early in several conditions including DLB, FTD and AD, challenging the assumption that AD is mainly a memory problem. Damage to any or all of these higher-level cognitive functions will impact everyday life, interfering with a wide range of activities. As examples, this may affect meal planning, shopping, route finding, bill paying, choosing clothes, remembering medication, and making appointments.

Closer inspection of meal planning, for instance, reveals that there are many steps (and sub-steps) involved that rely on different aspects of cognitive function: deciding what meal is desired, checking if the ingredients are available, shopping for missing items, preparing, cooking and serving the meal. Within one of these steps, such as cooking, there will also be many further smaller steps, such as finding a recipe, collecting and preparing the ingredients, finding the utensils and other equipment, following the recipe, operating the stove, etc. Each of these can be further broken down into a series of steps. Following a recipe, for example, requires multiple cognitive functions (italicized): *initiation* of activity relating to each line of the recipe instructions, *monitoring* that each line is carried out, *integrating* each of the lines of instruction, *keeping track* of the timing of each part of the recipe, and so on. Someone with dementia may lose the abilities to plan an activity, develop strategies for carrying it out, initiate the plan, or monitor its execution. These could all interfere with preparing meals at home and staying independent.

Faced with this situation, a range of possible solutions might be suggested. The easiest, but probably the most harmful for the person with dementia, is to simply provide meals for them. This would deprive them of the opportunity to keep exercising many important and meaningful skills, such as shopping, cooking, etc., which in turn will undermine their abilities further. Disabling people in excess of the difficulties produced by their current level of impairment is already a major problem for people with dementia. In addition, this places an unnecessary burden on family members or care services that could be delayed if the person could be supported to keep doing the activity through targeted interventions.

Living with Dementia

If people are to live a good life with dementia several conditions need to be in place. The first relates to the availability of interventions that can meet their specific needs and respond as these needs change over time. However, these can only be useful in the context of sensitive and appropriate care that can support people to live with their diagnosis and enable them to deal with their specific cognitive impairments. Finally, there needs to be a change in attitude towards dementia, to highlight that people can actually keep doing things and to stop disabling them unnecessarily. Technology has the potential to address all three of these and support people to live a good life with dementia.

Bespoke Technology

Technology-based interventions include both specific items, such as a day and date calendar, and systems that can provide monitoring and direct feedback or links to caregivers. There are currently very few specific items developed to meet the needs of people with dementia themselves. A search of the specialist websites provides a small list of items, including many that are low-tech, such as a large print address book and nightlights. Specific technology marketed for people with dementia includes item-locator devices, medication reminders and an easy-to-use television remote control. Some of these have been specifically developed for people with dementia while others are adapted from other fields.

Whilst many of the above can provide solutions to individual problems, there is scope for more advanced interventions that can maximize people's spared abilities and enable them to keep functioning for as long as possible. Also, there is a need to separate the priorities for interventions identified by families of people with dementia, such as safety and security (Astell 2006) from those targeting the specific difficulties experienced by people with a dementia diagnosis. One example is CIRCA (Computer Interactive Reminiscence and Conversation Aid; Alm et al. 2004), a touchscreen system developed to support conversation between people with dementia and caregivers.

Communication is often cited as a major problem in dementia care by both formal and family caregivers and is typically blamed on the dementia. However, people with dementia retain many of the component elements that are required to hold a conversation, such as being able to speak and desiring to engage in social interactions with other people. The challenge that CIRCA aimed to address was to make the most of their retained skills while finding a way round the impairments that make holding a conversation difficult.

CIRCA contains a database of photographs, short video clips and music designed to spark off recollections of events from earlier in life, which can form the basis of conversations.

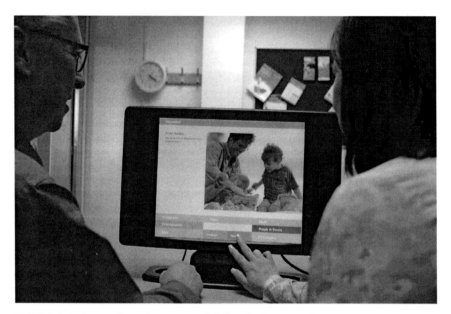

FIGURE 7.1 Screenshot of CIRCA – Childhood, photographs.

The touchscreen means there is no need for a mouse or keyboard and both people with dementia and caregivers can make choices about what they want to look at or listen to and these provide the topics of conversation. These combined elements of 'choice' and 'sharing' are very important for people with dementia and caregivers alike, and also impact on the relationship between them (Astell et al. 2010a). For people with dementia, being able to use the system, make choices and demonstrate their knowledge through recalling events from earlier in their lives is important for their sense of self and participation as an equal in conversation (Astell et al. 2010b). For family caregivers CIRCA prompts topics of conversation, lots of laughter and a shared experience, which helps keep them and their relatives with dementia speaking to each other. For staff in health and social care services CIRCA provides a shared activity for one-to-one or one-to-many sessions that enables them to get to know people better (Astell et al. 2010a). Seeing people with dementia use the computer also challenges their negative expectations about what people with dementia can do, enabling them to see the people they care for in a new light (Astell et al. 2009). Sometimes they even report having learnt something new from the interactions – either about the individual or about cultural history.

CIRCA was developed specifically to maximize the cognitive abilities of people with dementia that are less affected whilst minimizing the more impaired ones. It was primarily developed with people who have AD and as such was designed to address the problem they have with working memory. This is the cognitive process that underlies much of our day-to-day activity. Working memory is what allows us to keep in mind what we are doing and thus keep track of activities as we do them. In AD, working memory is affected very early (Baddeley et al. 1991) and as such people lose track of all sorts of daily activities. This is evident in events such as forgetting where they put items, such as keys, but also in their difficulties in holding conversations. Essentially, they cannot keep up with the thread of conversation, have difficulty answering direct questions and often repeat themselves as they forget what has already been said.

While working memory can be seen as the main problem in AD, there are other cognitive changes that contribute to difficulties holding conversation. These include impaired initiation and voluntary control of actions, which interferes with people's ability to initiate a topic of conversation and impaired metacognitive processes, which constitute our internal monitoring system, allowing us to reflect on and keep track of our cognitive activities. Alongside these impaired processes many skills are retained. Most importantly speech is retained far into the disease process in AD (Astell and Ellis 2006). Semantic knowledge, that is knowledge about the world, is retained along with memories from earlier in life that are stored in relatively unaffected long-term memory (Piolini et al. 2003). Finally, responsiveness to social interaction is retained, and actually lasts until the end of life, even after speech has finally gone (Ellis and Astell 2008). Other spared cognitive abilities include flexibility of the communication system and the natural tendency to compensate for deficits in functioning (Ripich et al. 1991). These allow people to find ways around the initial changes in functioning they experience but over time these abilities also decline, leading to a loss of confidence in social situations.

The challenge then in developing CIRCA was to supplement the retained processes, replace the impaired processes and create a novel system that required no learning or memory load. We adopted the model of a cognitive prosthesis whereby the aim is to use technology to extend or leverage the retained abilities. Subsequently CIRCA has been used by people with other types of dementia than AD and at different stages of the illness, and also by people with learning disabilities and people with cognitive impairment due to stroke. The intuitive interface and learning-free design mean that it is usable by many different groups. Additionally, the lessons learnt from creating and evaluating CIRCA have broader application for developing technological interventions to address other aspects of living with dementia.

Everyday Activities

CIRCA provides an example of developing a cognitive prosthesis for people with dementia to address a specific need (Astell et al. 2008). It serves as an illustration of how an analysis of the specific cognitive profile underlying a reported difficulty faced by people with dementia, in this case a communication problem, can be used to develop an effective intervention. In an effort to apply this approach to other activities that people find challenging, we recruited eight couples who were living with dementia and willing to participate in a project in their own homes. The aim of this project was to explore the sorts of problems that people with a dementia diagnosis want help with, to understand why these problems occur and what makes them challenging for the person with dementia and their partner to cope with. This knowledge could then be used to develop sensitive targeted interventions to support people to keep carrying out activities in their own homes and hopefully have a positive impact on their personal relationships.

The eight couples comprised five men and three women with a dementia diagnosis, two of whom were under 60 years of age, and their partners. At least two of the eight participants living with dementia had progressed quite considerably by the time we met them, as indicated by lower scores on a brief standardized measure of cognitive function, the Mini Mental State Examination (MMSE scores; Folstein et al. 1975). In addition, two of the participants with dementia were experiencing some anxiety and depression as indicated by their scores on the self-report Hospital Anxiety and Depression Scale (HADS; Zigmond and Snaith 1983).

The study also collected information from family caregivers about how they assisted their partner and their experience of burden, as well as a seven-day activity log and interview to explore the techniques the caregivers were currently using to support their relative to continue in their activities of daily life (further details of the study can be obtained from the author). Six couples completed the activity log and were asked to identify one activity the person with dementia wanted assistance to keep being able to do. One woman wanted to be able to prepare a meal and the other wanted to keep hanging out the washing. One man wanted to be reassured that he had taken his medication, one wanted to use his digital camera and two men wanted to use their remote controls for TV and digital programming systems independently.

Taking the meal preparation as an example, the types of problems that a person with dementia can experience when carrying out a multi-part sequenced task become apparent. This lady selected cooking as an activity that she carried out with no help from her husband. At the start of the study she found that when she was making meals she was getting confused about the timings of all the different parts of the meal and integrating these into the whole, for example, knowing how long to cook the meat, when to put the potatoes on to cook, when to make the gravy so that it did not go cold. She found that cooking was one activity that she could still engage in at home and wanted help to maintain her skills in this area. She was also very interested in computers and very much liked the idea of using technology to help her to do this.

After observing her making a full meal of mashed potatoes and minced beef it was decided to focus on understanding the components involved in just making mashed potatoes. This was broken down into seventeen separate steps that captured the way in which she carried out this task. Five of these steps involved locating items (1, 2, 6, 15, 16), e.g. 'Step 2 Find chopping board and peeler'; six involved making decisions (1, 4, 7, 11, 13, 16), e.g. 'Step 11 Add salt to water'; three involved sub-steps (5, 14, 16), e.g. 'Step 14 If done, pour water out into the sink, using the lid to hold back the potatoes'; and all except step 12 ('Wait until potatoes are ready') involved executing a combination of physical actions.

Each of these steps relies on a combination of cognitive and behavioural processes. Watching her carry out the task revealed that she was able to carry out the physical components of the tasks quite well, including those in multi-part sub-steps such as filling and boiling the kettle (Step 5). However, she had clear difficulties with the aspects of the task that relied more heavily on cognitive processes, particularly memory and those involved with planning, initiating and sequencing, i.e. executive functions. She could initiate steps in the task, such as finding the spatula or switching on the ring, but if these were not completed straight away, for instance because she could not immediately find the spatula or identify the correct dial to control the ring on the stove, she would become distracted and sent off task, i.e. 'de-railed'. At this point a cue or prompt would be needed to get her back on track.

From an analysis of both the cognitive and behavioural elements of the task we developed and tried a number of approaches to delivering prompts to support her continued activity. These revealed that it is possible to identify from her behaviour when she is being de-railed. This is an important consideration for developing automated support systems that need to be able to detect when the prompt is required from behaviour, including verbal signs. We tried delivering both visual and auditory prompts and found that this needs to have flexibility to accommodate unexpected changes to the sequence. For example, on one occasion the kettle had been switched off at the mains, which she did not realize until after peeling the potatoes and so the steps got out of sequence and she had to be put back on track. Also, we found that the sequence in which the various steps took place was not invariant, which is another challenge for developing automated support systems.

This study also highlighted a number of additional considerations for developing technology-enabled task support. For someone to complete the task independently the technology needs to be able to provide support for all aspects of the task. This requires an understanding of the cognitive aspects of the task – recognizing that the masher is required, initiating the behaviour to search for and locate the masher, knowing where the masher is kept, monitoring the progress of the search activity, identifying the masher, etc., – and the behavioural aspects – e.g. locating and picking up the potato masher. Understanding how these can go wrong, such as failing to locate the masher, picking up an alternate utensil or item, and why these problems occur, can then be used to develop an appropriate intervention.

Mainstream Technology

The list of activities people with dementia in the previous study wanted help with included commonplace activities in everyday life, including using everyday technology such as the television remote control or digital camera. There is increasing scope for the functionality of mainstream technologies to be beneficial for people with dementia, and indeed this could include delivery of prompts with tasks such as cooking. Understanding the specific cognitive difficulties that people with different types of dementia experience can also be used to inform this, especially in respect of supporting people to learn to use new devices or functions of devices they already use.

Brian's Blog

Brian was a 64-year-old man who had lived with a diagnosis of mixed Lewy Body and vascular dementia for the previous four years. Brian lived with his wife and had previously worked as a Social Care Officer, caring for older people with dementia for more than thirty years. He was referred to his local Alzheimer Scotland Resource Centre and typically attended there two or three times a week. We met him in the summer of 2012 as part of the COBALT (Challenging Obstacles and Barriers to Assisted Living Technologies) project, when we were seeking feedback on NANA (Astell et al. 2012), a novel technology developed for older adults to record daily information about their diet, cognitive function, mood and physical activity.

Brian provided extremely helpful and insightful feedback on NANA and expressed a huge interest in technology in general. He was keen to become involved in COBALT and, after discussion with his wife, offered to write a blog chronicling his experience for the COBALT website (www.cobaltproject.org). The following excerpts from his posts give a flavour of his personal experience of living with dementia, his attitudes both towards his illness and technology, as well as insights into some of the challenges he faces in day-to-day life. The posts have been edited for space but can be found in full at www.cobaltproject.org.

Brian's background information

Hello. My name is Brian. I am 63 years of age and I was given a diagnosis of Mixed Lewy Body and Vascular Dementia when I was 60 [.] Up until the age of 60 I considered myself to be competent in the use of my home computer. I was able to write letters and reports [...] I made all my own templates and [...] also enjoyed making and printing all my personal greeting cards. I was able to use the Internet and researched my Family History using contacts throughout the world. [...].

Unfortunately I completely lost these skills. For a time I was unable to stay in a room when the computer was switched on and would hallucinate quite badly if I was on my own at the computer. [...] I also had problems using my mobile phone and the remote control for the television. With a great amount of assistance from my wife S and my daughter J, I now have no fear of using any of the above equipment. Writing this short piece of work has taken me almost two hours and I relied very much on the Spelling and Grammar facility on the computer. I still have problems using the appropriate words and phrases.

Post 1

I went out shopping with my wife this afternoon and got a very unexpected gift from her. I am now the proud owner of a new iPhone. I have been able to fully charge it and can actually switch it on and off. That is as far as I can go at the moment but I am sure there is going to be opportunities for some lessons here and there. So, a very valuable and positive few days. I now believe good things are happening in my life once more.

Post 2

I could not wait to get the new iPhone out of the box this morning. Hit a problem right away. As I said yesterday, I had learned how to switch it on and off. Not quite true. When the box was opened, there was the phone switched on and lit up like a beacon. Ah well back to the drawing board. [...] S suggested that I should try working on the Sky remote control. I spent nearly an hour just pressing buttons to see what came on the screen. Between us we found at least twenty functions that we had not been using. So I continued to put this fairly new technology (well new to me) into practise and once more

I had proven to myself that despite the Dementia my brain is still able to take on board new information.

Post 4

J. dropped by today and we went through what I had learned yesterday. I still had problems remembering what she had shown me yesterday. We agreed that she would give me the instructions verbally and also write it down for me. This method definitely works for me as Maggie (COBALT researcher) proved when she was doing computer work with me, only one week ago. I look forward to the time when I can use my phone and computer independently. I am fully aware that this exercise will take some time but I am very happy how it is going just now.

Post 6

The phone is still in the box. I decided to go on to the computer just to see how much work I would be able to carry out. I started by sending out 3 E-Mails to friends and asked them to send me a reply when they received them. Within 1 hour I had 3 replies. I marked that up as another success. I then spent 2 hours on the Internet and did some Family research. I had some good results and was able to link up with people from Ireland, Australia, U.S.A. and England. This is after only a 1 hour lesson on the computer with Maggie. I really feel that my confidence is coming back. I also have a great sense of achievement. Yes, I am now able to go into a room alone and sit at the computer free from any anxiety.

Brian wrote with great clarity and openness about living with a dementia diagnosis. He was keen to engage with technology but was acutely aware of how his illness got in the way. He provided insight and illumination about the way in which his particular symptoms interfered with this life, for example problems with memory consolidation that interfere with new learning. Over eighteen months we worked with Brian to develop an approach to training and maintenance of skills to enable him to learn how to use the smart phone and more recently to re-learn the PC, which we wrote up jointly as a case study (Astell et al. 2014).

Brian's blog was based on his daily journal, which provided an aide-memoire for understanding the ups and downs of his life since his diagnosis. Like many people he had a 'mixed' dementia diagnosis, which interfered with his life in a number of ways. However, his experience showed how the functionality available in current technology can be of benefit to people with dementia if it is introduced, taught and the skills maintained in the right way. After joining the COBALT project Brian resumed many activities he had previously given up, such as independent travel and emailing. He regained his confidence and gave talks about his life with dementia before and after joining the COBALT project.

His determination and enthusiasm should serve as a clarion call for new interventions to be developed to support the increasing numbers of people living with dementia. Like the lady who wanted help with cooking, Brian was one of the growing numbers of people diagnosed with dementia at a younger age, so-called 'early onset' dementia. Smart, appropriately designed technological solutions, that reflect a thorough understanding of the cognitive challenges of the different types of dementia, can assist them to maintain their independence, reduce the burden on their families and ease demands on already overstretched health and social care services.

Moving Forward

To improve the lives of the millions of people currently and soon to be living with dementia, we need to stop focusing on the dementia label and take a much more objective view of the discrete problems individuals face. Key to this is an understanding of the cognitive processes involved in every aspect of everyday life. This should be the starting point for developing novel, targeted interventions for people living with dementia. Deconstructing tasks into their components and identifying the cognitive and behavioural aspects will also enable interventions to be made for the different types of dementia, i.e. someone with FTD may have problems initiating an activity, and someone with AD may have problems monitoring an activity once started.

CIRCA was created through deconstructing the communication problem in AD, and this has gone on to be successfully used in a range of dementia care settings in the UK and abroad. However, communication is just one problem faced by people with dementia, and the time is long overdue for bespoke interventions for the vast array of other difficulties faced by people with the many different types of dementia. The detailed account of one such everyday activity – making mashed potatoes – illustrates how to deconstruct such tasks and break them down into their cognitive and behavioural components. This approach can be applied to any activity to support development of creative interventions.

This can include novel applications of mainstream technologies currently available online and on the high street. For example calendar functions on smart phones can support people with memory problems to keep appointments. Brian's blogs illustrate the experience of one person with dementia with mainstream technology and his story can provide inspiration and hope for other people to take advantage of functionality that currently exists to improve their lives now. It should also serve to encourage researchers, developers and clinicians to look at creative applications of both current functionality and the potential for developing bespoke interventions to support the rapidly growing numbers of people with dementia.

These advances require a thorough analysis of currently available functionality, which then need to be matched up with the cognitive profiles of the main dementia subtypes. This would advance the adoption and integration of current technologies into people's lives. Alongside this we need to capture a whole range of user requirements to support the development of novel engineering and computerized solutions. This should include exploring the potential of voice-activated systems and visual-based ones alongside mixed media approaches. To meet these complex challenges we need multidisciplinary teams combining clinical, technical and social skills.

In putting forward this argument it has to be recognized that technology is not a panacea for all problems of people with dementia. There are some things that can be done with technology and done very well but others require the powers of human observation and evaluation. In figuring out how to adapt currently available technology or develop new bespoke interventions we need to have a good understanding of what functions technology can perform and its limitations. The potential application of technology also raises ethical issues, some of which, such as the use of GPS 'tagging' to prevent people with dementia getting lost, are more condition-specific (Astell 2006) – although the issue could also apply to children – whereas other ethical issues to do with surveillance, privacy, data storage and access apply to everyone who interacts with digital technology.

Conclusion

The growing numbers of people living with dementia can potentially benefit even more than the rest of the population from technology designed to respond to their specific profiles of spared and impaired cognitive processes. Technology can deliver satisfaction and achievement, maintain autonomy and improve quality of life of people with dementia. It can also improve relationships with family and formal caregivers and in turn improve their satisfaction with their caregiving role. More importantly, seeing people with dementia master technology, maintain their skills and achieve goals is a powerful tool for tackling negative perceptions and expectations about what people with dementia can do. This is currently the biggest obstacle to innovating for people to live a good life with dementia.

Acknowledgements

The CIRCA project was supported by grant number GR/R27013/01 to Astell from the Engineering and Physical Science Research Council. The dementia prompting project was supported by grant number ETAC-08-92018 to Astell from the Alzheimer's Association. NANA is supported by grant number ES/G008779/1 to Astell from the ESRC. COBALT is supported by grant number TS/I003010/1 to Astell from the Technology Strategy Board.

I am grateful to all of the people with dementia, their families, and the members of care staff that have given so much of their time and effort to support these projects. I am also indebted to Dr Maggie Ellis and the many other research staff and students for all of their assistance in carrying out these projects.

References

Alm, N., A. Astell, M. Ellis, R. Dye, G. Gowans and J. Campbell. 2004. 'A cognitive prosthesis and communication support for people with dementia', *Neuropsychological Rehabilitation* 14(1–2): 117–34. DOI: 10.1080/09602010343000147.

Alzheimer's Society. 2013. http://www.alzheimers.org.uk/statistics

Astell, A.J. 2006. 'Personhood and technology in dementia', *Quality in Ageing* 7(1): 15–25.

Astell, A.J. and M.P. Ellis. 2006. 'The social function of imitation in severe dementia', *Infant and Child Development* 15: 311–19.

Astell, A.J., N. Alm, G. Gowans, M.P. Ellis, R. Dye and J. Campbell. 2008. 'CIRCA: A communication prosthesis for dementia', in A. Mihailidas, L. Normie, H. Kautz and J. Boger (eds), *Technology and aging*. Amsterdam, Netherlands: IOS Press, pp. 67–78.

Astell, A.J., N. Alm, G. Gowans, M.P. Ellis, R. Dye and P. Vaughan. 2009. 'Involving older people with dementia and their carers in designing computer-based support systems: some methodological considerations', *Universal Access in the Information Society* 8(1): 49–59.

Astell, A.J., M.P. Ellis, L. Bernardi, N. Alm., R. Dye, G. Gowans, and J. Campbell. 2010a. 'Using a touch screen computer to support relationships between people with dementia and caregivers', *Interacting with Computers* 22: 267–75.

Astell, A.J., M.P. Ellis, N. Alm., R. Dye and G. Gowans. 2010b. 'Stimulating people with dementia to reminisce using personal and generic photographs', *International Journal of Computers in Health* 1(2): 177–98.

Astell, A.J., T.D. Adlam, F. Hwang, H. Khadra, L. MacLean, T. Smith, C. Timon and E.A. Williams. 2012. 'Validating NANA: novel assessment of nutrition and ageing', *Gerontechnology* 11(2): 243.

Astell, A.J., B. Malone, G. Williams, F. Hwang and M.P. Ellis. 2014. 'Leveraging everyday technology for people living with dementia: a case study', *Journal of Assistive Technology* 8(4): 164–76.

Baddeley, A.D., S. Bressi, S. Della Sala, R. Logie and H. Spinnler. 1991. 'The decline of working memory in Alzheimer's Disease', *Brain* 114: 2521–42.

Bayer, A. and S. Iliffe. 2011. 'What is vascular dementia?', http://alzheimers.org.uk/site/scripts/documents_info.php?documentID=161 (accessed 21 November 2012).

Bayer, A. and C. Metzler-Baddeley. 2012. 'Rarer causes of dementia', http://www.alzheimers.org.uk/site/scripts/documents_info.php?documentID=135 (accessed 21 November 2012).

Brunnström, H., L. Gustafson, U. Passant and E. Englund. 2009. 'Prevalence of dementia subtypes: a 30-year retrospective survey of neuropathological reports', *Archives of Gerontology and Geriatrics* 49(1): 146–49.

Ellis, M.P. and A.J. Astell. 2008. 'A case study of Adaptive Interaction: a new approach to communicating with people with advanced dementia', in S. Zeedyk (ed.), *Techniques for promoting social engagement in individuals with communicative impairments*. London: Jessica Kingsley Publishers, pp. 119–38.

Folstein, M.F., S.E. Folstein and P.R. McHugh. 1975. '"Mini-mental state": a practical method for grading the cognitive state of patients for the clinician', *Journal of Psychiatric Research* 12(3): 189–98.

Fox, N. 2012. 'What is fronto-temporal dementia (including Pick's disease)?', http://www.alzheimers.org.uk/site/scripts/documents_info.php?documentID=167 (accessed 21 November 2012).

Luengo-Fernandez, R., J. Leal and A. Gray. 2010. Dementia 2010. *The prevalence, economic cost and research funding of dementia compared with other major diseases*. A report produced by the Health Economics Research Centre, University of Oxford for the Alzheimer's Research Trust.

McKeith, I. 2010. 'What is dementia with Lewy bodies (DLB)?', http://www.alzheimers.org.uk/site/scripts/documents_info.php?documentID=113 (accessed 21 November 2012).

Piolini, P., B. Desgranges, S. Belliard, V. Matuszewski, C. Lalevee, V. De La Sayette and F. Eustache. 2003. 'Autobiographical memory and autonoetic consciousness: triple dissociation in neurodegenerative diseases', *Brain* 126(10): 2203–19.

Ripich, D.N., D. Vertes, P. Whitehouse, S. Fulton and B. Ekelman. 1991. 'Turn-taking and speech act patterns in the discourse of senile dementia of the Alzheimer's type patients', *Brain and Language* 40: 330–43.

Zigmond, A.S. and R.P. Snaith. 1983. 'The hospital anxiety and depression scale', *Acta Psychiatrica Scandanavica* 67(6): 361–70.

8. HOME TELEHEALTH
Industry Enthusiasm, Health System Resistance and Community Expectations
Sarah Delaney and Claire Somerville

THE ANNUAL MHEALTH SUMMIT IN Washington, DC is one of the many global events to arrive on the Digital Health calendar in recent years. Nearly five thousand enthusiastic delegates from industry and business to government and policy makers gather with health service providers and suppliers to listen to a prestigious line-up of visionary speakers and thought-leaders. They view over four hundred exhibits showcasing innovative devices, services, applications, tools and related solutions that promise improved patient access, better health outcomes, and increased cost savings while facilitating the provision of health to an ageing population. A vast range of new technologies facilitating patient-centric models of care, from home-based hubs to new generation smart health and wellbeing ecosystems, are displayed, discussed, demonstrated and modelled. Beneath the simulated care pathways depicting seamless interaction between health and ageing-in-place, one tries to imagine, from the perspective of frontline health and social care workers in stressed healthcare systems, how these innovations might become integrated into everyday health practice within the homes of ageing patient groups and within the existing service delivery architectures.

The observable gap of technology innovation between small-scale 'pilot' deployments of prototypes and fully functioning evaluated programmes at scale displays little immediate sign of closure. The assumed reasons and explanations for this persistent weakness to scale up pilots are as different as the various stakeholders involved but together produce a picture that suggests that something fundamental about the way we organize, engage, deliver and receive social and medical care is under reconstruction.

This chapter sets out to explore the dynamics of this change in the context of one particular field of home telehealth. We describe the positions of some of the key stakeholders engaged with home telehealth and explore some of the perceived barriers and facilitators to system-level change.

We draw these strands together to explore the process of mainstreaming or 'normalization' of home telehealth into everyday clinical and partner practice. These normalization processes are not necessarily confined to the context of older people. However, in this chapter we pick up and illustrate them with this age cohort in mind.

We start with the observation that innovation is happening and visions of a future where remote and home-based telehealth care provisions are commonplace. Business plans, care pathways and regulatory frameworks designed around telehealth are developing and rapidly transforming into policy initiatives. These technology innovations and plans for action expose a gap between visionary healthcare systems of the future and the sometimes fragile and always stressed healthcare systems of the present, as well as the everyday lives of older people. The discordance between what is possible, desirable and easy technologically, and what is possible, desirable and difficult in everyday social worlds of health and well-being is a recurring feature of the literature and evaluations of pilot telehealth programmes.

The plausibility of a recently developed theoretically based framework for analysing how and why complex health interventions become or do not become embedded in everyday life is accruing a level of empirical evidence worthy of attention in the light of the observation of discordance in innovation and wide-scale adoption of telehealth (Mair et al. 2012; May and Finch 2009; May, Montori and Mair 2009; Murray et al. 2011; Murray et al. 2010). Described as a middle-level theory by its developers, Normalization Process Theory (NPT) provides a means of exploring and framing the gap between research and implementation, technology innovation and mainstreaming. This chapter considers how the framing of the factors that facilitate and/or inhibit home telehealth mainstreaming are limited by stakeholder perspectives and whether NPT might enrich our understanding of why the technology industry anticipates significant expansion of home health technologies with correlated investment returns, that are not matched by health system, clinical enthusiasm and adoption by older people.

What Do We Mean by Home Telehealth?

One of the main areas of confusion in this field is the inconsistency with which different terms are used to describe aspects of information and communication technology (ICT) and health and social care. Various different terms and definitions are used, often interchangeably, in the literature giving rise to considerable confusion among consumers and stakeholders. For the purposes of this chapter, we will focus on home telehealth.

Home telehealth refers to the remote monitoring of a patient's medical condition, or the delivery of health care at a distance using an electronic means of communication (Department of Health UK 2009). There are a growing number of technological approaches to support people with long-term conditions, for instance vital sign monitoring technologies, life-style monitoring, reminder systems, telephone based care management programmes, kiosks for health and wellbeing, and others.

Typically these systems work on the basis of the user having a device in their own home which they use on a regular basis – weekly, daily or more frequently. Such devices often ask a range of pertinent health and quality of life questions which the user answers on a key pad or touch-sensitive screen. Additionally physiological data can be recorded, such as blood pressure, weight, lung function and blood glucose. Data is then transferred through the user's home or mobile telephone connection, or broadband internet connection, using encrypted messaging to a central computer server where it is compared against standardized profiles for each individual user. Any areas of concern can be reviewed through a secure internet connection by clinical staff who respond accordingly. Appropriate checks to ensure compliance with national and local data/IT standards are also conducted (Kubitschke and Cullen 2010).

As well as monitoring, some systems can also be used to try and increase the baseline, or targeted, knowledge of users by asking a range of 'educational' questions, such as 'what is the recommended amount of fluid you should drink per day?' A list of choices is then provided from which the user can select and feedback is provided as appropriate.

The lack of coherence of the field and what is meant by the term tele-health can be traced back to its development, from its origins in the 1970s and 1980s, through to the present day. The emergence of telehealth was driven by a number of institutions in the US (Darkins and Cary 2000), such as the US National Aeronautics and Space Agency (NASA), Antarctic survey stations, and the US military. In general, up until recently, telehealth systems were largely provided through these large institutions or organiza-tions, and delivered to a bounded, specific set of service users.

In contrast, the recent rapid expansion of home telehealth through a range of different sectors targeting 'the general public' in the last twelve to fifteen years can be seen as a response to a number of different problems facing healthcare systems in many developed countries (Koch 2006). These include an increasing pressure on health services due to demographic ageing and a concomitant increase in chronic disease, expanding demand on the part of service users for care that is accessible outside of the clinical setting, a focus on patient-centre and care management, equity of access to services, and increasing difficulties in the recruitment and retention of healthcare staff, particularly in community and home-based care for older people (Koch 2006). These challenges have been accompanied by rapid expansion of telecommunications technologies, along with provision of higher quality broadband services in many regions and the development of Cloud technology. ICT, internet and telecommunications providers have seen market opportunities not only in terms of demographic ageing and health service needs, but also the increased purchasing power of older people themselves.

Telehealth has moved over time from a relatively coherent, bounded service to a diverse market place, driven by different motivating factors, with multiple stakeholders who hold very different expectations of the function and role of telehealth. There is a multiplicity of providers entering the market, each of which may be developing different innovations and modes of delivery. The core home telehealth approach, that is, providing devices at home to users who can take readings (for example measure their body temperature or blood pressure) and send these to a triage centre (a centre where trained clinicians can view the data sent by users and measure it against specific limits set for each user), is now being supplemented in a number of ways. These include the use of health apps on android phones and tablets, the use of self-care apps without linking to a triage centre, user access to online health information, and advanced activity monitoring using internal activity sensors, radio frequency and GPS technology, that can provide sophisticated interpretation of the nature and level of activity (for example compliance with physiotherapy or other rehabilitation programmes).

In summary, then, we can see that there are several aspects to the development and expansion of home telehealth, from different sources, whose needs, wishes and expectations are not only very different but in some circumstances may even work against each other. This makes for a confusing picture that is hard to understand for many, if not all, of the actors in the field – policy makers, industry, researchers and potential customers such as older people.

Understanding the Gap between Innovation and Mainstreaming in Health Systems

Our discussion in this chapter primarily examines the gap between innovation and mainstreaming in health systems from three perspectives emerging from three key stakeholders: industry (the providers of technology), clinical (the gatekeepers of technology) and implementation (i.e. health systems). Each perspective illuminates a dimension of the wider picture and is framed within the concerns that one would probably expect given his or her stakeholder positioning in the field of health and technology. We also note additional factors in the case of older people that are most often related to usability and acceptance of telehealth technologies in the home.

Industry: The Barriers-Drivers Perspective

For industry, the gap between innovation capability and poorly scaled uptake has been framed within a barriers-drivers model. In this sense the telehealth landscape has been viewed from the perspectives of system set up, provision, funding and reimbursement of healthcare systems together with the processes and procedures these generate.

In a major study of the market potential for technology in the context of demographic ageing, Kubitschke and Cullen explored some of the key barriers and drivers to the mainstreaming of home telehealth, based on an analysis of the situation in sixteen countries (Kubitschke and Cullen 2010). Examples of the drivers identified included: an increasing body of research and evaluation; increased emphasis on chronic disease management and population ageing; the opening up of new funding streams; the presence of local 'champions' for home telehealth and product innovation in home healthcare devices and monitoring systems; and industry promotional efforts.

However, significant and persistent barriers were also highlighted. Lack of investment in technological infrastructure has hampered widespread distribution of systems that depend on reliable mobile phone networks and high-speed broadband. There are also persistent issues around the security, privacy and data protection implications of remotely collected and transmitted data. Kubitschke and Cullen also found that existing European healthcare systems are not configured in a manner that allows for a clear business case and value chain (Kubitschke and Cullen 2010). Interestingly, although research activities have increased in the field of home telehealth, there is still no clear picture of the clinical benefits or cost-effectiveness of home telehealth. Other important barriers identified include service barriers, such as the divisions between health and social care (which is a significant factor with older populations where social care packages often precede the introduction of more sophisticated telehealth systems); barriers to reimbursements (for example in the UK between social care and wellbeing as distinct from medical care needs); lack of clarity about information sharing protocols and responsibility structures; lack of inter-operability across devices and systems; and resistance on the part of medical professionals.

Research conducted according to the barriers-drivers model has tended towards finding a 'fit' for home telehealth within existing health system workflows and patient care pathways, as this approach is viewed by providers as a standardized means of improving service efficiency. The appeal of care pathways as an organizing model for understanding healthcare provision and implementation has been explained by its effectiveness in reconciling clinical and management interests in a single solution (Allen 2010a; Allen 2010b). However, it has been argued (Pinder et al. 2005) that the care pathway metaphor can be misleading in that 'care pathways' can exist in an ideal form in the abstract, only to lose coherence in concrete application. They therefore hover between fact and fiction, and it is suggested that an over-reliance on the care pathway model may inhibit our ability to fully understand the mechanisms of implementation of health interventions and programmes. Pinder et al. (2005) found, for example, little evidence in practice for the assumption that a patient is an active participant at the centre of a pathway. This is frequently a problem in relation to older people, whose care trajectory may weave a path across primary and secondary medical care and social care systems. For example, an older individual may be admitted to hospital as a result of a fall, discharged home and transferred to a social care worker who arranges services for him or her. These include emergency alert systems from commercial suppliers, and also visits to their general practitioner for chronic disease monitoring. In this scenario, the older person therefore interfaces with four delivery systems that are not necessarily well connected at the hub.

The policy and industry level search for a 'fit' with the care pathway model may not be the most appropriate model on which to expand and accelerate the roll-out of telehealth programmes and may require more innovative models to enable telehealth potential to be realized, particularly as it pertains to the links between community and home-based monitoring and care providers located elsewhere. Communication technologies in health will exist far beyond the lifespan of the care pathway model; stakeholders need to begin to envision and design more innovative tools for managing the quality and standardization of outcomes in healthcare systems to better reflect the complex reality of implementing change in the delivery of services beyond the clinic and into the homes of older people.

Clinical: The Evidence-Base Perspective

From a clinical perspective, the gap between technology innovation and wide-scale adoption within healthcare systems has mainly been framed as relating to the lack of a clinically-valued evidence base.

The challenges to evaluation of telehealth have been well-documented (Broens et al. 2007). A number of systematic reviews have drawn attention to the relative lack of evidence of the benefits of telehealth in terms of clinical outcomes, cost effectiveness and patient satisfaction (Currell et al. 2000; Barlow et al. 2007). From this evidence-base perspective, the lack of a unified vision among the key stakeholders may be a factor inhibiting the evaluability of health technology programmes (Leviton et al. 2010). The design and form of a telehealth programme may be questioned in further depth and an assessment made of the feasibility of a programme achieving the desired results during pilot phases. This form of assessment can shed light on the types of stakeholder conflicts identified by Greenhalgh (Greenhalgh et al. 2012) as well as the logic, goals and performance criteria of programme effectiveness. Calls for the adoption of more comprehensive evaluation methods that address a number of outcomes connected to the multi-stakeholder context of telehealth and the co-adaptive interaction between users are gathering momentum (Kramer et al. 2012). Such initiatives hope to promote the development of a firmer empirical base and provide a framework for more multi-disciplinary research that integrates the measurement of the constellation of achievable outcomes and impacts.

In attempting to explain the observed time lag between technology, innovation and wide-scale adoption, the perspectives described above focus on the structural assumptions that underlie the way in which healthcare systems operate and the nature of what constitutes measurable success. However, neither of them provides a whole-system explanation of the relationship between the rapid innovation in home telehealth, with mainstream implementation lagging behind, and very low public awareness and uptake either in terms of private purchase or via third-party providers (such as health care intermediaries). Another way of viewing the divergence between innovation, research and mainstreamed telehealth is to view clinically effective practice through the lens of implementation research (Eccles et al. 2009; May et al. 2009). It is to this that we now turn.

Implementation and the Health System: Normalization Process Theory

The study of factors that promote or inhibit the uptake of research findings into routine practice is a growing field in response to the unpredictable and often haphazard transfer of findings from pilot to scaled delivery. More simply, but importantly, an increasing body of work is focusing on a 'middle range theory' (Merton 1957) of implementation and mainstreaming. Middle range theory aims to integrate theory with empirical research.

Normalization Process Theory (NPT), developed from an earlier model (NPM – Normalization Process Model) (May et al. 2007), which aimed at providing a framework for understanding how and whether complex interventions become routinely embedded in health-care practice (normalized) (MacFarlane and O'Reilly-de Brún 2012). The theory deals mainly with normalization into the professional side of healthcare systems, for example gaining support from staff to integrate new technologies in care pathways. However, we believe there is also scope for the theory to have useful application at the community level with older people.

As it was initially conceptualized, NPM did not explain how interventions are formed in ways that are sustained, how actors are enrolled into them, and how new interventions are appraised. NPM was later extended to a middle range theory, NPT (Morrison and Mair 2011), covering the social organization of implementation and the elements that contribute to making new practices routine. In its new form, NPT focuses on what people do – on their contributions to the social processes by which innovations are implemented, embedded and integrated in their social contexts. 'NPT is concerned with "implementation" and has sociological significance because it characterizes human attempts to impose order and direction on contending, conflicting, contingent, and sometimes very turbulent patterns of social action and relations, and their distribution across social time and space' (May 2013: 26). As such, we suggest that it may have potential for understanding the different or similar ways in which older people adopt, embed and integrate telehealth into their lives as well as for understanding the systems of implementation in their homes.

NPT builds from four propositions: firstly, that material practices become routinely embedded in social contexts as the result of people working, individually and collectively, to implement them; secondly, that the work of implementation is operationalized through four mechanisms – coherence, cognitive participation, collective action and reflexive monitoring; thirdly, that the production and reproduction of a material practice requires continuous investment by agents in ensembles of action that carry forward in time and space; and finally, that actors' investments in material practices and implementation, and the work that flows from their investments, are themselves affected by the play of power and by changing social contexts (May and Finch 2009).

If it is assumed that a telehealth programme is a complex intervention that comprises a number of components acting independently and inter-dependently, then an NPT approach may offer a theoretically-derived methodology to help understand the factors that enable successful implementation and integration into routine work (normalization) as well as an explanatory framework.

NPT, Appraisal and the Evidence Base for Telehealth

A NPT approach begins with an examination of how a practice is conceptualized and understood by participants, and how this understanding 'coheres', or holds together in action. When we apply this to home telehealth, the divergent conceptualizations and understandings of stakeholders potentially results in a lack of coherence within the practice of home telehealth, the motivations for implementing it and the expected outcomes. Different stakeholders have disparate, and sometimes competing, expectations of what these systems are and what they have to offer. For older people it might be the hope that they can travel less frequently to distant clinics, or a sense of wellbeing and connectedness gained from the knowledge that they are being monitored and cared for, albeit at a distance.

Another key component of NPT which is of potential utility in helping us to understand the complexities surrounding the mainstreaming of home telehealth is that of reflexive monitoring (May and Finch 2009). Reflexive monitoring describes the process by which actors are able to appraise and reflect on their work. Of interest here is the exploration of factors that promote or inhibit the appraisal of a practice. May and Finch (2009) argue that the ability to appraise, and the degree of formality of that appraisal, is a key factor in the embedding or normalization of a practice. An interesting point is made regarding the formality of appraisal. Contrary to what one might expect, according to NPT, relatively informal approaches to appraisal, seen by actors as clinical experience, appear to be associated with successful normalization (Finch et al. 2007). On the other hand, highly formal and strictly defined modes of evaluation, such as randomized controlled trials (RCTs), seem to be less valuable as research tools to integrate experiential or qualitative aspects of implementation.

The intense scrutiny on the quality of the evidence base for home telehealth, and the focus on RCTs and systematic reviews, may therefore be a factor which inhibits the mainstreaming of home telehealth. The history of the research and development of an evidence base for the efficacy and cost effectiveness of telehealth has been characterized by the difficulties associated with aligning stakeholders whose aims, objectives and vision differ greatly and with formulating mixed method approaches to research and development that meet shared expectations of outputs and outcomes.

A number of factors contribute to this situation. Firstly, there are particular challenges in conducting research on innovation in health service delivery in general, where interventions tend to be diffuse, complex and difficult to define (Fulop et al. 2001) and where studies are necessarily multi-disciplinary. This is especially the case with older populations whose health needs are often more complex and pressing, and the opportunities for experimental research more limited. This makes it more difficult to implement the innovation and evaluate its effects (Barlow et al. 2006). Secondly, in the case of telehealth, 'user needs' are especially complex because of the wide variety of stakeholders and their diffuse requirements (Sixsmith and Sixsmith 2000). As well as medical efficacy, these include cost efficiency, acceptability for patients, technical reliability and fulfilment of legal requirements, and compatibility with the health and social care system (Barlow et al. 2006) and, in the case of older people, competing demands and needs that cross social and clinical health systems that are not always harmonized. Thirdly, the existing literature on the evaluation of home telehealth is organized around studies that are often methodologically and scientifically unsound and which therefore do not provide reliable evidence for practice (Williams et al. 2003).

The discourse of informal appraisal based on everyday experience of working with home telehealth has been relatively invisible in comparison with the vocal and highly visible search for 'gold standard' evidence. Voices from the clinical world have been calling for evidence that complies with the methodological frameworks and rigour of the RCT. However, the majority of research until recently has consisted of small pilot projects, very few of which make it past the early research stage for reasons that are still widely debated in the literature (Broens et al. 2007; McCartney 2012; Paré et al. 2007; Greenhalgh et al. 2012; Murray et al. 2011). This is despite the notable enthusiasm of some telehealth champions (Cleland et al. 2009) and policy initiatives (e.g. ThreeMillionLives 2012)[1] that commit to ambitious plans.

So, how can this focus on formal appraisal act to inhibit normalization of home telehealth? One possible explanation is that the informal experience of individuals who are working in the area is being lost in the wider debate about 'formal' evidence. More recent analysis of the organizing vision and high-level strategy on home telehealth elucidates five conflicting and overlapping discourses that cluster around the key stakeholders: policy; industry; social science and nursing researchers; the political economy of academics and clinicians; and, finally, front-line implementers. Interestingly, older people, as one of the fastest growing user groups for telehealth, are missing from this list of key stakeholders.

Those stakeholders that are analysed reflect different disciplinary and stakeholder assumptions that drive each sector (Greenhalgh et al. 2012). Telehealth, like many technologies in healthcare, requires the different values and worldviews held by each stakeholder group to intersect and the measures of success, be they clinical outcomes from RCTs, patient satisfaction, cost effectiveness or efficiency and investment return, to align in some way. Evaluation has therefore proven to be a challenge since a telehealth intervention typically includes a mix of elements and commitment from all these groups.

As discussed briefly above, home telehealth deployments in Europe were initially based around small research trials and pilot studies but have begun to grow in scale in recent years, particularly in the UK (for example the Whole Systems Demonstrator), and the potential for EU-wide deployments have increased with the establishment of funding initiatives such asHorizon 2020. Cross-industry partnerships have emerged, e-health and telehealth research centres have been established and there remains among policy and industry stakeholders a view that Europe is on the verge of a tipping point towards the wide-scale adoption of telehealth interventions and service delivery.

Conclusion

Telehealth today remains locked into a space where stakeholders with differing expectations and interests have difficulty in reaching a shared vision and the potential and desired outcomes of mainstreaming. Clinicians, older people, healthcare providers and technology innovators still have some way to go to construct a platform of evidence, efficacy and efficiency that satisfies multiple needs and expectations. The gap between health technology innovation and mainstreamed implementation is well recognized. Multiple explanations for this are offered within the academic and grey literature. In this chapter we have focused on three that are most usefully informed by our experience in telehealth and our backgrounds in social sciences and anthropology.

This chapter has summarized the already well-documented explanations for the failure to mainstream the initiatives proffered by industry and clinical stakeholders. For industry the explanatory models are framed around a drivers and barriers model of understanding health systems and change. We have looked at the model through which healthcare systems are managed and questioned how sustainable the care pathway is in the light of predicted changes in the way societies will access, deliver and pay for healthcare in the coming decades and in ageing populations. From the clinical perspective the explanatory reasoning is understood against the normative framework of a credible evidence-base – a necessary step to all health intervention. Whilst both explanations make sense within their own frames of reference, neither extends the reasoning beyond their hermeneutic foundation. A third integrative perspective was explored where the focus shifted to how telehealth innovations are implemented and embedded into everyday practice. We looked at this emerging theoretical perspective that focuses on the dynamic processes of implementation and wondered whether this approach might reveal more about how healthcare systems and the culture of work practice form barriers to change, particularly noting how this perspective might help understanding of implementation among older people.

To predict, if it were possible, what e-health might look like thirty years from now one has to imagine for a moment what it is that we ourselves might demand of a system. For some people today who might be labelled as 'quantitative selves' (*The Economist*, March 2012)[2] – those people who have their Nike running shoes linked up to an app on their smart phone – in-home or at-a-distance health monitoring will almost certainly become normalized, a circadian rhythm that indexes the passing of days against visibly measurable indicators of sustainable wellbeing. For the majority, the trajectory of engagement with self-monitoring via e-health solutions will be akin to the January spike in new gym memberships that plummets by March. Sustainable solutions need to override user fatigue, and, as in all new interventions in health and medicine, attain some user compliance.

Notes

1. http://www.dh.gov.uk/health/files/2012/01/Concordat-3-million-lives.pdf.
2. http://www.economist.com/node/21548493.

References

Allen, D. 2010a. 'Care pathways: an ethnographic description of the field', International Journal of Care Pathways 14(1): 4–9. doi: 10.1258/jicp.2009.009015.
———. 2010b. 'Care pathways: some social scientific observations on the field', *International Journal of Care Pathways* 14(2): 47–51. doi: 10.1258/jicp.2009.009016.
Barlow, J., S. Bayer and R. Curry. 2006. 'Implementing complex innovations in fluid multi-stakeholder environments: experiences of "telecare"', *Technovation* 26: 396–406.
———. 2007. 'A systematic review of the benefits of home telecare for frail elderly people and those with long-term conditions', *Journal of Telemedicine & Telecare* 13: 172–79.
Broens, T.H.F., et al. 2007. 'Determinants of successful telemedicine implementations: a literature study', *Journal of Telemedicine and Telecare* 13(6): 303–9. doi: 10.1258/135763307781644951.
Cleland, J.G.F., C. Lewinter and K.M. Goode. 2009. 'Telemonitoring for heart failure: the only feasible option for good universal care?', *European Journal of Heart Failure* 11(3): 227–28. doi: 10.1093/eurjhf/hfp027.
Currell, R., et al. 2000. 'Telemedicine versus face-to-face patient care: effects on professional practice and health care outcomes', *Cochrane Database of Systematic Reviews* 2 (CD002098).

Darkins, A. and M.A. Cary. 2000. *Telemedicine and telehealth: principles, policies, performances and pitfalls*. New York: Springer.

Department of Health UK. 2009. *Whole systems demonstrators: an overview of telecare and telehealth*. London: Department of Health.

Eccles, M., et al. 2009. 'An implementation research agenda', *Implementation Science* 4(1): 18.

Finch, T.L., F.S. Mair and C.R. May. 2007. 'Teledermatology in the UK: lessons in service innovation', *British Journal of Dermatology* 156(3): 521–27.

Fulop, N., et al. (eds). 2001. *Studying the organisation and delivery of health services: research methods*. London: Routledge.

Greenhalgh, T., et al. 2012. 'The organising vision for telehealth and telecare: discourse analysis', *British Medical Journal Open* (4). doi: 10.1136/bmjopen-2012-001574.

Koch, S. 2006. 'Home telehealth – current state and future trends', *International Journal of Medical Informatics* 75: 565–76. doi: 10.1016/j.ijmedinf.2005.09.002.

Kramer, G.M., et al. 2012. 'A standard telemental health evaluation model: the time is now', *Telemedicine Journal and e-health* 18(4): 309–13. doi: 10.1089/tmj.2011.0149.

Kubitschke, L. and K. Cullen. 2010. *ICT and ageing: European study on users, markets and technologies. Final report*. Brussels: European Commission: Directorate General for Information Society and Media.

Leviton, L.C., et al. 2010. 'Evaluability assessment to improve public health policies, programs, and practices', *Annual Review of Public Health* 31(1): 213–33.

MacFarlane, A. and M. O'Reilly-de Brún. 2012. 'Using a theory-driven conceptual framework in qualitative health research', *Qualitative Health Research* 22(5): 607–18. doi: 10.1177/1049732311431898.

Mair, F.S., et al. 2012. 'Factors that promote or inhibit the implementation of e-health systems: an explanatory systematic review', *Bulletin of the World Health Organization* 90: 357–64.

May, C. 2013. 'Agency and implementation: understanding the embedding of healthcare innovations in practice', *Social Science and Medicine* 78: 26–33.

May, C., et al. 2007. 'Understanding the implementation of complex interventions in health care: the normalization process model', *BMC Health Services Research* 7(1): 148.

May, C.R., et al. 2009. 'Development of a theory of implementation and integration: Normalization Process Theory', *Implementation Science* 4: 29. doi: 10.1186/1748-5908-4-29.

May, C. and T. Finch. 2009. 'Implementing, embedding, and integrating practices: an outline of Normalization Process Theory', *Sociology* 43(3): 535–54. doi: 10.1177/0038038509103208.

May, C., V.M. Montori and F.S. Mair. 2009. 'We need minimally disruptive medicine', *British Medical Journal* 339(7719): 485–87. doi: 10.1136/bmj.b2803.

McCartney, Margaret. 2012. 'Show us the evidence for telehealth', *British Medical Journal* 344: e469. doi: 10.1136/bmj.e469.

Merton, R.K. 1957. *Social theory and social structure*. New York: The Free Press.

Morrison, D. and F.S. Mair. 2011. 'Telehealth in practice: using Normalisation Process Theory to bridge the translational gap', *Primary Care Respiratory Journal* 20(4): 351–52.

Murray, E., et al. 2010. 'Normalisation process theory: a framework for developing, evaluating and implementing complex interventions', *BMC Medicine* 8: 63. doi: 10.1186/1741-7015-8-63.

———. 2011. 'Why is it difficult to implement e-health initiatives? A qualitative study', *Implementation Science* 6(1): 6.

Paré, G., M. Jaana and C. Sicotte. 2007. 'Systematic review of home telemonitoring for chronic diseases: the evidence base', *Journal of the American Medical Informatics Association* 14(3): 269–77. doi: 10.1197/jamia.M2270.

Pinder, R., et al. 2005. 'What's in a care pathway? Towards a cultural cartography of the new NHS', *Sociology of Health & Illness* 27(6): 759–79. doi: 10.1111/j.1467-9566.2005.00473.x.

Sixsmith, A. and J. Sixsmith. 2000. 'Smart care technologies: meeting whose need?', *Journal of Telemedicine & Telecare* 6: 190–92.

Williams, T., et al. 2003. 'Normative models of health technology assessment and the social production of evidence about telehealth care', *Health Policy* 64(1): 39–54.

9. ANALYSING HANDS-ON-TECH CARE WORK IN TELECARE INSTALLATIONS
Frictional Encounters with Gerontechnological Designs

Daniel López and Tomás Sánchez-Criado

IN THE PAST TWENTY YEARS gerontechnological technologies have been marketed as plug-and-play solutions to complex and costly care necessities. They are expected to reduce the cost of traditional forms of hands-on-care. Science and Technology Studies (STS) have contributed to discussing this idea (for an overall perspective, see Schillmeier and Domenech 2010) by pointing at important transformations in the care arrangements where these technologies are implemented. Instead of just 'plug-and-play' solutions, transformations are found in protagonists, their roles and functions, and more importantly in redefining care.

This chapter seeks to add new nuances to the definition of care in these scenarios by paying attention to what we term 'hands-on-tech care work'. This terminology refers to the practices, usually undertaken by technicians (installation, repair and maintenance), which hold together the silent infrastructures that are now considered to be suitable and sustainable forms of care work for ageing societies. Hands-on-tech care work is usually hidden from most of the discussions concerning new care technologies for older people. On the one hand this is because installation, repair and maintenance work on telecare devices is considered as a mere technical procedure, i.e. not considered to be part of care work. On the other hand it is because of the widespread view that if technologies are well designed, installing them is simply a matter of 'plug-and-play'. However, if we look carefully into the installation process, these concepts are easily refuted. This is because these technologies need to be continually welcomed, tuned, adjusted, tweaked, personalized, updated and installed.

We shall consider ethnographic observations of the installation process of a social alarm (consisting of a pendant and a phone hub) for older people living at home in Catalonia and Madrid. We intend to question not only the concept of care technologies as a plug-and-play solution, but also to examine the common understanding of what care work is in these technologically-based care scenarios.

For the purpose of this chapter, we have limited the data to installation of telecare devices, excluding technical checks or repairs. During the installation, various moments of friction occur. These moments of friction and uncertainty are worth careful analysis since they are not supposed to be within the scope of the service. Paying attention to these frictions during installation allows us to see the process of handling this gerontechnology. Its possibilities and practicalities can be explored and tested (Hasu 2000). Such frictions usually make visible a greater number of possibilities for technology than those currently assumed by the designers (Hyysalo 2004). In that sense, the 'success' of a technology or a design has to face the 'creative integrations' required by their users (Suchman et al. 1999). This cannot always happen without the help and care of the service technicians.

These frictions reveal the 'hands-on-tech' care work conducted by installers as a particular form of care work. By mixing technical, spatial and relational elements, the service's function and the protagonists involved are redefined, thus making the technology useful for the users and operational for the services. In this regard, 'hands-on-tech' care work entails a constant tinkering (Mol 2008; Mol et al. 2010b), adjusting the particularities of every home to the predispositions (and impositions) of the service and its devices.

In this vein, delving into the 'hands-on-tech' care work carried out by telecare technicians will enable us to frame the debate about care technologies for older people, taking into account the double aspect of the care work performed by telecare technicians, who not only take care of the material aspects but also of their very users and their relations with close relatives, neighbours, caregivers and friends. We would like to suggest that acknowledging such care work might open up a new approach to care technologies. Rather than focusing on design and use, which implies seeing these technologies as products to be consumed, we propose taking into account the problems encountered when installing new care devices. This places onto centre stage questions concerning the lives of older people. The installation phase may trigger changes in habits and routines that are essential for people to live their lives as they wish. It is essential to find out what adjustments may help or improve their lives or, on the contrary, put them at risk. The diverse forms of 'hands-on-tech' care work lead to diverse forms of dealing with this ethical concern. We believe this should underpin innovation policies for ageing societies.

Challenging Plug-and-Play Attitudes in Care Technologies

What is at stake in most of the debates about ICT solutions for active ageing is whether these promising innovations may finally result in more sustainable health and social care systems or not. Alternatively it may be that this urge to reduce costs may lead to more precarious caring and thereby to more vulnerability for those needing care. Whereas researchers adhering to the latter criticize new care technologies as a way to support traditional hands-on-care together with its humane values (such as empathy, reciprocity and understanding), those adhering to the former would be in favour of care-at-a-distance technologies as a way of increasing the system's efficiency, whilst enhancing the independence and wellbeing of older people (Mort et al. 2011).

However, despite their differences the arguments used by both the geron-technological believers and the critics turn around the same point: be they 'for' or 'against', these technologies are defined as 'plug-and-play' solutions. This plug-and-play image reinforces the misleading distinction between 'warm' and 'cold' care solutions (Pols and Moser 2009), the former being more human-based and the latter more technical-based. Moreover, when we look at hands-on-care or care-at-a-distance, the material care practices tend to be approached as a mere technical issue. As a result of this the activity of caring using the technologies of these care practices is regarded as even more disconnected from the actual practices of care giving.

Even though nowadays care is a social and political concern (Daly 2002) as well as an object of theoretical discussions and sociological and ethical classifications (Tronto 1993), the material aspects of care have not received the same attention as the political economy of care work. This is precisely the argument that Julia Twigg (2002) puts forward in her ethnographic approach to home care tasks such as bathing. According to Twigg, the material aspects of care have traditionally been silent and hidden from both public gaze and social inquiry. To do otherwise, she argues, would challenge our modern, secular model of citizenship. This model is based on the idea of an independent, autonomous and disembodied rational subject, detached from 'his' worldly needs. This model carries with it very subtle and mundane mechanisms that by making dependency and frailty invisible, together with its gendered distribution of labour, lead to gender exploitation and subordination (Kittay et al. 2005). Twigg shows how these distinctions are enacted in the care workers' everyday lives. In her account, care work is split in two, on the one hand, dealing with what is publicly defined as care (comprising both relational work and practical and emotional competences), and on the other hand, bodywork as detached from care work, which is downplayed not only by managers and policy-makers but also by care workers themselves (see also Timonen et al. 2006). The former relational and emotional aspects are emphasized in public, whilst the dirtiness and filthiness of physical work is usually kept away from view.[1] This could be done because of its low wages (the tasks are usually delegated to lower-level staff) or because it is unnamed by care workers themselves. The care workers themselves do not or cannot allocate time to explicitly share their complaints and know-how, thus keeping it out of the public sphere.

According to the work of Roberts and Mort (2009), telecare can make care work more invisible, reinforcing a threefold division of labour:[2] (1) physical work (mostly performed by home care services, according to users' needs – cleaning, shopping or personal care, usually outsourced to specialized services or to migrant workers); (2) emotional work (mainly performed by relatives and friends who care about the users); and (3) monitoring (a supervising role allocated to telecare services, which needs, in order to properly function, a clear-cut distinction from the other areas).

Rather than disembodying care, this monitoring role of telecare and the threefold division of labour required entails a redefinition of 'what counts as care' and its material aspects (Pols 2012). The assumption that care consists exclusively of bodywork, with emotional support being its specific feature, leads to reductionist accounts of care practice and care technologies (Mol et al. 2010a). As we tried to show in our studies on home telecare, operators' active-listening practices constitute care work (see López et al. 2010; Roberts et al. 2011).[3] In any case, both Twigg's (2002) vindication of bodywork and the consideration of 'hidden' tele-operators' active-listening practices (López et al. 2010; Roberts et al. 2011) are too often regarded as invisible forms of care work. They are thus taken for granted rather than given proper public recognition.

Switch on the Lights for the Installers

However, as we would like to show in this chapter, care studies have forgotten to pay attention to another invisible yet essential form of care work in technological settings. Despite the growing influence of STS studies in the understanding of technocare systems (Mol et al. 2010b; Oudshoorn 2011; see for example, Pols 2012; Schillmeier and Domenech 2010), little or no attention has been paid to the study of what we would call 'hands-on-tech' care work. This is the care work performed by the technicians in charge of installing, repairing and maintaining care-at-a-distance technological services, such as telecare.

As a way of amending this situation with installation, repair and maintenance technicians, our suggestion would be to redirect our attention to interesting developments in workplace studies and ethnographies of infrastructures (Lampland and Star 2009; Star 2002). Such literature tends to make visible the important efforts needed to keep infrastructures working smoothly as well as the 'need' for such work to remain invisible. As Henke explains, 'if the everyday routines of work are so dependent on repair for the continued maintenance of social order, we would expect that repair skills should be highly visible in their practice. Paradoxically, however, those things which are most vital for basic aspects of social interaction tend to be the things that are most invisible' (Henke 1999: 69).

By showing their importance through ethnography, these works seek to invert the widespread and historical invisibility of operators and technical workers' 'manipulation' (Mort 2002; Orr 1996; Shapin 1989), in stark contrast with the public recognition of engineers' 'vision' or designers' 'invention'.

Indeed, Henke's (1999) representation of repair technicians' work highlights its mixture of bodies, discourses and space. It also considers the distributed and contextual nature of its know-how and its on-going and constant basis: work, that, as Denis and Pontille (2013) put it in their study of the Paris metro maintenance technicians, has to do with taking care of things that are unstable and plural so as to constantly put order back in place, thus showing the workings of others and making it visible.

We believe that such a framework could help us to tackle the specific aspects of the double invisibility affecting telecare installers' 'hands-on-tech' care work. This would allow us to interfere with and problematize the common 'plug-and-play' presentation of gerontechnologies as 'solutions'.

Tense Encounters within the Installation Process

In the following section we will show several excerpts from installation processes that took place in the regions of Catalonia and Madrid (Spain), from two different telecare services from autumn 2008 to summer 2009. Our two ethnographies were carried out in a supervised, fly-on-the-wall mode only interacting with telecare users in the company of the services' staff . Even though there are several slight organizational differences between the two organizations, they may be considered broadly speaking as analogous in size and structure. Both rely mainly on public-funded users, therefore they have to comply with the service standards put in place by the Spanish Institute for Older People and Social Services.

In both services, telecare installers have to wire and plug in the devices. They then configure them and later check if the pendant and terminal are working correctly. They also check that the communication with the tele-operators is smooth and if the details of the user are correctly recorded in the service's database. Their job usually starts with a user petition form sent to the repair and maintenance department by the commercial office of the telecare service that contains the user data. From that moment an appointment has to be made by the service's social workers, contacting the future user by phone.

The following excerpts show different situations of friction at different points of the process. These are instances of the intricate singularities that installers might come across whenever they cross the user home's threshold during an installation appointment. They will help us show the 'hands-on-tech' care work skills that they have to perform for the installation to take place, almost always capable of avoiding the pitfalls when moving between the Scylla and Charybdis of every installation job.

Friction One: Who Is the User?

The installers we shadowed usually say that 'you cannot install it if the user refuses'. Even if the service has been requested by another person (such as one of the user's children), the installation always requires a certain degree of active collaboration on the part of the user, be it at the beginning (in order to access the house) or at the end (signing the contract that authorizes them as a service user). In fact, it is not that unlikely for users to slam the door in the technicians' face or to refuse to open the door.

What seems to be an ethical and practical requirement for the installers becomes difficult to discern throughout the process of installing the device. Assuming that having asked for the service is the same as wanting the service turns out to be extremely problematic:

> We are in Ciudad del Sur,[4] a medium-sized municipality forty minutes south-bound of Madrid, to undertake an installation in a middle-class block of apartments. The older person's daughter opens the door. The future user looks extremely quiet and worried, sitting in the living room's sofa, saying: 'they insist that I should have the device, as if I want it...' It appears that the service has been requested by the daughter in her name after she had a fall. However, the older woman is not exactly rejecting us. Joaquín, the installer (who has to perform a given ratio of installations), talks to her saying, 'But we are not here because you cannot manage yourself', and then goes on, jokingly, explaining the virtues of the service simulating a cheesy commercial from the 1960s. The daughter adds that she cannot be at home all the time to take care of her. But the older woman is stubborn in her reluctance, 'But if

they have come from Madrid ... I have to be useless'. Joaquín, who is already setting up the hub nearby the living room's phone answers her from the floor, 'we have a station in town'.

The older woman remains unconvinced and starts murmuring that the pendant would disturb her when washing the dishes. Joaquín laughs off her complaints, playing, very respectfully, with her, turning on and off the social alarm pendant around her neck, making her laugh, and explaining to her how the device works. 'Red button engages the call... and look, this clothes-pin in the back could be useful to avoid problems when washing the dishes... so it is not always necessary to have it around your neck'. She laughs but she is still worried, 'What if I fall and I hurt my hands and I cannot press?' which makes Joaquín laugh out loud: 'That would be bad luck'. They laugh together. Still a bit worried but much more relaxed, the user says that she had accepted the device, through clenched teeth, because she would like to have some company. At the same time giving a very unconvincing look at the pendant she has recently been given.

When Joaquín finishes the technical part of the installation he cries out in a funny voice: 'I need signatures!' opening up a blue cardboard folder with the service's forms. The daughter springs into the living room: 'Me or her?' but Joaquín turns kindly to her mother offering her the pen, 'Don't worry, this is not a test!' Writing proves to be difficult for the new user. After that they do a quick 'first call check' with the lady being engaged by Joaquín throughout the process. Do this, do that, 'wear it always, even under the shower'. She has fun with Joaquín's comic explanation but Joaquín is in a hurry, 'We need to get going!' When leaving the house Joaquín winks at her with a smiling face saying, 'You know, if you need something, bang!' He mimics a button-press.

In many situations it is crystal clear who wants it. Frequently, it is the older users who live alone and do not have a nearby relative or carer at hand. When that happens, she or he requests the service and there is no need to negotiate with third parties. Then again, many installers recall situations like the one we have just witnessed. Even though access to the home is relatively easy and the user-installer interaction can be fluid, the whole installation setting turns into a sort of ambivalent theatre, where many underlying and opposed interests, as well as mixed expectations on how everyone should behave, are exposed.

In those cases, the question of who wants it is no longer easy to establish and it is during the installations that the problem emerges. This is manifested through silent gestures and slight boycotts or in open quarrels. Sometimes intervention from relatives or carers is needed to put an end to it and thus facilitate the installation. But most of the time the installer has to play along in the uncertain and strange terrain of the user's home. They have to deploy all of their skills to navigate the tide. They have to act (as Joaquín did in the case above) as a sort of dance teacher, grabbing the user by the hand and making her try the first steps of the installation tune, offering more or less convincing arguments of different kinds (sometimes technical but also, as in this case, non-topical small-talk or jokes to prevent the user's confrontation with the whole process) with the sole purpose of setting up the installation and vanishing from the scene, running off to the next appointment.

In fact, installers know they cannot simply ignore these ebbs and flows when they happen, no matter how much they would prefer a smooth installation. Installations require a great deal of collaboration from the part of the yet-to-become users that may be sometimes supplemented by the efforts of the relatives or carers to convince them. Even though installers wish the process to go smoothly, installations are not mere 'plug-and-play' moments, where all they have to do is set up a device and make it work. Installations involve affective and kinship relations, responsibilities and expectations, which must be successfully interwoven in such a way as to enable the locating of the device in the most technically-suitable place in the user's home, as well as a demonstration and the completion of all the needed paperwork for the service contract between the user and telecare company.

As we will show with further examples, such interactions during installation need a particular 'hands-on-tech' care work by the installers, care work that is only visible by watching them perform. In order to grasp its importance, in the subsequent ethnographic material we would like to focus on two key moments of friction in every installation process: (1) 'where should it be placed?' – the moment when the exact location of the device is determined; and (2) 'what counts as a contact?' – when installers gather the user data required by the service.

In each of these frictional encounters the installers' 'hands-on-tech' care work is needed, indeed is indispensable for telecare to take place in the smoothest possible way. This leaves everyone with the impression that it is a mere 'plug-and-play' task simply because they vanish after every installation, only returning when they are needed to take care of the whole setting.

Friction Two: Where Should it Be Placed?

Most of the installations begin with a short interview. The installers ask the users the same set of questions in approximately the same order. 'How many telephones are there in the house?', 'Where do you spend most of the time?', 'Do you have any hearing difficulties?' With these questions, the technicians make sure that the house infrastructure complies with the minimal technical conditions for the service to work properly and identify the appropriate location for the telecare terminal's placement.

Telecare services require the users to provide an installed base in the house where they can work. There must be a working power supply (which means that the user has to pay the bills, otherwise the device would run out of battery after six hours and the user would remain helpless from that moment on) and there must be at least one fully functional phone landline, digital or analogue, which is essential so the terminals can make the calls to the alarm centre.

However, at the same time as attending to the house's technical infrastructure, they also need to deal with users' dwelling behaviours.

> In between installations one of us talks to Oriol, an installer from one of the local offices of the Catalan service we are observing. He tells us that the placement of the hub's location depends on the supervision of the rooms the older users use the most. However, they also have to take into account if there is, for instance, a child of the older user who comes to spend the night as this would make it important to understand which spaces are being used more during daylight. One of us asks him if the users have aesthetic preferences. Oriol answers that there are people who do not want installers to drill holes in the walls or too much wire in the flat, but in this local office if they do not want to 'rely on' the phone line the user has to sign a disclaimer.[5] Furthermore, kitchen installations are not recommended so as to avoid interferences from other electrical equipment. Likewise proximity to the TV set is also not recommended so that the tele-operators can hear clearly in the case of an emergency. In a nutshell, the location of the device in the house must provide the teleoperators on the other side of the line with good quality sound so as to understand what is going on in the case of an emergency.[6]

Given that the ability to move around often reduces with age, some users spend most of their time in a few rooms (mainly the living room during the day and the bedroom at night). The installers are encouraged to plug the telecare device into the telephone closest to these areas, so that the tele-operators can easily hear what is going in most parts of the house. As we will see in the following case, finding the right site to install the telecare terminal involves complying with the above mentioned infrastructural requirements but none of these requirements are merely technical nor can they be handled without taking into account non-technical criteria.

> Francesc and one of us arrive at Filomena's flat. She is seventy-five, living alone. When entering the home we notice the excessive and extreme care in every detail of the house's decoration, great mirrors, crystal figurines, golden frames, paintings, vases, curtains whose pattern matches those of

the table doilies and immense artificial plants. We have to move with extreme care around the house so as to not break anything. It is a museum/house with an exhibition of objects.

Filomena presents herself dressed with a high-quality dressing gown, a hairstylist coiffure and makeup. She starts talking about the ceiling leaks from a neighbour's flat and shows us through the house pointing out the green mould she will have to have repaired. Francesc asks her about the number of phones in the house, and if any of them are cordless.[7] Filomena points at three phones: one in the bedroom, another one in the study and a third one in the living room. Checking the space Francesc says that the most central room is the entrance hall and that the device should be installed there on a low table which has a couple of statues, vases and an artificial plant.

When he starts placing the device on the table she insistently asks if it is going to remain in there and if there couldn't be a better place for the thing. Taking a look at it amongst the luxurious pieces of decoration the ugly and bizarre plastic hub is a bit incongruous and would be the first thing one sees when entering the house. Although not opposing forthrightly the placement Filomena suggests that we accompany her to the adjacent room, the study, pointing at a bookshelf where there is an empty spot. She tells us that this was the previous location of the thing and that the device should go there. It is a place somewhat hidden from view but central enough, as Francesc remarks. He nods but insists that he would have to drill through the wall to wire up the device, something he cannot do today because he doesn't have the drill with him. Hence, he will make a provisional installation in the living room directly plugging it into one of the phones.

In this excerpt a clear point of friction can be seen at the intersection of two ways of handling the hub's placement. One is techno-centric (Francesc's choice, taking into account the service's needs for optimal functioning) and the other is user-centric (taking into account the user's preferences and Filomena's modes of dwelling). In Filomena's case the point of conflict comes to the fore through a quiet negotiation: the entrance hall (together with the living room) is one of the 'public' sites of her house where she welcomes her guests, hence it is an essential part of the 'presentation of herself' (Goffman 1959) strategies. Placing the device in such a place might endanger her social image as she perceives it; she is unwilling to accept that position perhaps because she does not want to be seen as someone in need of care. Eventually, the friction was resolved by Francesc because her chosen spot did not contradict the technical requirements of the service. Even though Francesc's and Filomena's principles are mismatched, she only wants it in a place hidden from view whilst he needs a place in compliance with the service's needs (even if it requires a drill).

In similar situations installers try to solve the problem by carrying out an installation in parallel to avoid drillings and extra wire. As installer Apolinio explains: 'Everyone has the right to have a neat and tidy house... You can't just go in there and place a plainly visible ugly wire if the user doesn't want to'. In such cases frictions regarding the hub's placement arise in the form of slight aesthetic clashes. However, at other times it is the terminal's radio range that is brought to the fore as a problem because of the older person's use expectations. This happens with very active older people who move around a lot and would like to have protection outdoors, in houses with gardens, in the apartment block's stairway or upstairs in houses with more than one level. Similarly, people with slight hearing problems want the device to be installed as close as possible to the places where they usually dwell. This poses some problems to the technician's criterion of central location and requires installers to handle the situation carefully – another form of 'hands-on-tech' care – in order to reach a workable compromise (see Figure 9.1).

FIGURE 9.1 'Provisional installation'.

Scene of a 'provisional installation', a trick performed by Lorenzo to show an older woman who was slightly hard of hearing that she could be heard from a central point of the house even if she was in her room with the doors closed. Observed by one of the authors in Madrid (November 2008). Picture taken and used with permission.

Friction Three: What Counts as a Contact?

Once the terminal has been placed installers become data-gatherers, checking if the existing data collected in the installation request form is correct. They also need to fill in several forms on site – some to be communicated to the tele-operators when doing the 'first-call check' but mostly to be recorded in the database in the service offices later. Amongst the important paperwork to be filled in, such as the key-custody form, is the 'contact data' form.

Practices surrounding writing down the contacts details give rise to one of the most important points of friction in the process: that is, making decisions on who the contacts are and who would be an appropriate person for such a role according to the users' and the services' differing criteria, e.g. a close person in emotional terms vs. someone who would be easily reachable if anything happened to the older user.

One of the sources of this friction in the installation process lies in the different criteria in the contact selection process. This opens up to closer scrutiny the sorts of relations that older people maintain with those who are supposedly closest to them (relatives, friends and neighbours). In most of the cases contacts are selected from users' kin. This may be for reasons of true affection, filial obligation or a mixture of the two.

One day when witnessing the installation in Caterina's flat, Lucía, the installer, asked her to give her the names of the contacts. Complaining that her children were 'a bit far away', dispersed around different provinces of Catalonia but no farther than an hour drive, she began listing all of them; they all had mobile phones and almost all of them had keys to access her flat. The son who was present during the installation had planned to take the keys the older woman had prepared for the service's custody. They began searching for keys. During the conversation they spoke several times of a close neighbour and long-time family friend, called Manu. Despite the fact that he had keys to access the flat and could be a more useful contact in an emergency, he was discarded as a contact. In this case Lucía did not intervene, but in other cases, as in the following one, some users who maintained a close relationship of mutual support with neighbours brought up the question of the suitability of including relatives as contacts:

> When Amparo, the social worker, asks the user who the contacts would be, she explains that she lives on her own and if anything bad happens to her the service should contact her cousin, who has keys to access and lives in the very same industrial town on the Llobregat river in Barcelona. But then she goes on to name Montserrat, a long-time friend from the sewing factory, and Encarna, a long-time friend who is in her will. When Amparo asks her if she is a relative or a friend, the user hesitates and goes on to explain that neither

of the two are, but both are 'someone I trust'. The user says that she wouldn't be a good main contact because Encarna is working all day.

However, when the users we observed have close relatives nearby (very often their children) the question of who should be the appropriate contact turns into something of a 'love test': who would you like, or who could come should an emergency occur? Who is responsible? Who takes care of you? Who cares? Who do you trust the most? Who do you feel closer to? An interesting instance of this was narrated to us by the technician Oriol whilst driving towards an appointment we had. He explained that certain users want all of their children included as contacts, and recalled laughing about a user who wanted her son in Almería (800km far from Barcelona) to be included. 'It simply couldn't be done', he said, because such a person would be useless as a main contact but they solved the problem by including her son as a contact and then scribbling a memo for the alarm centre tele-operators stating that they should only contact him for information purposes.

The user's definition of a 'close' contact person often contrasts with the services' definition. As far as the services are concerned, a good contact is, to put it simply, anyone the user trusts who would be free to help the services attend the user or open the door in case of a quick intervention being needed. However, as we have seen the selection process is usually complex because of 'vagueness' about the category of 'contact' which can in fact include many sorts of relationships. The installers need to translate these relationships into the services' terms.

This makes evident another strand of 'hands-on-tech' care work by the installers: the ability to be able to finalize the paperwork having established a compromise between the interests of the users and those of the services. In some cases, as we have seen in the previous story with the technician Lucía, the installer understands that this is something that needs to be negotiated with the user's relatives and steps aside. In others, the installer defends the functional definition of the contact over family concerns but with sensitivity, as in the case recounted by Oriol in the car where he was able to compromise by including her far-away son as a contact but 'deactivating' him as an option in cases of emergency.

Rethinking Care Technologies through 'Hands-on-Tech' Care Work

As we have seen throughout the various frictions described, the main duty of the installer is not only to 'join together' the functionalities of the terminal and the pendant with the particular configuration of power supply and phone wires. Installing the telecare device also requires the 'joining together' of domestic architectures, dwelling practices and aesthetic preferences together with acoustic ranges and free-noise zones.

What at first sight would seem to be very clearly defined turns out to be a matter of complex negotiation. The definition of 'the user', the way in which the telecare service might be used, the expectations and will to use it, and the people who are going to aid the user are all debated throughout the process. In fact, even the personal and intimate feelings that 'join together' the user with other people they feel close to can be put to test during the installation process.

Handling these situations is not always easy and sometimes the installers use the 'technicalities' jargon or 'geek-tricks' to avoid getting trapped in the 'way too personal' dramas of some users. However, in many cases it is indeed necessary to plunge into such personal dramas, to dive skilfully into their relational and emotional density in order to get the installation done. A successful installation may depend on the installer's skills in 'joining together' the expectations, needs, conflicts and desires of all of the participants. And as we have seen, not only do they have to deal with the controversial spatial configurations of the technology but these must be 'joined together' with the distributions of tasks and responsibilities derived from enacting particular forms of kinship, neighbourhood, 'mutual-aidness' or friendship relationships.

In sum, there is no such thing as a 'plug-and-play' situation. The frictions mentioned above show installation to be the flash point of particular heterogeneous arrangements in which the service might become functional (or fail to do so). The tricky part is that this arrangement is neither contained in the technical settings of the devices nor could be naturally deployed by strictly following 'protocols of installation'. This 'joint-togetherness' must be made up by the installer: '[...] each another next first time', using Garfinkel's (2002: 98) expression. This is precisely the caring side of their work. These installations are contextually produced and therefore depend on the elements they articulate. They are fragile and their production is fallible.

The fragility and fallibility of this joint-togetherness is precisely what the 'plug-and-play' discourse hides from view. Taking into account such a doubly invisible hands-on-tech care work and its importance in handling the frictions we have seen above allows us to grasp how these technologies are at stake every time the installers have to perform an installation in a house. This is because they might fail at any time throughout the process, either when entering the home, in their placement of the device, or in the subsequent paperwork. Considered in this light, installations become sociomaterial processes of constant negotiation, taking place in an alien setting in which every installer has to use his or her best 'negotiation skills' to take care of the practical setting that such technologies and services need, what they are useful for and to whom (Akrich 2002; Ciborra 2002).

Telecare and home care technologies bring with them the promise of a transformation in the relationships of care-giving and care-receiving in conditions of budgetary efficacy and enhancement of self-care. In the presentation of these promises the design of such gerontechnologies usually takes front-stage. The argument goes that a mere placement would instantly show benefits. In this chapter we have ethnographically shown and analysed several frictional encounters that the technicians of two Spanish telecare services had to face when visiting the users' homes to complete the installations. Grounding our research in a review of the social studies of care and technology practices, we have tried to interfere with the 'plug-and-play' discourse contained in the promises of these innovations. What image of such innovations would be brought about if we made visible the doubly invisible technicians' 'hands-on-tech' care work, which remains concealed from public gaze as part of the background activities of care delivery and the maintenance of its infrastructures? We would like to conclude by pointing out some possible scenarios such a research programme might open up.

Thinking and designing innovations based on their installation and placement practices brings to light the necessary negotiations and the constant repair and maintenance work they require. This gives us a very different image from the 'plug-and-play' presentations (where devices are treated as finished-and-usable objects). Thinking about installers' 'hands-on-tech' care work could bring with it the promise of a renewal of the anthropological understanding of such technocare settings, offering more than two possible points of entry (either design or use) and allowing for a more nuanced view than the 'pro/con technology' framework. By paying more attention to the frictions of the implementation processes we might be able to give more detailed descriptions of the skills required to navigate through them, which, as our observations indicate, extend far beyond the reach of merely taking care of technologies: 'hands-on-tech' care work is about constantly emplacing and underpinning the materiality of the devices and concrete user configurations for these later-life services to work (Sánchez-Criado et al. 2014).

Turning our attention from the promise of design as a space of ready-made and clear-cut 'solutions' to such constant underpinnings could also affect gerontechnological innovation policies and strategies. We believe that paying attention to 'hands-on-tech' care work would be of great interest as a new issue in the current trend of participatory and co-creation strategies, allowing us to counter the engineer-centric processes of design by putting at the centre the work and know-how of those in charge of their implementation and maintenance (López 2014). Paying attention to 'hands-on-tech' might introduce the need to conceive of care work and its materiality in a more open-ended, 'repairable' fashion, placing at its very centre the on-going collective process of tinkering with problems rather than the production of closed-down and commoditized care 'solutions'.

Acknowledgements

This work was funded by the FP7 European Project 'Ethical Frameworks for Telecare Technologies' (Ref. 217787) and the project 'Experticia, Democracia y Movilización Social' (CSO2011-29749-C02-02), funded by the Spanish Ministerio de Economía y Competitividad. For the writing of this chapter Tomás Sánchez Criado has also received the support of an *Alliance 4 Universities* post-doctoral fellowship at Universitat Autònoma de Barcelona. We would like to acknowledge the work of all of our colleagues on this project; their intellectual contributions to this work are inestimable. We would also like to thank the installers and managers of the telecare services for their generosity.

Notes

1. The 'invisibilization' of care as 'dirty work' is also an 'achievement' to which many home technologies have contributed, as several feminist studies have documented (see for example Cockburn and Ormrod 1993 on microwaves or washing machines, and Oldenziel and Zachmann 2009 on kitchen architecture). In this new technological space the users are thought of as 'managers' rather than as 'workers': when for instance, cooking becomes a clean, eminently cognitive activity in which food is processed according to formal procedures of calculus, much of the important and painful work of cooking (preparation and care for the process) goes under the radar (see also Giedion 1955).
2. This fragmentation however, does not lead to a change in the hegemonic sexual division of labour by which women (i.e., wives and daughters, or lowly paid migrant carers) are still the main care providers (Gutiérrez Rodríguez 2010; Hoch- schild 2000).
3. Operators' assignment is to correctly code and align the incoming calls, stick- ing to the protocols of interaction throughout the whole process but need- ing to 'break these guidelines to be able to attend to the calls' slight nuances. This allows them to detect hidden or unexpressed needs that require a special response.
4. Names of people and places have been slightly transformed for the sake of anonymity.

5. Telecare devices can be connected to the phone landline by a single cable – which is what S refers to as 'relying on it' – or in parallel. Single-cable installations allow the telecare devices to 'take control' of the line hence ensuring a higher efficacy in cases of emergency. In some cases telecare devices installed in parallel cannot complete the call because the phone has been left off the hook.
6. Indeed, the good placement of the terminal can turn a troublesome situation like an alarm call without response from the user into one that is much easier to handle. By changing the audio system of the device's transmission, the tele-operator can hear the user breathe or cry out even if he or she is lying down in any of the adjacent rooms, thereby identifying what kind of situation they are facing. In any case, when doubt arises during an installation, the phone connectivity of the telecare device must prevail over audibility.
7. Cordless phones very often remain 'off the hook', hence creating difficulties for telecare devices in case of an emergency. In such cases telecare devices 'must come first' in the single-cable installation as they are able to take control of the line.

References

Akrich, M. 2002. 'A gazogene in Costa Rica: an experiment in techno-sociology', in Pierre Lemonnier (ed.), *Technological choices. Transformation in material cultures since the Neolithic*. London: Routledge, pp. 289–37.

Ciborra, C. 2002. 'Xenia: hosting an innovation', in Claudio Ciborra (ed.), *The labyrinths of information: challenging the wisdom of systems*. Oxford: Oxford University Press, pp. 103–18.

Cockburn, C. and S. Ormrod. 1993. *Gender and technology in the making*. Thousand Oaks, CA: Sage.

Daly, M. 2002. 'Care as a good for social policy', *Journal of Social Policy* 31(2): 251–70.

Denis, J. and D. Pontille. (2013). 'Material orderings and the care of things', *CSI Working Paper Series* 34. Available at http://www.csi.ensmp.fr/working-papers/WP/WP_CSI_034.pdf (accessed 25 November 2013).

Garfinkel, H. 2002. *Ethnomethodology's program: working out Durkeim's aphorism*. Lanham, MD: Rowman & Littlefield Publishers.

Giedion, S. 1955. *Mechanization takes command*. New York: Oxford University Press.

Goffman, E. 1959. *The presentation of self in everyday life*. New York: Doubleday.

Gutiérrez Rodríguez, E. 2010. *Migration, domestic work and affect: a decolonial approach on value and the feminization of labor*. New York: Routledge.

Hasu, M. 2000. 'Blind men and the elephant', *Outlines. Critical Practice Studies* 2(1): 5–41.

Henke, C.R. 1999. 'The mechanics of workplace order: toward a sociology of repair', *Berkeley Journal of Sociology* 44: 55–81.

Hochschild, A.R. 2000. 'Global care chains and emotional surplus value', in Will Hutton and Anthony Giddens (eds), *On the edge: living with global capitalism*. London: Jonathan Cape, pp. 130–46.

Hyysalo, S. 2004. 'Technology nurtured: collectives in maintaining and implementing technology for elderly care', *Science Studies* 17(2): 23–43.

Kittay, E.F., B. Jennings and A.A. Wasunna. 2005. 'Dependency, difference and the global ethic of longterm care', *Journal of Political Philosophy* 13(4): 443–69.

Lampland, M. and S.L. Star. 2009. *Standards and their stories: how quantifying, classifying, and formalizing practices shape everyday life.* Ithaca, NY: Cornell University Press.

López, D., B. Callén, F. Tirado and M. Domènech. 2010. 'How to become a guardian angel? Providing safety in a home telecare service', in Annemarie Mol, Ingunn Moser and Jeannette Pols (eds), *Care in practice. On tinkering in clinics, homes and farms.* Bielefeld: Transcript, pp. 73–91.

López, D. 2014. 'Little arrangements that matter. Rethinking autonomy-enabling innovations for later life', *Technological Forecasting and Social Change* (In Press). doi:10.1016/j.techfore.2014.02.01

Mol, A. 2008. *The logic of care.* London: Routledge.

Mol, A., I. Moser and J. Pols. 2010a. 'Care: putting practice into theory', in Annemarie Mol, Ingunn Moser and Jeannette Pols (eds), *Care in practice: on tinkering in clinics, homes and farms,* Bielefeld: Transcript, pp. 7–27.

Mol, A., I. Moser and J. Pols. (eds). 2010b. *Care in practice: on tinkering in clinics, homes and farms.* Bielefeld: Transcript.

Mort, M. 2002. *Building the trident network.* Cambridge, MA: MIT Press.

Mort, M., C. Roberts and C. Milligan. 2011. 'Telecare and older people: re-ordering social relations', in René von Schomberg (ed.), *Towards responsible research and innovation in the information and communication technologies and security technologies fields.* Luxemburg: Publications Office of the European Union, pp. 149–64.

Oldenziel, R. and K. Zachmann. 2009. *Cold war kitchen.* Cambridge, MA: MIT Press.

Orr, J.E. 1996. *Talking about machines: an ethnography of a modern job.* Ithaca, NY: ILR Press.

Oudshoorn, N. 2011. *Telecare technologies and the transformation of healthcare.* New York: Palgrave Macmillan.

Pols, J. 2012. *Care at a distance: on the closeness of technology.* Amsterdam: Amsterdam University Press.

Pols, J. and I. Moser. 2009. 'Cold technologies versus warm care? On affective and social relations with and through care technologies', *ALTER – European Journal of Disability Research* 3(2): 159–78.

Roberts, C. and M. Mort. 2009. 'Reshaping what counts as care: older people, work and new technologies', *ALTER – European Journal of Disability Research* 3(2): 138–58.

Roberts, C., M. Mort and C. Milligan. 2011. 'Calling for care: "disembodied" work, tele-operators and older people living at home', *Sociology* 46(3): 490–506.

Sánchez Criado, T., D. López, C. Roberts and M. Domènech. 2014. 'Installing telec-are, installing users: felicity conditions for the instauration of usership', *Science, Technology & Human Values* 39(5): 694–719.

Schillmeier, M. and M. Domenech. (eds). 2010. *New technologies and emerging spaces of care.* Burlington: Ashgate.

Shapin, S. 1989. 'The invisible technician', *American Scientist* 77(6): 554–63.

Star, S.L. 2002. 'Infrastructure and ethnographic practice', *Scandinavian Journal of Information Systems* 14(2): 107–22.

Suchman, L., J. Blomberg, J. Orr and R. Trigg. 1999. 'Reconstructing technologies as social practice', *American Behavioral Scientist* 43(3): 392–408.

Timonen, V., M. Doyle and D. Prendergast. 2006. *No place like home: domiciliary care services for older people in Ireland*. Dublin: Liffey Press.

Tronto, J.C. 1993. *Moral boundaries: a political argument for an ethic of care*. London: Routledge.

Twigg, J. 2002. 'Care work and bodywork', in B. Bytheway, V. Bacigalupo, J. Bornat, J. Johnson and S. Spurr (eds), *Understanding care, welfare and community*. London: Routledge, pp. 285–98.

PART THREE
Life Course Transitions

MAJOR IDENTITY AND EXPERIENTIAL CHANGES occur as we move across boundaries from one life course state to another: from perceiving ourselves as healthy to being sick, from being mobile and independent to giving up our driving licenses, from working to being retired, from being a couple to being alone, from being alive to being dead. Older adults are frequently regarded as being at the margins of technological change, yet the later life course is filled with moments of intense learning, information sifting and flexible transition management. This happens often, and not always happily, within digital landscapes as technologies provide new opportunities for visualizing and accessing services, for building or retaining relationships and managing our lifestyles.

The first chapter in this section discusses the important transition of becoming caregiver (and also care receiver) while we age. The older we grow the more likely it is that we will need support to perform certain tasks. This support can come from formal (e.g. paid) or informal (e.g. friends, neighbours and family) workers, the latter frequently older people themselves. As highlighted by Iris and Berman, the challenge here lies, in part, in the fact that people often have difficulties in identifying with being a caregiver, since for many people caregiving is associated with paid professionals. Once again, as in several other chapters in this book, timely access to comprehensible and targeted information is a critical issue. The internet carries great potential for the effective delivery of information, albeit with the risk of information overload. Through the example of E-Careonline in the US, the authors discuss some of the key questions people have and the obstacles they face when looking for information regarding caregiving.

The sharing and accessing of information as part of a community plays a key role also in the shaping of identity and the practicalities discussed in the following chapter. Ono presents her ethnography-based work which explores two concurrent important transitions in the life of older Japanese adults: that of becoming a retiree from work and migrant at the same time. The focus of the chapter is on the phenomenon occurring among relatively affluent baby boomers of migrating in the hope of a better life in Southeast Asian countries with warmer climates and a lower cost of living. This is part of an identity shift that never fully occurs (e.g. people define themselves more like long-stay tourists than migrants), and of a renegotiation of previous family and community ties (e.g. how to deal with filial duty and caregiving to older parents still alive). Key to this transition is gaining access to information to become part of a new virtual community that is shaped around storytelling in blogs and other forms of media.

The theme of engagement with new technologically mediated identities is continued by De Schutter and colleagues in their exploration of the emerging field of gaming development for and usage by older adults. This chapter describes the adoption of gaming and becoming 'a gamer' among older populations, the motivation to remain a gamer, and finally their content preferences and tastes in gaming choices. Awareness of some of the commonalities, but most importantly, diversity among players is key for developers to provide viable options for this expanding community of users.

We decided to conclude this section and the book with a chapter exploring the fascinating topic of what happens to our digital traces at the end of the life course and beyond. Wendy Moncur discusses differences between physical, social and digital deaths and what happens to our data when we (physically) die or lose direct agency. As she suggests, the data we leave behind has legal, emotional, personal and economic implications, and technologies are not, yet at least, designed to acknowledge or engage with the death of their user or the needs of those left behind.

10. CAREGIVING IN THE DIGITAL ERA

Madelyn Iris and Rebecca Berman

MEETING THE NEEDS OF OLDER adults who are 'ageing in place' has emerged as an important social and health policy issue in the US and around the world, in both developed as well as developing nations (Hayward and Zhang 2001; Mukherjee 2008; United Nations 2002; Walker 2005). This issue is driven by the anticipated expansion of the older population over the next thirty years, along with an extended life expectancy (Haub 2008). For example, in the US the percentage of persons 65 and older is expected to rise to approximately 19 per cent by 2030, with the greatest growth in the number of persons 80 and over (US Administration on Aging 2011). In the US, to help older adults maintain their independence and continue living in their own homes despite possible decline and impairment, the formal service system (often called 'the ageing network') has evolved with a growing emphasis on home and community-based services. However, spouses, family members and friends, who may be older themselves, are also providing a significant share of personal assistance and support, especially with respect to the social emotional dimensions of care (Polivka 2009).

In this chapter, we use the term 'caregivers' to refer to non-paid, family carers, such as spouses, adult children, other relatives, friends and neighbours. A survey of caregivers conducted in 2010 by the Pew Research Center (Fox and Brenner 2012) found that approximately 27 per cent of Americans were already providing care for an older adult each year. The website CarersUK (2009) reports that in the UK nearly 6 million people, or about 12 per cent of the adult population, provides unpaid care to an ill, frail or disabled person. This trend is likely to continue over the next three to four decades, as the world's population ages. In the US the MetLife Foundation's 2009 study of caregiving found that 66 per cent of caregivers were female, with an average age of 48 years. Most caregivers

(86 per cent) assisted a relative and over one-third were taking care of a parent (National Alliance for Caregiving 2009).

As caregivers, spouses, family members and friends are often motivated by a desire to enhance the quality of life of those for whom they care (hereafter referred to as 'care receivers'). To help them, caregivers need easy access to information and education about caregiving and connections to resources and assistive services (Iris 2003). With the advent of the 'digital era', the internet has become a well-accepted avenue for seeking information, resources and education about caregiving and age-related health issues. Over the last decade, as internet connectivity and use has expanded, a variety of evidence-based psychosocial interventions aimed at enhancing knowledge, skills and support have made use of digital technology to provide caregivers with the assistance they seek, all delivered electronically. For example, Boise, Congleton and Shannon (2005) refer to an electronic version of their education program 'Powerful Tools for Caregivers' and Pierce, Steiner, Khuder, Govoni and Horn (2009) developed and tested a web-based intervention that provided education and support to caregivers of stroke survivors. In addition, general informational sites, such as those hosted by the Rosalyn Carter Institute for Caregiving[1] and the National Alliance for Caregiving,[2] provide links to other sites, information about programmes, and educational materials. Possibilities for online information gathering are rapidly expanding at the same time that caregivers are better able to access the World Wide Web via high-speed internet connections on computers as well as mobile devices (Rainie 2012). Thus, the internet has given caregivers access to a global network of information and created an international 'marketplace' for caregiver support and in response to growing demand, both for-profit businesses and non-profit organizations alike have developed products and tools targeting the caregiving market.

This chapter focuses on internet-based information, resources and guides that caregivers can use to improve the care they provide, increase their care receivers' quality of life, and learn techniques and methods to care for themselves as well. We briefly review the field of electronic enhancements to caregiving, hereafter referred to as 'the digital domain for caregivers' and present a case example of the development and testing of a website that was grounded in caregivers' perspectives. Our goal is to identify and address common facilitators and inhibitors that caregivers face as users of digital resources.

The State of the Digital Domain for Caregivers

Technological advances continue to shape the rapid development of internet and web-based resources, the content and format of websites, and the ways in which internet users access digital information. In this section we provide a snapshot of the 'state' of the digital domain for caregivers based on a review of websites targeted to this audience.[3] We examine how caregivers' needs and preferences for information and resources are met via the digital domain, and characterize the types of information caregivers tend to seek out. However, given the diversity of caregivers and the particular problems they may experience due to their care receiver's needs, as well as the ever-changing content of the World Wide Web, this review should not be viewed as comprehensive.

Family members caring for older adults frequently turn to the internet for information and resources to help them deal with a wide range of health care and caregiving issues (Fox and Brenner 2012). In fact, caregivers are among the most likely groups to look for online health information (Fox 2011). For example, in an assessment of caregiver needs, Iris (2006) found that approximately one third reported seeking support via the internet. The internet is particularly valuable to caregivers as they are not always able to leave the care receiver alone, especially if that person has dementia, and thus they can have difficulty getting to appointments to sign up for assistance or attend educational events. As a result, navigating the internet may seem more convenient. Among caregivers, internet users tend to be more educated than non-users, but as Fox and Brenner (2012) found, simply being a caregiver increases the likelihood of using the internet. In addition, compared to other internet users, caregivers are also more likely to use social tools and search for online reviews of health care treatments or providers (Fox and Brenner 2012). Motivation for seeking health information on the internet may include the desire for more information than was given by healthcare providers, getting alternative information without pursuing a second opinion from a healthcare provider, and communicating with others who are experiencing similar health issues (Metcalf, Tanner and Coulehan 2001).

Research evidence suggests that online resources and educational interventions can be beneficial for caregivers. For example, caregivers who used online informational and supportive resources, including a videoconference support group, experienced reduced stress (Marziali and Donahue 2006). A qualitative pilot study of a web-based intervention for caregivers of stroke survivors suggests that receiving online encouragement from an expert, as well as online support among caregivers, may facilitate caregivers' ability to learn and manage the caring role (Thompson et al. 2004).

Preliminary evaluation of AlzOnline's Positive Caregiving classes documented increases in caregiving self-efficacy and decreases in caregiving burden among twenty-one caregivers (Glueckauf et al. 2004). Use of the website, 'The Caregiver's Friend', tested as a worksite-based programme, also produced improvements in caregivers' self-efficacy, anxiety, and depression (Beauchamp et al. 2005).

There is currently an abundance of web-based information and tools for caregivers. In the US alone providers of online information and resources (hereafter referred to as providers) are highly varied, and include: federal, state, and local governmental entities and agencies; caregiver organizations, networks or coalitions; disease-specific organizations, networks or coalitions; educational institutions; healthcare providers, service providers (non-profit and for-profit), long-term care facilities and residential providers; and businesses such as pharmaceutical companies, insurance companies, legal firms and financial organizations. For example, at the time of writing the website www.usa.gov has an entire section devoted to caregiver resources and the websites of organizations such as the National Alliance for Caregivers and the National Family Caregivers Association[4] provide a wealth of information and resources specifically targeted to caregivers.

Despite this volume of information or perhaps due to it, navigating online information can be complicated and a variety of factors influence access to and use of the internet including, but not limited to, income, education, age, geographic location and ethnicity (Fox 2011). For example, while both internet use and the number of caregivers is growing among ethnic groups, the majority of web-based information targeting caregivers is available in English only or via automated translation tools. The ways in which people choose to seek out information and navigate the web are also shaped by cultural beliefs about issues such as privacy or the trustworthiness of information.

In addition, lay conceptualizations of caregiving and caregivers can also affect access. For example, many family members do not think of themselves as caregivers, even though they may be providing a great deal of personal care, such as assistance with bathing, dressing, toileting, etc. As evaluators for the project 'Caring Together, Living Better' (CTLB), developed to build a faith-based network of support for African-American caregivers in several low-income Chicago suburbs,[5] we learned that church volunteers and others caring for older family members thought 'caregiver' was a term reserved for paid caregivers. They did not associate the concept of caregiving with their own roles as care providers for spouses, family members or friends. After nearly two years of outreach using carefully crafted language, the targeted communities in the CTLB project became more familiar with the idea of unpaid caregiving as a recognized role, evidenced by stories we collected from volunteers and caregivers about how the project changed individual and community awareness of caregiving (Iris and Berman 2010).

During the project's strategic planning session caregivers shared stories that revealed a desire for easier access to web-based information that they could easily understand and relate to in terms of their caregiving situation. They told us that when caregivers are looking for understandable, trustworthy answers to complex questions they often have only a short period of time to search the web, and following the maze of internal site links and hyperlinks across sites can easily become frustrating. For example, caregivers repeatedly emphasized that they are short of time and energy, need information quickly, and do not know what they are searching for until they find the 'right' questions to ask. Knowing what to ask was especially important at times of abrupt 'care transitions', such as when there is a sudden decline in a care receiver's functional abilities, when a caregiver starts living with the care receiver, or when another individual assisting with care dies or moves away, such as a spouse or sibling. Consequently, the challenge for website sponsors and content developers is to make the search for web-based material as user-friendly as possible and to identify and rectify possible mismatches between their own perspective on what is needed and that of caregivers.

Based on the findings of several research and evaluation projects, including our own experience with the development and testing of a caregiver website, and by working with caregivers in other settings, we believe that caregivers learn how to find information and resources by finding out what they don't know and they often didn't know what to ask until they had more experience. They described a fragmented process of information seeking that involved a great deal of trial and error, as well as frustration (Iris and Berman 2010).

Figure 10.1 illustrates common caregiver questions framed within what is essentially a nonlinear, iterative process of information seeking. These questions derive from caregivers' perceptions of their care receivers' needs as well as their own needs, including: understanding the care situation; learning about resource options; exploring specific alternatives; assessing and selecting what are believed to be the most appropriate resources for specific situation; validating knowledge, decisions or actions; identifying new questions; and planning for the future.

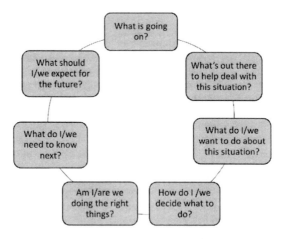

FIGURE 10.1   Questions caregivers ask.

Early on in the development of websites targeted to caregivers, most were organized around programmes and services for the purpose of outreach to potential clients, as well as the marketing of products. As the digital domain has expanded and evolved, more websites now organize information around issues that caregivers face, such as enhancing care and quality of life for an older adult, supporting the caregiver, and planning for the future care of a parent. Figure 10.2 provides a sampling of the types of information and resources that providers make available to caregivers.

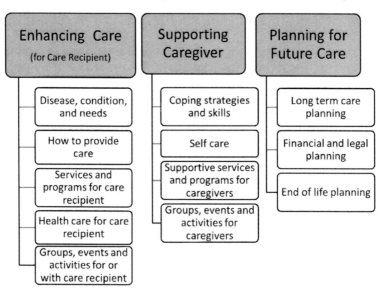

FIGURE 10.2   Examples of online information.

However, to find these websites, users must first identify with being a caregiver, which remains a continuing challenge. Furthermore, the language providers use to describe their categories of information does not always match a particular caregiver's questions and thus the information and resources that are available may not be perceived as relevant. For example, some providers include categories of information and resources that target subgroups of caregivers engaged in 'long-distance caregiving', not a search phrase that immediately comes to the mind of an adult son or daughter who is worried about a mother who lives far away.

Information and resources for caregivers are currently provided in a variety of ways, including websites with content and downloadable materials; sites that serve as portals to other sites; multi-purpose or complex websites; and web-based tools for specific purposes. Figure 10.3 provides an overview of the modes by which caregivers can access information and resources.

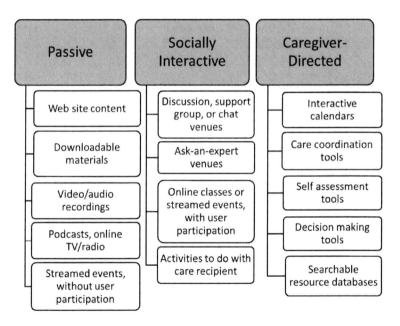

FIGURE 10.3 Modes of access.

The most common mode is passive, as when a caregiver reads, views or listens to information and, at most, clicks on links to audio or video presentations or tools. The second mode includes socially interactive sites that provide participatory online support, information and resources, such as 'ask an expert features', message boards, chat rooms, online support groups and caregiver classes. For example, the Family Caregiver Alliance website[6] provides links to a variety of moderated and non-moderated online support groups.

As technology has advanced, a third mode of access has evolved, that includes web-based tools. These sites allow the caregiver to actively direct the sharing and use of information via online surveys, templates or software. For instance, the Area Agency on Aging 1B[7] website in Michigan offers an online 'Caregiver Self Assessment' questionnaire (http://www. aaa1b.com/caregiver-resources/caregiver-self-assessment), which, when completed and submitted, is scored and provides the caregiver with an assessment of their level of stress, along with recommended actions the caregiver can take to reduce stress or get more help. The Alzheimer's Association website[8] offers customized action steps to help guide caregivers through decisions about care options, based on their answers to an online 'Alzheimer's Navigator' survey. Caregivers can also use online templates or software to control the content or presentation of information, some of which include socially interactive features. Lotsa Helping Hands[9] and Share the Care[10] offer calendars and other tools for coordinating a 'caring community' to assist with care. Caregivers can also use free personal websites, such as Caring Bridge,[11] or general social media sites (e.g., Facebook), to post updates on a family member's health for family and friends, who can then share their supportive comments.

As technology becomes yet more sophisticated, the growth in more interactive and user-directed options for caregivers is likely to continue and evolve. In addition, the availability of online activities for homebound older adults and persons with dementia is growing. For example, the Social Care Institute for Excellence provides a guide to using information and communication technology with people with dementia.[12]

In the case example that follows, we emphasize the importance of understanding the caregivers' perspectives and the factors that affect their ability to participate in this domain. Critical reflection on our experience with developing a multi-component caregiver website that provided multiple modes for accessing information and other resources is used to highlight key principles for those designing digital resources for caregivers in the future.

E-Careonline: A Digital Caregiver Resource

E-Careonline was a web-based, interactive resource for caregivers of older adults, developed and evaluated between 2005 and 2008 by the authors at CJE SeniorLife in Chicago. CJE SeniorLife is a multi-service organization serving older adults and their family members through a wide variety of programmes and services, including transportation, subsidized housing, long-term care, assisted living, healthy ageing programmes, home delivered meals, etc. Founded over forty years ago, it now serves over 20,000 older adults each year. The E-Careonline project evolved out of an earlier study directed at caregiver education and assistance, using video-phone technology (Finkel et al. 2007). A second project focused on educating caregivers about depression and falls, but utilized print materials only (Iris 2005). Funding for ECareonline was provided by the Fund for Innovations in Health of the Jewish Federation of Metropolitan Chicago, and the Braun Fund at CJE SeniorLife.

E-Careonline was conceived as an 'on demand' web-based educational intervention for caregivers, offering knowledge and resources to assist them in carrying out their caregiving responsibilities, improve the quality of care provided, decrease the sense of burden and increase users' confidence in their ability to provide care for their loved ones. One important aim of the project was to document participants' satisfaction with the intervention, based on their assessments of the site's usefulness and by tracking their use. We also sought to elicit ideas for the future design of the site and throughout the process of developing, testing and seeking participants' feedback we utilized elements of participatory research. Each phase of the project was approved by the Institutional Review Board at Mount Sinai Health Systems in Chicago.

E-Careonline incorporated a number of features considered innovative at the time. The most unique was a set of modules with videos and text in four skill areas: lifting and transferring, preventing falls, communicating with individuals with dementia, and identifying and managing depression in the care receiver. The video 'clips' were developed in collaboration with Terra Nova Films Inc., a visual media distribution and production company based in Chicago. Full-length videos were reviewed, and selected sections were edited down to create brief (3–5 minutes) demonstrations of techniques. For example, the task breakdown video clip demonstrated how to improve and enhance communication around various activities of daily living such as grooming, tooth-brushing, preparing a simple meal, etc. The clip on lifting and transferring demonstrated techniques for working with care receivers with significant mobility impairments, in order to prevent injury to both the care receiver and the caregiver.

A unique feature of the site was an interactive message board where participants could post questions and comments. The message board was monitored by a CJE social worker who was able to offer assistance and referrals when necessary. Another area of the site, called 'A Moment for Yourself', had video and audio modules on breathing and relaxation exercises, poetry, writing exercises and examples of other resources for coping or reflection (e.g., books, films and links to self-care resources). More passive aspects of the site included a set of text-only educational modules that provided tips and downloadable forms for managing day-to-day health care tasks, communicating with visitors, hiring in-home caregivers, making financial and legal decisions, making end of life decisions, and selecting an assisted living facility or nursing home. The Resources section included local, state and national resources, as well as information about specific diseases or topics covered in the educational modules.

Feasibility Phase

In the first phase of the project, an initial version of the website was developed and piloted with eight family caregivers, recruited using convenience sampling: six of the eight had participated in a caregiver educational intervention previously conducted by CJE SeniorLife. Seven were white and one was African-American. Their economic status varied, as did their caregiving situations: three were wives caring for husbands, three were sons caring for mothers, and two were daughters caring for parents. The average age of the group was approximately 65 (based on estimates of individual age). Six of the nine care receivers had some form of dementia, one had impairments resulting from a stroke and one had Parkinson's disease. All but one participant had their own computers and half had high-speed internet connectivity. A laptop computer was lent to the one person without a computer; dial-up connections were paid for by the project, when needed.

During this phase the site hosted two videos (task breakdown and lifting and transferring) as well as related text-based content. The project assistant met individually with each caregiver (at his or her home) to orient the participant to the E-Careonline project and use of the site. The caregivers were then given six weeks to try out the site. They were asked to view each video clip at least twice and were given a binder of materials that included the textual content of the site as well as a notes section, where they were to record their use of the site and their thoughts about utilization and recommendations for improvement. At the end of the six weeks we conducted a semi-structured interview with each participant. Each participant had suggestions for improvements regarding both content and design, including building a page specifically for caregivers who were new to caregiving or were about to become caregivers. They also suggested that the text materials be shortened and organized under very specific topics and they wanted to see more specific instructions on the 'How to Use This Site' page. One important finding from these interviews highlighted the necessity of being able to review and assimilate information in short periods of time, which became a core principle for subsequent design of the text, video and audio content of the full website. All of these recommendations were addressed prior to the implementation of the randomized trial of the site, described below.

Randomized Trial of E-Careonline

To determine the efficacy of the site, and measure its success in meeting the stated objectives of the project, i.e. assisting caregivers in fulfilling their caring responsibilities, improving quality of care, decreasing burden and increasing caregiving self-efficacy, in 2006 we implemented a one-year randomized trial. For the purpose of the randomized trial, we defined a caregiver as anyone who felt she/he was 'providing assistance or care' to a person over the age of 60 and whose care receiver was living in a community setting. We recruited broadly through a number of networks and distributed information about the project and how to participate via flyers, newsletter announcements, bulletins, and presentations to approximately ninety different organizational or individual contacts such as adult day centres, caregiver support groups, home health programmes, the Northwestern University Alzheimer's Disease Center Research Registry, etc. In addition, we disseminated public service announcements via the local media (e.g. radio stations and newspapers).

Volunteers were randomly assigned to either the internet-based intervention group (treatment) or to a waitlist comparison group (control). Intervention group participants were instructed to access E-Careonline once a week for three months. Comparison group participants were provided with access to E-Careonline after a three-month waiting period. We anticipated that caregivers who used E-Careonline would experience more positive outcomes than those who did not, in the following areas: general self-efficacy (i.e., beliefs or confidence in one's own ability to complete tasks or reach goals), caregiving self-efficacy (e.g., confidence in ability to provide care and seek support), sense of burden due to caregiving, anxiety and depression. All participants completed a set of validated, standardized measures to assess each of these domains before using the website and again after using the website for three months.[13]

In addition, participants were asked to complete a satisfaction survey during a follow-up interview. The survey addressed navigability and overall helpfulness of the site, participants' assessment of their use of the various content components and to what degree each component was helpful. They were also asked about their use of other resources provided via hyperlinks on the resources page. The satisfaction survey included two questions about caregivers' confidence in their ability to provide care and get information that would help them provide care, and how this was affected by using E-Careonline.

Fifty-seven caregivers participated (31 were assigned to the intervention group and 26 to the comparison group), ranging in age from 39 to 86, with a mean age of 61.1 years. The characteristics of those who participated in the study reflected overall gender trends among caregivers. Over three-quarters were women, and fewer than 10 per cent had less than 12 years of education. Two-thirds reported incomes of $50,000 or more (67.3 per cent). Most participants were white (75.4 per cent), although 19.3 per cent were African-American and 5.3 per cent were Asian. These caregivers represented a variety of caregiving situations: 41 per cent were caring for spouses, 54.1 per cent were caring for parents or parents-in-law, and a few were caring for other relatives. The majority (88.3 per cent) reported that the care receiver had a cognitive impairment or memory disorder. More than two-thirds of the participants spent considerable time providing care: 69.6 per cent estimated that they were providing 20 or more hours of care per week, with half of the total sample providing 30 or more hours of care. More than 90 per cent of participants had previous experience using the internet and 83.6 per cent reported having accessed information about caregiving over the web.

Participant Outcomes

Statistical analysis of the participants' responses on the assessed outcomes showed that, on average, at baseline participants from both the intervention and comparison groups tended to be confident in their ability to complete tasks and goals, including those related to caregiving, and they reported experiencing low levels of burden, anxiety and depression. Thus, the study would have been unlikely to demonstrate improvement in the selected outcomes areas for those who used the intervention due to this 'ceiling effect'. As expected, statistical analysis of participants' responses after three months showed that caregiver burden stayed relatively steady for the intervention group, and increased only slightly for those in the comparison group. This suggests that the use of the web intervention might at least have helped caregivers maintain low levels of burden. There was no change in levels of anxiety and depression, which remained low for both groups. Despite the high levels of self-efficacy at baseline, caregivers' self-efficacy still improved among those who were exposed to the intervention, while it decreased among those in the comparison group. In other words, caregivers who used the website gained more confidence in their ability to take care of their older relatives, in particular in the area of community support service use. These results suggest that the use of E-Careonline may have had a positive impact on participants' confidence in their ability to provide care and to find and arrange for supportive services in the community.

We also tracked participants' activities when visiting the site, via user statistics features of the website administrative software. Participants visited the site anywhere from 1 to 36 times over three months, with an average of 9.7 visits. Visits occurred at all times of the day and night, averaging around 15 minutes in duration. The Message Board was visited more consistently during the first six months of the project. The second most visited page was the 'Moment for Yourself', particularly the breathing exercise. Other frequently visited pages included 'Resources, Tips and Tools' (the downloadable items), and the videos on Task Breakdown and Depression. In the second six months of the project, participants more often visited the Task Breakdown, Lifting and Transferring and Falls videos, along with their associated text modules.

Participant Satisfaction and Use of the Site

During the post-project interviews participants expressed high levels of satisfaction with E-Careonline. Overall, almost all of the 22 participants who completed a satisfaction survey reported that using the site made them more confident in their ability to care for a loved one and more confident in their ability to get information that would help them care for a loved one. The site also provided them with a sense of comfort and confidence. They viewed the site as a source of 'validation' for their role as caregivers, in that someone was thinking about their needs in a way they made them feel recognized. Over 90 per cent of study participants found it easy to navigate within the site and noted that its primary benefit was that it was a 'one-stop' website with comprehensive information, convenience, ease of use and professional sponsorship. Caregivers from outlying areas of suburban Chicago were particularly enthusiastic about having access to a web-based intervention.

Following completion of the randomized trial of E-Careonline project, the site was revised to incorporate recommendations made by study participants before opening it to the public. We used what we learned from the caregivers to refine the content and appearance of the website and to make recommendations to CJE SeniorLife's marketing department relative to site design, content and word choices. We also asked the participants in the randomized trial for suggestions for a permanent name for the site. Once the site was made public, we continued to monitor site usage data to identify outreach strategies for dissemination of information about the public launch of the site.

During the first few months of public access we asked users to complete a voluntary online survey. After responding to caregivers' feedback and making further revisions, the site was handed off by the researchers to a programme department at CJE SeniorLife for on-going updating and management. The site, now called Caregivinghelp.org, includes six components: Caregiving Circle, Perspectives, Safety, Plan Ahead, a Resource Directory, and Learn about Us. The video clips developed for E-Careonline were still operational at the time of writing, as were the self-care exercises for caregivers, including breathing and relaxation exercises. At the time the site was handed over to the programme department there had been approximately 761 unique users. By the end of 2012, there were a total of 3,708 visits tracked, and just over 3,000 unique visitors. Of these, 84.12 per cent were new to the site.

Conclusion: Translation to Practice

Digital resources are important portals of information and education about the caregiving experience. Findings from the E-Careonline project showed that the content of the site was helpful to caregivers, as evidenced by small reductions in caregiver burden scores, and improvements in self-efficacy scores, particularly with regards to their ability to find information needed to help them with caregiving. The frequency of visits to the site can be interpreted in several ways: first, the breadth and depth of information provided was more than an individual could absorb in a single visit; and second, that caregivers found it helpful to revisit various pages to validate their knowledge, look for updates and check out new postings to the message board. The psychological benefits, expressed as validation for the role of a caregiver, were particularly meaningful.

One of the important lessons learned from the development and testing of E-Careonline is that understanding the ways in which caregivers use a website is critical for developing a successful web-based intervention. Our experiences with E-Careonline demonstrate how a web-based intervention can be an efficient and effective venue for dissemination of education and resources to a population that has limited time and competing responsibilities (e.g., child care, employment, cooking, cleaning, laundry, etc.). E-Careonline brought educational and other resources to caregivers wherever and whenever they chose to access the internet. It provided multiple modes of learning that were amenable to caregivers' different preferences, needs and attention levels. The site was sensitive to the time constraints of caregiving in that information was provided in the form of brief web pages and downloadable documents, 3–5 minute video clips, and brief audio exercises that could be completed in 10 minutes or less. We also learned that there is a particular need for comprehensive web-based education and informational resources in geographic areas with fewer or less accessible community-based resources for caregivers.

In addition, during presentations of E-Careonline at local, state and national conferences, there was substantial interest from a variety of professionals, such as occupational therapists, programme planners and supervisors. A number of individuals commented that the site would complement their efforts at educating and training family caregivers, thereby making their work easier and improving the quality of care. Thus, web-based educational interventions may also be a valuable tool for professionals seeking to support caregivers, and ultimately allowing care receivers to receive the best care possible, for as long as possible.

Based on our cumulative experiences with conducting caregiver research and evaluation of caregiver support projects, including E-Careonline, we suggest several overall guiding principles for those who wish to develop and/or improve the relevance and usefulness of digital resources for family caregivers of older adults. First and foremost, it is critical that content be provided in a way that is sensitive to variation in caregiving perspectives and experiences. A common approach has been to focus digital content on particular types of caregiving relationships (e.g., spouse vs. adult children) or caregiving experiences, such as care for persons with a specific illness (e.g., dementia, stroke, Parkinson's disease, etc.) or living arrangement of the caregiver (e.g., long distance, co-resident, etc.). While this targeted approach responds to legitimate needs, we encourage developers of web-based resources to acknowledge caregiving as a process of change, and provide and organize digital content around key transitions that both caregivers and/or care receivers may move through over time, including end of life transitions.

Second, the potential demands of providing care (which can include limited time, variable attention and emotional stress) have implications for the design and format of digital resources. Information should be written so that it can be easily reviewed in short time spans, organized in a way that reduces frustration, and offered in multiple learning modes. Finally, digital information providers must continue to improve their understanding of how caregivers identify themselves, the language they use when conducting online searches, and the types of questions caregivers ask when they are unfamiliar with a problem or option they are just beginning to explore.

The extensive body of research on the experience of caregiving, including interventional as well as qualitative research, provides a rich source of information for those developing websites. Throughout the process of developing and improving a web-based resource, the most valuable sources of information are the caregivers themselves. It is imperative to include their perspectives by providing options for meaningful input on content, language, organization of information and design elements, using feedback strategies such as email, message boards, webinar focus group, brief online surveys and other communication modes.

Providing digital information to caregivers can also serve as a window for learning more about how caregivers use information in this realm. Those who monitor website use may benefit from posing their own 'research questions' to user statistics generated through website tools, in order to learn more about how people use a particular site. Research that improves our understanding of caregivers' search strategies and use of key words or phrases would provide valuable information for website development as well as tools that caregivers are more likely to find and use. Furthermore, there is a particular need for research on how caregivers' use of web-based resources and other digital information tools changes over time in response to the shifting tasks of caregiving. Future research on how caregivers incorporate digital information into their overall information seeking strategies would also be of value, including examinations of caregivers' perceptions of the trustworthiness of information. Finally, investigations into the use of social media, such as Twitter or Facebook, as well as interactive web tools or mobile apps intended to promote social interaction for impaired older adults, would provide insights into how caregivers build their information-seeking networks and social support systems.

Digital strategies present few limits on geographic reach and accessibility and thus are uniquely effective for global dissemination. As access to electronic information continues to expand and as product development opens new avenues for access, such as smart phones and tablets, caregivers will be more and more likely to turn to the 'digital domain' for information, assistance, supportive interventions and resources to enhance the care receivers' quality of life and social networks. Professionals who work with older adults and their caregivers will need to be attentive to the variety of modes for accessing web-based resources and be skilled in the use of such resources themselves so that they can more proactively assist caregivers. Perhaps most importantly, providers of web-based resources must be sensitive to the unique constraints and needs of caregivers, meeting them where they are at in their caregiving experience, both in terms of web content and design.

Acknowledgements

E-Careonline was developed with funding from the Braun Fund at CJE SeniorLife, and the Fund for Innovations in Health, Jewish Federation of Metropolitan Chicago. Our thanks to Molly Haroz for her contributions to the design and development of E-Careonline.

Notes

1. http://www.rosalynncarter.org.
2. www.caregiving.org.
3. This brief overview of the state of the digital domain presented below does not include the rapidly burgeoning field of Mobile Health applications (mHealth), Remote Patient Monitoring or Medication Optimization technologies to help manage, dispense or track medication (Center for Technology and Aging 2012) as these products benefit both the older adult as well as his or her caregiver.
4. www.caregiveraction.org.
5. Caring Together Living Better was a three-year project of AgeOptions, an Area Agency on Aging (see note below) covering the suburban Cook County, IL region. The project, funded by the Harry and Jeannette Weinberg Foundation, and was one of fourteen projects supported by the foundation. More information about all the projects can be found at www.hjweinbergfoundation.org.
6. www.caregiver.org.
7. Area Agencies on Aging (AAA) are regional planning and service organizations authorized by the US Older Americans Act and covering all fifty states in the US. Each AAA operates independently, and may provide direct services to older adults and their family members living within their geographic boundaries, such as information and referral to other programmes, as well as serving as a contracting organization with more localized agencies for services such as assessment and provision of home and community based services, including home delivered meals, personal care, transportation, respite, etc. In addition, some AAAs are engaged in the development of new, innovative services and programmes, such as the Caring Together Living Better programme described in this chapter.
8. www.alz.org.
9. www.lotsahelpinghands.com.
10. www.sharethecare.org.
11. www.caringbridge.org.
12. www.scie.org.uk/publications/ictfordementia/.
13. Detailed information on the measures used and results of the pre/post assessments can be found in the final project report. Copies can be obtained by contacting Madelyn Iris at micki.iris@cje.net.

References

Beauchamp, N., A.B. Irvine, J. Seeley and B. Johnson. 2005. 'Worksite-based internet multi-media program for family caregivers of persons with dementia', *The Gerontologist* 45(6): 793–801.

Boise, L., L. Congleton and K. Shannon. 2005. 'Empowering family caregivers: the powerful tools for caregiving program', *Educational Gerontology* 31(7): 573–86.

CarersUK. June 2009. 'Facts about carers'. Available at http://www.carersuk.org/professionals/resources (accessed 8 November 2012).

Center for Technology and Aging. 2012. 'Programs'. Available at http://www.techandaging.org (accessed 8 November 2012).

Family Caregiver Alliance. 2012. 'Women and caregiving: facts and figures'. Available at http://www.caregiver.org/caregiver/jsp/content_node.jsp?nodeid=892 (accessed 11 November 2012).

Finkel, S., S.J. Czaja, R. Schulz, Z. Martinovich, C. Harris and D. Pezzuto. 2007. 'E-care: a telecommunications technology intervention for family caregivers of dementia patients', *American Journal of Geriatric Psychiatry* 15(5): 443–48.

Fox, S. 2011. 'Accessing health topics on the internet'. Pew Internet and American Life Project. Available at http://pewresearch.org/pubs/1875/Internet-health-topics-accessing-updated-data (accessed 8 November 2012).

Fox, S. and J. Brenner. 2012. 'Family caregivers online'. Pew Internet and American Life Project. Available at http://pewInternet.org/~/media//Files/Reports/2012/PIP_Family_Caregivers_Online.pdf (accessed 7 November 2012).

Glueckauf, R.L., T.U. Ketterson, J.S. Loomis and P. Dages. 2004. 'Online support and education for dementia caregivers: overview, utilization, and initial program evaluation', *Telemedicine Journal and e-Health* 10(2): 223–32.

Haub, C. 2008. 'Global aging and the demographic divide. Population Reference Bureau'. Available at http://www.prb.org/Publications/Articles/2008/globalaging.aspx (accessed 20 November 2014).

Hayward, M. and Z. Zhang. 2001. 'Demography and aging: a century of global change, 1950–2050', in R.H. Binstock and L.K. George (eds), *Handbook of aging and the social sciences*, 5th ed. San Diego: Academic Press, pp. 70–85.

Iris, M. 2003. 'Final report: caregiver needs assessment and evaluation: national family caregiver resource program'. AgeOptions (Suburban Area Agency on Aging), Oak Park, IL.

———. 2005. 'Caregiver initiative to prevent falls and treat depression: year two final report and year three proposal'. Chicago, IL: Fund for Innovation in Health, Jewish Federation of Metropolitan Chicago.

———. 2006. 'E-care feasibility study final report to the Braun Committee'. Chicago, IL: CJE SeniorLife.

Iris, M and R. Berman. 2010. 'Innovative methodologies for evaluating the development of a caregiver support partnership', Annual Meetings of the Gerontological Society of America, November 2010.

Marziali, E. and P. Donahue. 2006. 'Caring for others: internet video-conferencing group intervention for family caregivers of older adults with neurodegenerative disease', *The Gerontologist* 46(3): 398–403.

Metcalf, M.P., T.B. Tanner and M.B. Coulehan. 2001. 'Empowered decision making: using the internet for health care information and beyond', *Caring* 20(5): 42–44.

Mukherjee, D. 2008. 'Globalization without social protection: challenges for aging societies across developing nations', *The Global Studies Journal* 1(3): 21–27.

National Alliance for Caregiving (in collaboration with AARP). 2009. 'Caregiving in the US: executive summary'. Available at http://www.caregiving.org/pdf/research/CaregivingUSAllAgesExecSum.pdf (accessed 5 November 2012).

Pierce, L., V. Steiner, S. Khuder, A. Govoni and L. Horn. 2009. 'The effect of a web-based stroke intervention on carers' well-being and survivors' use of healthcare services', *Disability and Rehabilitation* 31(20): 1676–84.

Polivka, L. 2009. 'The global Florida: long-term care in postindustrial countries', in J. Sokolovsky (ed.), *The cultural context of aging: worldwide perspective*. Westport, CT: Praeger, pp. 576–88.

Rainie, L. 2012. 'Changes to the way we identify internet users'. Pew Internet and American Life Project. Available at http://www.pewInternet.org/Reports/2012/Counting-Internet-users.aspx (accessed 3 October 2012).

Thompson, T.C., L.L. Pierce, V. Steiner, A.L. Govoni, B. Hicks and M.-L. Friedemann. 2004. 'What happened to normal? Learning the role of caregiver', *Online Journal of Nursing Informatics* 8(2). Available at http://www.eaa-knowledge.com/ojni/ni/8_2/caregiver.htm (accessed 2 May 2007).

United Nations. 2002. 'International plan of action on ageing 2002'. *Global Action on Ageing*. Available at http://undesadspd.org/Ageing/Resources/MadridInternationalPlanofActiononAgeing.aspx (accessed 20 November 2014).

US Administration on Aging. 2011. 'A profile of older Americans 2011'. Available at http://www.aoa.gov/Aging_Statistics/Profile/2011/docs/2011profile.pdf (accessed 20 November 2014).

Walker, A. 2005. 'Towards an international political economy of ageing', *Aging & Society* 25: 815–30.

11. DIGITAL STORYTELLING AND THE TRANSNATIONAL RETIREMENT NETWORKS OF OLDER JAPANESE ADULTS

Mayumi Ono

Introduction

Within the 'super aged society' of Japan, increasing numbers of Japanese pensioners are becoming interested in retiring abroad. The emerging transnational mobility of Japanese retirees illustrates the transformations in experiences and expectations around the later life course in contemporary Japanese society. The everyday life of older Japanese adults, which has conventionally been represented as static and passive, is in a dynamic state of transformation. This has not been brought about by their transnational mobility but by a new social environment generated by the greater opportunities for mobility. This chapter examines how older Japanese people relate to each other through migration, how they establish their social environments, and how they recreate communities by utilizing information and communication technology, such as websites, weblogs and social networking services. In particular, it will explore how online communication mediates retirement mobility to Malaysia and how it affects the life of Japanese retirees migrating there.

Ageing is one of the most significant socio-economic and cultural factors for the outflow of retirees from Japan. The declining birth rate, combined with the increased percentage of people over 65 years old, is substantially affecting the demographic structure of Japan and accelerating the labour shortage. Japan has been defined as a 'super ageing' society where, in 2011, approximately 29,750,000 people, or 23.3 per cent of the total population of 127,800,000, were 65 years old and above (Cabinet Office 2012). It is estimated that this will increase to 39.9 per cent of the total population in 2060 (NIPSSR 2012).

Increased longevity has influenced the life of older Japanese adults in numerous ways. The Japanese super-ageing trend has created a phenomenon of what may be labelled 'cross-generational ageing'. An increasing number of relatively 'young' older individuals (60–74 years old) find themselves in the position of caregiver for the 'older' elderly (75 years old and above). They thus have to be concerned with the care arrangement for their parents as well as their own long-term financial security for the next few decades (Toyota and Ono 2012).

The super-ageing society, however, has produced not only older adults in need of care but also relatively young and healthy retirees who are actively seeking to build a second life by means of their retirement pension and savings. Although Japan has been experiencing economic stagnation since the 1990s, the baby boom generation had a chance to benefit from the remarkable economic growth of the past. As a result, it is reported that the average amount of savings of an household with members who are 65 and older is 23,050,000 yen, 1.4 times more than the national average (Cabinet Office 2011: 23). Healthy adults around retirement age are therefore expected to have significant purchasing power potential and are targeted as new consumers by various industries, including leisure and tourism. International retirement migration to affordable destinations appears to be an economically appealing choice of lifestyle for healthy, older Japanese people.

Pensioners' transnational mobility and migration is a relatively new phenomena in both Japan and wider Asia in comparison to the long established and well-studied retirement migrations from northern Europe to the Mediterranean since the 1970s (King et al. 2000). It is only since the late 1990s that increasing numbers of Japanese older adults have been taking advantage of retirement packages offered to foreign retirees by Southeast Asian countries, such as Malaysia, Thailand, Philippines and Indonesia, when it was commercialized as a form of long-stay tourism (Toyota 2006; Ono 2008; Ono 2009; Ono 2010; Yamashita 2009; Toyota and Ono 2012). It was originally part of a government-led project, known as the 'Silver Columbia Plan '92', launched by the former Ministry of International Trade and Industry in 1986. The plan received criticism that the government was 'exporting' its older population, and, as a result, the private sector took charge of the project and established the 'Long Stay Foundation' in 1992. This reformed the plan by moving from the migration of older individuals to a new style of leisure applicable to a wider audience. Because of this switch, the simple term 'long-stay' (*rongusutei*) was introduced to refer to a 'residential-type overseas leisure' (*kaigaitaizaigatayoka*) available to Japanese individuals.

As in the European case, the major destination countries for Japanese international retirement migration are also located to the south, namely in Southeast Asia and Oceania. Older Japanese adults are motivated to move abroad after retirement in order to make their post-retirement life more meaningful with new experiences by exposing themselves to different cultures, as well as taking advantage of lower living costs which make their retirement financially sustainable. The government of Malaysia, the country which has been recognized as the most desirable destination among Japanese, has implemented a tourism policy, the 'Malaysia My Second Home Programme' (MM2H), which attracts affluent foreign retirees in order to stimulate the economy. Although Japanese international retirement migration is mostly conducted by healthy retirees around 60 years of age, it also includes older adults who suffer from chronic conditions. These schemes are popular despite the fact that their visas do not guarantee permanent resident status but rather that of a visitor with multiple entries.

Lifestyle Migration and the Encumbrance of Social Relations

Retirees' ambition to seek better ways of life through seasonal or perma-nent transnational migration is an emerging global phenomenon and has largely been studied in the fields of tourism and migration. Michaela Benson and Karen O'Reilly (2009) conceptualize this mobility as lifestyle migration. Examining cases of European mobility within Europe, Benson and O'Reilly define lifestyle migration as 'the spatial mobility of relatively affluent individuals of all ages, moving either part-time or full-time to places that are meaningful because, for various reasons, they offer the potential of a better quality of life' (Benson and O'Reilly 2009: 2). Furthermore, the authors argue that lifestyle migration is about escape, not only away from somewhere and/or something but towards self-fulfilment and a new source of recreation, restoration, and/or rediscovery of one's own potential or 'true' desire (Benson and O'Reilly 2009: 3).

Similar to the cases of Europeans, international retirement migra-tion of older Japanese is also a form of lifestyle migration. For example, it takes place in 'unfamiliar' destination countries for Japanese older people where they do not have family or an established social infrastructure apart from their original communities. However, it is not necessary for Japanese retirement migrants to regard their social relations prior to migration as indispensable to their next phase of life. Rather, many Japanese retirees tend to perceive their previous social relations such as family, colleagues, friends and their local communities as negative constraints, or *shigarami*.[1] These constraints may form social capital and identity, but they also pro-foundly affect the outbound mobility of the retirees' post-retirement lives. Therefore, international retirement migration is not only a lifestyle change but also an 'escape' from constraints. Negative aspects of the pre-migra-tory lives of mobile individuals are recognized as significant causes for their desire to seek out better places to live abroad. As Robert D. Putnam (2000) indicates, it has been the conventional argument on communal ties that social capital does not necessarily reconcile with freedom or tolerance.

Community can both restrict freedom and promote tolerance, a relationship that composes the 'dark side of social capital' (Putnam 2000). Locally embedded social relations encumber individuals with various sorts of socio-cultural obligations and duties, which in turn results in people feeling burdened and constrained. Because the desire to escape from constraints at home motivates retirees to move abroad, some retirement migrants are willing to live in their destination country as long as possible to be apart from their family, such as their older parents and children, who conventionally have constituted the modern family in Japanese society. David W. Plath (1980) argues that Japanese seek 'long engagements' with others as their 'consociates' or as their 'convoy' to enable themselves to grow and mature into their old age. Plath demonstrates that these consociates, people with whom one exhibits some degree of intimacy over time, such as friends, lovers, kin, colleagues and classmates, are the primary social resources and restraints who are empanelled as a special jury to examine the course of an individual's being and becoming (Plath 1980: 8). Such a negative view of social relations as constraints implies that family no longer comprises the absolute convoy for the individuals concerned, and this has partly resulted in facilitating this retirement mobility of Japanese older adults into a new place. The individual pursuit of the good life by way of lifestyle migration is a social phenomenon where each individual involved is tactically seeking to solve their issues elsewhere, even though the solutions they find may only provide temporary changes to their lives. These individualized lifestyles and escapist strategies through migration, however, do not necessarily mean that migrants do not seek any new social relations or new communities.

The eagerness to create new social relations and be associated with to migrants' social networking is linked with the desire to obtain information about the destination countries and to meet those who share the same interests with regards to retirement migration. Reciprocal social relationships do not necessarily require long-term accumulations of trust. Putnam argues that reciprocity as a continuing relationship of exchange with mutual expectations is a highly productive component of social capital based on individual acts and characterized by a combination of what one might call short-term altruism and long-term self-interest (1993: 172). The norm of such reciprocal relationships reconciles self-interest and solidarity and therefore facilitates cooperation (Putnam 1993: 172). Reciprocity works amongst those who share the same interests, regardless of how long they have known each other or the levels of accumulated trust among them. In the example discussed here, Japanese older adults have created reciprocal relationships between themselves and Japanese retirement migrants abroad by developing social networks through both physical space and the internet.

Planning Retirement Migration through Social Networks

ICT and Digital Literacy of Retired Japanese

In order to learn about the new lifestyle proposed by transnational migration, Japanese people of retirement age often need to begin by understanding how to communicate with others over the internet so that they can participate in related social networks. It is therefore indispensable for the development of Japanese international retirement migration for older Japanese to have ICT skills.

The information and communications technology (ICT) infrastructural environment in Japan has become more robust and more personalized over the last few decades. More people perceive the internet as important in a wide variety of situations and as a vital means of obtaining information. Surfing the internet is also considered a hobby or leisure activity. The evolution of ICT infrastructure has resulted in lifestyle changes within Japanese society (MIAC 2011). It has been shown that 78.2 per cent of the total Japanese population of 127.80 million in 2011 used the internet, with more than 90 per cent of the individuals between the ages of 13 to 49 utilizing it. The older age groups of 65–69 (57.0 per cent), 70–79 (39.2 per cent), and 80 and older (20.3 per cent) were comprised of individuals who used the internet less (MIAC 2012) but were still involved in considerable numbers. Furthermore, it was shown that higher income groups by household display higher percentages of internet use (MIAC 2012). It is apparent that older people and those with lower incomes tend to be less digitally active than other demographic groups. However, the data also indicates that the diversity in digital literacy and access exists within the older adult category as well.

Non-profit Organizations, Voluntary Associations and ICT for Japanese Migrants

Non-profit organizations (NPOs) and voluntary associations have played important roles in the dissemination and development of international retirement migration in Japan through ICT. Since the late 1980s, when the idea of international retirement migration was introduced to Japanese society as a new way of life for older people, voluntary associations for the international retirement migration of older people have been established in various parts of Japan. These voluntary associations and NPOs, such as *Nangoku Kurashi no Kai* (an NPO for living in tropical resorts), aim to create virtual and social networks among those interested in international retirement migration in order to share information and facilitate successful transition between cultures and lifestyles.

ICT has helped to establish social networks among Japanese retirees, connecting international retirement migrants to distant potential migrants in ways that would be difficult with face-to-face communication. NPOs and voluntary associations for international retirement migration therefore make use of the internet in order to establish their social infrastructure. Members of these groups are mostly older retirees who generally do not have a wealth of ICT experience or capabilities. Therefore, many of these NPOs organize classes for this population to acquire the necessary skills in order to learn how to utilize digital devices to be a part of a community. NPOs and voluntary associations use social networking services (SNS), internet blogs, sites of individual retirement migrants, and related organizations in order to create networks for mutual assistance and for nurturing friendship among the members.

The following sections describe how, through the use of internet, social networks and the role played by the media, Malaysia has come to be recognized as a preferred destination for Japanese retirement migration while examining the role that mass media plays in this process. This is explored through an ethnographic study conducted from August 2006 to January 2009 and through further research conducted in February, March and April 2011. Ethnographic observation of Japanese retirement migrants at their home, as well as at field sites like the Japan Club of Kuala Lumpur, was conducted in order to follow participants' trajectories both online and offline. Moreover, semi-structured interviews were conducted with specific participants.

Malaysia, Migration and the Media

As noted earlier, the Japanese case has a number of similarities to the European case, especially in terms of choosing the destination based on climate, lower cost of living, cultural proximity, and familiarity. While Western destinations, such as Hawaii, Canada, Australia, the West Coast of the US, and New Zealand, were the preferred long-stay destinations for Japanese retirees in 1992, the most desirable destinations since 2006 have shifted away from Western locations to the Asian countries of Malaysia and Thailand – which rank in the top five destinations – and the Philippines and Indonesia – which rank in the top ten (Long Stay Foundation 2011). This new trend in transnational mobility has been made possible by policies and socio-economic changes in both the original home and host societies involved, as well as a shift in individual motivations facilitated by the use of social networks and media.[2] Malaysia has become an important recipient country upon the implementation of the Malaysia My Second Home Program (MM2H). This was implemented in 2002 in the wake of the Asian Financial Crisis of 1997 in order to attract affluent foreign retirees in the hope that they could help stimulate the suffering Malaysian economy (Chee 2007). According to statistical data obtained from the Malaysian Ministry of Tourism, from the beginning of the initiative in 2002 to October 2011, Malaysia received 16,608 participants from more than 75 countries. Japanese individuals comprised a large percentage of the successful applicants, with 1,512, following those from China (2,733), Bangladesh (2,027) and the United Kingdom (1,754) (Ministry of Tourism 2013). The statistics on approved MM2H applications show households ranging from sole residency, to couples, to families, some of which include an older dependent person or children under 21.

The presence of Japanese retirees has been growing in Malaysia, especially in the Cameron Highlands, Penang and Kuala Lumpur, since the implementation of MM2H. Since the 1980s, Penang has attracted Japanese long-stay tourists and retirement migrants because the area was known for expatriates' residences as well as being a major Japanese tourist destination with beach resorts. However, the popularity of Kuala Lumpur has been growing gradually since the mid-2000s, and Penang has experienced an outflow of Japanese retirees to Kuala Lumpur and back to Japan. One of the reasons for this movement is that Japanese retirees cherish the freedom and flexibility of being a temporary resident and being able to use 'pendulum mobility' between Malaysia and Japan to their advantage (Toyota and Ono 2012). However, it is noteworthy that the development of a retirement network initiated by Japanese retirement migrants in Kuala Lumpur has played a significant role in attracting more residents moving from Penang as well as newcomers from Japan.

Statistical data shows that 20,444 Japanese nationals were living in Malaysia and around half, 10,310, in Kuala Lumpur in October 2012 (MOFA 2013). It is important to note, however, that there is no accurate statistical data on Japanese retirees in Malaysia due to the fact that not everyone with an MM2H visa currently resides within Malaysia and that not all Japanese individuals apply for the special visa because many Japanese retirees stay on a regular three-month tourist visas without settling.

The Role of the Media and of Digital Storytelling

Due to limitations that many Japanese migrants have with the languages commonly used locally, such as English and Malay, and because of a desire for a general sense of security, many tend to live within Japanese retirement communities and build reciprocal relationships with each other. As previously mentioned, in the case of Japanese retirement migrants in Malaysia, NPOs and voluntary associations for retirement migration have played an important role in encouraging inexperienced, older Japanese members to go abroad and live in foreign countries. These new travellers then take short visits to the destinations and ask their peers for advice as they seek to test out the new lifestyle. Older people from various parts of Japan learn about these associations via different types of media, such as books, magazines, news articles, TV shows, and websites, and then participate and interact with other members virtually in order to arrange seasonal visits or to relocate in the future. Personal experiences, life stories and narratives of earlier migrants in the digital and print media are used to present convincing portrayals of international retirement migration as a worthwhile way of realizing the 'true' self. Joseph Dominick (1999) argues that personal web pages allow individuals to transcend from media consumers to media producers. Web authors are not merely sharing information with others, they are also engaged in establishing a sense of self on virtual terrain (Papacharissi 2002: 346). Knut Lundby (2008) uses the term 'digital storytelling' or 'mediatized stories' to describe the necessary competences that 'amateurs' and 'ordinary people' develop to tell their own stories with new digital tools. Furthermore, storytelling implies the shaping of the story as well as the sharing of it with others afterwards (Lundby 2008: 3). It is therefore not just self-fulfilment but communal and public practice.

These ideas of identity and self-fulfilment are tangled up with increased media attention given to the serious public concern for creating individuals' strategies for surviving old age in a society where traditional household formations and retirement practices are rapidly changing. Japanese sociologist Chizuko Ueno (2007), for example, writes about how to prepare for surviving alone in old age. In a similar vein, in 2000 Yasuhiko Sakamoto and his wife, a couple of pioneer Japanese retirement migrants in Malaysia, began to send messages and information about retirement migration to Malaysia via a mailing list. They then developed an internet bulletin board, and finally created their own website in 2004, which resulted in a printed publication in 2006. In 2007, when the baby boomers were approaching retirement, Sakamoto wrote a guidebook entitled *Rewarded life in Malaysia: shall we live in Malaysia after retirement?* This text introduced the Sakamotos' experiences of retirement life in Malaysia, now being updated to the third edition, and was widely read by many Japanese who were planning to move to Malaysia or were interested in travelling there after retirement. The following three case studies illustrate the effect that pioneer retirement migrants' narratives can have on the decisions made by others.

Digitalized Self-Stories, Social Networks and the Role of ICT

Penguin and Goby

Following the creation of a Malaysian programme to accept foreign retirees, the Sakamotos moved to Kuala Lumpur in 2000 while keeping their house in Japan. Mr Sakamoto had lived there for seven years as an expatriate worker for a trading company some thirty years before and liked the city. It was originally his idea and initiative to move to Kuala Lumpur while his wife was reluctant to leave their house in Japan. Slightly stooped when he walks, Sakamoto was given the nickname Penguin by his friends. He called his wife as Goby because she tries everything in the same way a goby fish bites anything.

The couple's own experiences with storytelling started as a group message sent via email to their friends in order to eliminate the burden to write everyone individually. A few years later in 2004, the collections of autobiographical email stories about their everyday life in Malaysia were published on their own website tilted *Malaysian Penguin and Goby*. Below is Goby's first group email entitled *The First Mail from Malaysia* from April 2000.

> Hi everyone, it has been a while since I wrote to you last time. My apologies to write you back all at once. One month has passed since we arrived in Malaysia and I did not feel it because I was busy everyday (omit the latter part of the sentence).
>
> Asking myself 'why suddenly?', 'why Malaysia?', and 'for how long?' and also answering myself 'I don't know' in my heart with a sleepy face, I just followed my husband, however now I can tell the reasons with smiles.
>
> That's because Malaysia is a wonderful place. Although it is often said that home is where you make it, I have never known Malaysia as such a nice place. To explain why it is nice, I cannot say in a single word.
>
> The country is affluent. The city is full of energy. People are friendly. Climate is nice. It is full of fruits that are cheap. Golfing, playing tennis, and swimming is part of the everyday. Eating out is cheap and delicious. Various kinds of ethnic food are available and cheap. There are many beautiful trees and flowers. You don't worry about hay fever. (Sakamoto online: yokofiles. html).

In her storytelling, she explains how her life in Malaysia has begun by following her husband and describes how her personal feeling has changed to the point of liking her new life. As a wife, she describes how nice living in Malaysia can be for various reasons. She also expresses the shifting of her feelings and personal experience from doubt to being convinced about their migratory decision. Reading through the digitalized stories by Penguin and Goby, readers learn about the process through which earlier retirement migrants became assured of their decision to migrate, while in the process collecting detailed practical information about the MM2H program.

The website also provides information and an online booking tool for a series of voluntary seminars run by the Sakamotos and others on long-stay and retirement migration to Malaysia. These are regularly held twice a week at the Japan Club of Kuala Lumpur and have attracted attention not only from potential retirement migrants but also print and televised media outlets keen to interview the couple. Sakamotos' digitalized narratives have been distributed as online information as well as a PDF file available for downloading. Proliferation of their digitalized textual self-portraits has further been expanded by their publication as a printed guidebook in 2006 from a Japanese publisher that focuses on genres such as long-stay tourism, migration, and studying abroad of affected Japanese retirees. The title of the book has been chosen from one of Sakamoto's article on the website, *Rewarded life in Malaysia*.

Since the mid-2000s, as both media coverage and personalized digital storytelling of Japanese retirement migrants in Malaysia has increased, more Japanese older people began to visit and move to the city of Kuala Lumpur. The following section explores in more detail, the case of The Japan Club of Kuala Lumpur; an example of how ICT and digital storytelling have played a significant role in developing the communities of Japanese retirement migrants in Malaysia.

Building Social Networks among Retirement Migrants in Malaysia and Beyond

The Japan Club of Kuala Lumpur was a non-profit organization which was originally established for expatriate workers and their families in 1963. In recent years it has undergone a unique transformation due to increasing number of Japanese retirement migrants and long-stay tourists to Malaysia. The club realized the increasing presence of retirement migrants and felt the responsibility to function as a 'safety net' available to all Japanese residents in Malaysia.

The club itself gained increasing recognition as a centre of gravity for retirement migrants following the establishment of the mutual assistance group and seminars created by members of the club, including the Sakamatos. The volunteer members consisted of Japanese retirees, participants of MM2H programme, Japanese wives married to local Malaysian men, Japanese entrepreneurs, and licensed MM2H visa agents. The volunteer group created a website with a bulletin board in order to communicate with potential retirement migrants and among existing retirement migrants in Kuala Lumpur. Some of the retirees did not have ICT skills; therefore the volunteer group began also a computer class. In the words of Mr Sakamato, 'There are three important skills necessary for retirees in order to have a rewarded life after retirement. One is communication skill in English language. Second is communication skill with internet. Third is the ability to drive a car.' The volunteers' group was later expanded into a successful online community by creating its own social networking service (SNS) on the web. The network grew, tying people in Japan and Malaysia with others all over the world, and now has more than 2,700 members.

Sakamoto (2006) in his book claims that Malaysia is the best place in the world for retirement, and that he plans to live there permanently. He also states that 'making Malaysia a paradise for elderly care' is his dream, going as far as suggesting that leaving Japan to move to Malaysia as a family is one solution for families with older members who require nursing care (Sakamoto 2006). He claims that Malaysia has potential as an 'eldercare paradise' due to its MM2H retirement visa system, warmer climate, spatial housing arrangements, and availability of reasonably priced domestic workers (Sakamoto 2006). This view received a lot of attention and as a result Sakamoto's digital stories have influenced the migration decision making of a number of Japanese retirees with older parents in need of care.

Filial Piety and Caring for the Elderly

In 2008 a Japanese older couple, who has been lived in Kuala Lumpur for several years under the MM2H scheme, decided to relocate their 91-year-old mother suffering from severe dementia, from a retirement home in Japan to live with them in Kuala Lumpur. For over a year, they took care of her by themselves during the day and brought her to a local nursing home at night until her death of natural causes. During the months they took care of the mother, the couple kept a weblog entitled *The Journal on Vernal Life in Malaysia*, which describes their daily activities and experiences taking care of their mother as migrants. During an ethnographic interview in 2009, the husband explained why he created his weblog and his personal feeling about bringing his mother to Malaysia.

It was my wife who strongly wanted to bring my mother to live with us in Malaysia. Although we were paying for the cost of our mother's nursing home in Japan, our other siblings and relatives accused us of having foregone filial responsibility as 'the first son and his wife' by moving to Malaysia. I thought that this would be the last chance for me to be a 'good son' to my mother and do 'oyakoukou' (filial piety) by bringing her over to Malaysia to be with us. I made the weblog and write about my mother so that my brothers and sisters in Japan can access to read about how she lives and how she is taken care of anytime.

The couple's experience of taking care of an aged mother in Kuala Lumpur gradually came to be known, and was later published in a magazine article describing him as a pioneer who had experimented with a new form of elderly care. In the magazine article, he once again states,

Although I was born to be the first son of the family and moved to Malaysia while leaving my mother in a nursing home in Japan, I have felt something weigh on my conscience. My wife, especially, has felt that strongly. As soon as we came to know this information (about Malaysian government has allowed to bring older parents of the family as attendee), my wife said to me 'we shall bring your mother right away'. (Long Stay Foundation 2012)

Subsequent media coverage and applause has encouraged the couple to act as advisors for others considering bringing their aged parents in need of care to Malaysia. One interviewee who followed their example explained:

We contacted them sending a message via SNS for the first time and visited them to meet up for the second time. They helped us and taught us many things. I am expecting that more people who need eldercare will come to Malaysia soon so that the eldercare service available here will improve. I feel a dilemma writing about how we take care of our mother here because it is all about private issues. However, I want more people to move to Malaysia so I write about us just as we are. Anything we speak out, people will read on SNS.

Similar to the previous case, these migrants regard writing their digital self-storytelling as an important responsibility. In this sense, ICT and use of blogs create public space for Japanese retirement migrants. Moreover, their migration story is reported in an article of a major newspaper company, Asahi Shinbun Company (14 April 2013) as well as digitalized in other forms. As can be seen in the above quote, they feel that distributing their story attracts more care-led migrants so that the care business for Japanese clients may develop faster and better. Accounts of their everyday life with their older mother are uploaded to the SNS of the Japanese retirement community. Consequently, this reciprocity among Japanese retirement migrants, especially among those who migrate to Malaysia with older parents in need of nursing care, further enables the local retirement industry to better cater to Japanese clients. It is noteworthy that the chain of digital storytelling of retirement migrants creates a conversation that is helping to shape the lifestyle of older Japanese adults seeking new ways of life. Having already sold their houses in Japan and settled in Malaysia, some individuals are determined to stay for the rest of their lives, despite their visas not guaranteeing status as permanent residents. They can remain in Malaysia as long as the Malaysian government approves the renewal of their visas. The case of Japanese retirement migrants in Malaysia shows that continued international retirement migration through the mediatized autobiographical stories and narratives of migrants facilitates a new pattern of retirement migration, such as the transnational mobility of older patients and adults in need of nursing care. Indeed, ICT mediates digitalized personal experiences and life-stories among Japanese retirement migrants in Malaysia and potential retirement migrants in Japan who otherwise would have never known each other. Through their transnational mobility, Japanese migrants reconcile their motivations to realize their desired self and address cultural norms of filial piety. ICT brings post-retirement life of these Japanese retirement migrants into public space, making their ways of lives and life-stories 'texts' of reference for others who are seeking their own story of how they live their old age.

Conclusion

Information and communication technology has played a significant role in the development of Japanese international retirement migration. Japanese retirees utilize online social networks to gain insight into the practicalities around international retirement opportunities by obtaining an alternative space for communication. By learning and utilizing ICT, older Japanese adults communicate with people outside their established networks and create a community for those who share interest in retirement migration. Within this social network, Japanese retirees share personal stories and exchange ideas and information about the benefits and challenges of this lifestyle option. Narratives often focus on how Japan's state welfare policy no longer guarantees security in later life and convincingly advocates retiring to the South as a reasonable life strategy. In this sense, the network of retirement migrants is a community of practice, searching for the 'small stories' that outline and mutually reinforce how its members successfully live and navigate an alternative third and fourth age together. Ethnographic observation assured that the ICT facilitates not only networking and community building of retirement migrants but also reciprocity of information and support and sharing of anxiety and expectation of their on-going life, which leads to the create a new way of life.

Notes

1. According to the Daijirin and Daijisen dictionaries, *shigarami* refers to obstacles which disturb or obstruct the flow of something and things which constrain the body and are difficult to sever.
2. Japanese retirees began to move to Southeast Asia in the early 1990s when the receiving countries started issuing special visas for foreign retirees, such as the 'non-immigrant "o-a" (long stay)' and 'non-immigrant "o" (pension)' visas in Thailand, the 'Special Resident Retiree's Visa (SRRV)' in the Philippines, and the lansia or lanjutusia (retirement) visa in Indonesia (Ono 2008, 2009).

References

Appadurai, A. 1990. *Modernity at large: cultural dimensions of globalization*. Minneapolis: University of Minnesota Press.

Asahi Shinbun Company. 2013, April 14. *Maleshia Tsui No Sumika, Umi Koete* (Final Home across the Ocean), http://digital.asahi.com/articles/TKY201304160573.html?ref=comkiji_txt_end_s_kjid_TKY201304160573, retrieved 17 August 2013.

Benson, M. and K. O'Reilly. 2009. *Lifestyle migration: expectations, aspirations and experiences*. England: Ashgate Publishing.

Bernal, V. 2006. 'Diaspora, cyberspace and political imagination: the Eritrean diaspora online', *Global Networks* 6(2): 161–79.

Cabinet Office, Japan. 2011. White Paper on Aging Society. http://www8.cao.go.jp/kourei/whitepaper/w-2011/zenbun/pdf/1s2s_2.pdf, retrieved 20 April 2013.

———. 2012. White Paper on Aging Society. http://www8.cao.go.jp/kourei/whitepaper/w-2012/zenbun/, retrieved 20 April 2013.

Casado-Diaz, M. A. 2009. 'Social capital in the sun: bonding and bridging social capital among British retirees', in Michaela Benson and Karen O'Reilly (eds.), *Lifestyle migration: expectations, aspirations and experiences*. England: Ashgate Publishing, pp. 87–102.

Chee, H. L. 2007. 'Medical tourism in Malaysia: international movement of healthcare consumers and the commodification of healthcare', Working Paper in National University of Singapore's Asia Research Institute Working Paper Series No. 83, January 2007.

Chizuko U. 2007. *Ohitori Sama no Rogo* (Retirement of the Singles). Tokyo: Hoken.

Dominick, J. R. 1999. 'Who do you think you are? Personal home pages and self-presentation on the world wide web', *Journalism and Mass Communication Quarterly* 76: 646–58.

King, R., T. Warnes and A. Williams. 2000. *Sunset lives? British retirement migration to the Mediterranean*. Oxford and New York: Berg.

Long Stay Foundation. 2011. Long Sutei Chosa Tokei 2011 (Statistic data on long-stay 2011). Tokyo: Long Stay Foundation.

———. 2012. LONGSTAY 2012 Nen Fuyu Go (Long-stay 2012 Vol. Winter). Long Stay Foundation: Tokyo.

Lundby, K. (ed). 2008. *Digital storytelling, mediatized stories: self-representations in new media*. New York: Peter Lang Publishing.

NIPSSR (National Institute of Population and Social Security Research). 2012. http://www.ipss.go.jp/syoushika/tohkei/newest04/sh2401top.html.

MIAC (Ministry of Internal Affairs and Communications, Japan). 2011. 2011 White Paper Information and Communications in Japan, http://www.soumu.go.jp/johotsusintokei/whitepaper/eng/WP2011/2011-outline.pdf, retrieved 8 February 2013.

———. 2012. White paper Information and Communications in Japan, http://www.soumu.go.jp/johotsusintokei/whitepaper/eng/WP2012/2012-outline.pdf, retrieved on 8 February 2013.

Ministry of Tourism, Malaysia. 2013. Top 10 Participating Countries From 2002 – November 2012 Malaysia My Second Home (MM2H) Programme, http://www.mm2h.gov.my/statistic.php, retrieved 14 April 2013.

MOFA (Ministry of Foreign Affairs, Japan). 2013. Annual Report of Statistics on Japanese Nationals Overseas, http://www.mofa.go.jp/mofaj/files/000017472.pdf, retrieved 21 March 2014.

Ono, M. 2008. 'Long-stay tourism and international retirement migration: Japanese retirees in Malaysia', *Senri Ethnological Reports* 77: 151–62.

———. 2009. 'Japanese lifestyle migration/tourism in Southeast Asia', *Japanese Review of Cultural Anthropology* 10: 43–52.

———. 2010. 'Long-stay tourism: Japanese elderly tourists in the Cameron Highlands, Malaysia', *Senri Ethnological Studies* 76: 95–110.

O'Reilly, K. 2000. *The British on the Costa del Sol: transnational identities and local communities*. London and New York: Routledge.

Papacharissi, Z. 2002. 'The self online: the utility of personal home pages', *Journal of Broadcasting & Electronic Media* 46(3): 346–68.

Plath, D. W. 1980. *Long engagements: maturity in modern Japan*. Stanford: Stanford University Press.

Putnam, R. D. 1993. *Making democracy work: civic tradition in Modern Italy*. Princeton: Princeton University Press.

———. 2000. *Bowling alone: the collapse and revival of American community*. Simon & Schuster.

Sakamoto, Y. 2006. *Gohobi Jinsei Mareishia* (Rewarded life in Malaysia). Tokyo: Ikarosu Shuppan.

Sakamoto, Y. & Yoko. 'Malaysian Penguin and Dabohaze', http://www.geocities.jp/hikosakamotojp/index.html, retrieved 17 August 2013.

Toyota, M. 2006. 'Ageing and transnational householding: Japanese retirees in Southeast Asia', *International Development Planning Review* 28(4): 515–31.

Toyota, M. and M. Ono. 2012. 'Building a temporary second home: Japanese long-stay retirees in Penang', in Francis Hutchinson and Johan Saravanamuttu (eds), *Catching the wind: Penang in a rising Asia*. Singapore: ISEAS, pp. 167–85.

Yamashita, S. 2009. *Kanko Jinruigaku No Chosen: 'Atarashii Chikyu' No Ikikata* (Challenge of anthropology of tourism: a way of living in 'a new planet'). Tokyo: Kodansha.

12. DIGITAL GAMES IN THE LIVES OF OLDER ADULTS

Bob De Schutter, Julie A. Brown and Henk Herman Nap

ACCORDING TO THE LATEST ACADEMIC literature on the topic, the advent of digital games[1] dates back to the early 1950s. In 1951, the British computer company Ferranti showcased the Nimrod Digital Computer – an imposing machine, 11.5 x 5 x 10 feet in size – by featuring the mathematical game, *Nim*. It would take twenty-four more years for Atari to launch Pong, the first digital game to achieve commercial success.

The history of digital games within the formative years of today's seniors can be characterized by and traced to a variety of technological evolutions. First, digital games have become a rich audio-visual experience. While early games were displayed with only a handful of computer pixels, contemporary games feature high-definition illustrations and three-dimensional photorealistic imagery (Wilson and DeMaria 2002). The same can be said of in-game audio. While the synthetic computer sounds from the days of Pong certainly had a charm of their own, modern game sound tracks feature symphonic orchestras, popular musicians or the beats of high-profile DJs.

The way in which players manually interact with digital games has also evolved over the years. Even though the joystick, gamepad and keyboard/mouse are still regarded as the holy trinity of input devices for avid game players, a new generation of embodied and direct input devices has taken the digital gaming market by storm. Successful products – such as EyeToy (2000), *Nintendo Wii* (2006), *Singstar* (2004), *Guitar Hero* (2005), *Dance Dance Revolution* (1998), *iPhone* (2007), and *Microsoft Kinect* (2010) – have led to a wide range of alternative input devices that are accessible to audiences who are less skilled or unfamiliar with traditional game controllers.

Digital gaming has become a rich audio-visual embodied gaming experience and the player experience is further enhanced by the rise of mediated play via the internet. The standalone arcade hall games have been replaced by a wide variety of online games. On one side of the spectrum there are MMORPGs (Massive Multiplayer Online Role-Playing Games), in which millions of people play together. For example, *World of Warcraft* (2004) has been estimated to have over 10 million subscribers (Karmali 2012). On the other side, there are social games that tie into social networking sites such as Facebook and Google Plus. These are less demanding in terms of a learning curve and some are extremely popular. For example, *Farmville 2* is currently estimated to have 40 million active monthly users (AppData 2013).

In line with the Web 2.0 movement, end-users have become media producers of digital gaming, as evidenced by a wide range of games that are designed to evoke player creativity, as well as the formation of online 'modding' communities whose members modify parts of existing games into completely new games (Edge Magazine 2003). Players can nowadays create their own game content and can play these modified games wherever they want since game devices have become ubiquitous. Although portable gaming consoles became popular during the 1980s (e.g. Nintendo Gameboy), the current mobile gaming market is booming because of the upcoming of affordable and high-spec smartphones and tablet PCs. These ubiquitous devices provide the end-users with an online game library (e.g., Google Play Store and Apple iTunes) of hundreds of thousands of free and low-cost digital games.

In summary, due to technological advancements, digital games have become a collaborative, ubiquitous and accessible medium.[2] The digital game audience expanded from children and young males with a fascination for computer technology (Fromme 2003; Williams 2006) with new categories of users like 'casual gamers'. Casual gamers are a group of gamers who are less inclined to spend hours learning to play a game or to master a complex set of controls. In contrast to 'hardcore' gamers, casual gamers search for games that provide instant gratification or are socially supported (Juul 2008). The typical casual gamer is female and digital games have become increasingly popular among this group of gamers: Nielsen-Net Ratings reported that women between 35 and 49 years of age are the largest demographic group of players in the world (Nielsen-Net Ratings 2004). Casual games are also increasingly popular among older age cohorts who now have a strong foothold in digital gaming. The annual gaming market assessment released by the Entertainment Software Association (2012) reported that the 'age 50+' segment represents 29 per cent of the gamer market in the US; this is a 20 per cent increase since 1999. Games have also gained popularity among older adults in Europe. A study by the British Broadcasting Corporation (BBC; Pratchett 2005) reported that 6.5 per cent of all British digital game players are over the age of 50, a percentage that roughly corresponds to 18 per cent of all British adults between 50 and 65 years of age. The National Gamers Surveys by TNS/Newzoo (Hagoort and Hautvast 2009) provided a broader perspective on the matter by assessing and comparing data from various countries. Their market research indicated that female players are more prevalent than male players in the 50 to 65 age group, and that of the six countries that were surveyed, the US has the largest percentage of older adults within its gaming audience. Based on these market studies, it can be inferred that digital games have become a popular activity in the lives of a considerable percentage of older adults in Western societies.

TABLE 12.1   Percentage of population playing digital games and time spent (Hagoort and Hautvast 2009).

	Male (50–65)		Female (50–65)	
	Pct.	Hrs/Week	Pct.	Hrs/Week
Belgium	37	4,2	53	5,3
France	33	3,9	44	4,5
Germany	37	2,5	42	3,5
The Netherlands	45	3,2	59	3,7
United Kingdom	41	3,5	43	3,8
USA	72	4,9	72	7,5

Despite the increased prevalence of digital game play among older populations, research specifically probing the characteristics of this burgeoning market segment is still in its infancy. Pioneering research on digital game players is presented in the following sections divided into three categories: effect, design and audience studies.

Category I – Effect Studies

The first category concerns effect studies that assess digital games as a catalyst for potential benefits among older users. These studies focus on the extent to which digital games can help maintain or improve specific cognitive, perceptual and motor abilities, or aspects of overall life quality. The vast majority of these studies are experiments with non-digital game playing seniors who are often recruited from congregate living facilities or as volunteer patients within a clinical setting. Overall, the results from these studies indicate that older adult use of digital games can be 1) beneficial as a therapeutic or medical intervention (e.g. Beasley 1989; Riddick et al. 1987), 2) a means to improve social and emotional wellbeing and entertainment (e.g. Goldstein et al. 1997; McGuire 1984), 3) related to an increased interest in and eagerness to learn about technology (e.g. Bailey 1989; Hollander and Plummer 1986), and 4) a tool to potentially improve particular cognitive, perceptual, and motor skills (e.g. Basak, Boot, Voss and Kramer 2008; Clark, Lanphear and Riddick 1987; Drew and Waters 1986; Dustman, Emmerson, Steinhaus, Shearer and Dustman 1992; Goldstein et al. 1997; Miller 2005).

Category II – Design Studies

A second line of research on digital games for an older audience focuses on the design of digital games for and/or by older adults and the potential adoption of them. The rationale prompting these studies is often the same as those in the first category; digital games are regarded as a potential means to improve the quality of life of older game users. However, for seniors to experience such benefits, it is essential that games be designed to appropriately suit their game preferences and ability level. Furthermore, as an additional design consideration, assessments must be made to identify factors that influence the adoption of this technology.

While the methodology behind these studies varies from usability testing (e.g. Nacke, Nacke and Lindley 2009; Neufeldt 2009; Van Gils, Derboven and Poels 2008; White, Harley, Axelrod, McAllister and Latham 2009), design research (e.g. Aison, Davis, Milner and Targum 2002; De Schutter and Vanden Abeele 2008; Dogruel and Jöckel 2008; Gerling, Schulte and Masuch 2011) to literature reviews (e.g., IJsselsteijn, Nap, de Kort and Poels 2007; Gamberini, Mariano and Barresi 2006), the results of these studies are game design suggestions that address normative age-related impairments (such as vision, hearing, tactile sensitivity, cognitive processing and motor skills), and provide guidance with regards to maximizing the appeal of digital games to older adults. One group of studies within this category specifically focuses upon game design within the context of intergenerational play – games that encourage interaction between different generations, such as grandparents and grandchildren (e.g. Kern, Stringer, Fitzpatrick and Schmidt 2006; Khoo and Cheok 2006; Tarling 2005; Vanden Abeele, De Schutter, Husson, Vos and Annema 2008; Vetere, Nolan and Raman 2006).

Category III – Audience Studies

While the first two categories emphasize older adults as the target audience, actively playing older adults are not the focus of these studies, as their samples consist exclusively of non-playing older people. Reflecting the increased use of digital games among older adults, a third and final category has emerged: audience studies. These studies focus upon the use of digital games by older adults and the motives that prompt and support their game play. In contrast to the previous two categories, the studies within this category sought out active game playing older adults and specifically focused on how games may be integrated within the context of their daily life. The results of these explorative studies provided insight as to how digital games are intertwined within the time expenditure of older adults (e.g., Quandt, Grueniger and Wimmer 2009), how games are experienced and evaluated within their social context (e.g., Nap, de Kort and IJsselsteijn 2009), and how older adults are motivated to play (or to have started playing) digital games (e.g. De Schutter 2011; O'Brien, Knapp, Thompson, Craig and Barrett 2013).

This chapter continues with an in-depth review of audience studies on seniors who are active digital game players. A unique insight is given in the exploration of the factors that play a role in the interaction of older age cohorts with digital games. The research findings that are highlighted and categorized herein provide a foundational perspective of how digital games can become an integral and beneficial component within the lives of game playing seniors. For an overview of the state of the art of the first and second category of studies on older adults and games, please refer to the work of Nap and Diaz-Orueta (2012) and Marston and Smith (2012).

Adoption: Taking a First Step on the Road to Becoming a Gamer

Game play is framed as a common and acceptable leisure activity for young adults yet, to a far lesser extent, for older adults. Today's younger generations have grown up with digital technologies and therefore, have had greater exposure. However, this is not the case for older generations. Exposure to and engagement with technologies, such as digital games, is varied among members of older generations and increases the heterogeneity of the player characteristics. This includes, but is not limited to age-related functional abilities, preferences, and experience. One of the underpinnings of developing a theoretical framework for older adult digital gaming is to gain an understanding about why and how older people started playing games.

When examining the rationales for older adults to start playing games, most studies reported that social factors contributed to the adoption of game play in their lives. Playing digital games often started with an introduction from other people, such as partners, children, grandchildren, friends or colleagues. For example, Pearce (2008) described how a husband with a passion for first-person shooter games encouraged his 59-year-old wife to play *Myst* adventure games, and how she would eventually get her adult daughter to join her in playing the games she loved. Quandt et al. (2009) described how the senior participants often inherited the old PCs of their adult children as a gift, which often included pre-installed digital games. This handing down of and exposure to gaming technology from generation to generation was further exhibited when grandchildren were introduced into the mixture, as grandparents tend to enjoy spending time with them, which can spark a bit of playful competition (Haddon and Silverstone 1996).

One reason for the socially inspired adoption of digital games could be related to older adults not having enough knowledge about the medium. Pearce's (2008) sample of participants (recruited through gaming sites) were already at a stage in their gaming careers where gaming forums, online reviews, and even developer websites or print magazines were used to find out about new games, whereas older players in related studies typically described how they had difficulty in finding suitable games for themselves. For example, Woldberg (2008) reported that 58 per cent of her sample of 404 actively playing participants felt that they did not have enough knowledge about digital games to seek out and purchase games for themselves. Therefore, the majority of her respondents relied upon friends and family to tell them what to buy and for technical support when assistance was needed within the game.

For other participants, however, the adoption of digital games was spurred by exposure to games that were provided as a package deal that came with their personal computers. For example, Quandt et al. (2009), Nap et al. (2009), and Pearce (2008) found that some of their participants became aware of digital games because they already owned a computer for work-related purposes. Consequently, they stumbled upon the games accidentally because they were already pre-installed or because they came across them while surfing the internet.

The earliest example of how pre-installed games lure older adults into playing digital games was reported by Haddon and Silverstone (1996) who described a couple who bought a television set and were introduced to digital games through an electronic game that was offered along with the television. For older adults like these, it seems that games were regarded as inexpensive, which was reflected in their game purchasing habits.

However, Copier (2002), Pearce (2008) and Nap et al. (2009) found that many of their participants sought out free games online, bought used or price-reduced games, borrowed games from friends, played gifted games, or even obtained pirated versions from friends or family.

Another case of game adoption was reported by Quandt et al. (2009) in which two cases described how life-changing illnesses – including a loss of control and mobility – triggered a computer gaming career. De Schutter (2011) confirmed this as one precursor for game adoption, with multiple examples of participants (mostly homebound) who had either temporary or permanent illnesses that led to digital game play.

In addition, actively playing older adults are often introduced to digital games through coincidental factors simply because they interested them. For example, Nap et al. (2009) described older adults with a passion for airplanes and rally driving who turned to digital games to simulate these passions. However, Copier (2002) found that many of her respondents seemed to have an unquestionable passion for playing games. The former group of participants followed their passion into playing digital games, while for the latter, digital games were simply a continuation of their passion for games.

Considering the various roads that lead to adopting digital games as a potentially meaningful pastime in later life, the literature is lacking in studies that assess the role of social networking sites as a catalyst to gaming. Although studies suggest that exposure to online games can lead to playing digital games, it is not yet known how online social games, such as Facebook's *Farmville* or online poker, lead to a gamer lifestyle. However, some have argued that these so-called social games – with *Farmville* as its poster child – are not actually games (e.g., see Liszkiewicz 2010). While more research into this topic is recommended, this could be a tentative explanation for why the gap between *Farmville* and the more stereotypical genres of games is still a large one.

Motivation: The Reasons Why Older Adults Keep Playing

Not everybody who plays a digital game makes it a regular part of his or her life. However, for those that do, there is that special 'something' that prompts them to return to a beloved game or to explore new ones. Motivation is a key consideration to examine within game studies, yet what are the mechanisms that motivate older players? This is a challenging question to pose, as older adults are by default of nature heterogeneous – the attributes that characterize the aging population span a greater range of diversity than younger cohorts. Thus, it is crucial to identify influential factors that lead to understanding, instead of making generalized assumptions about older players' motivations. In turn, an insight in the influential factors could provide a basis for developing games that suit the particular needs and preferences of this growing niche market.

Like much of the research literature that examines older players, there is discontinuity with respect to population (participant) characteristics. Nonetheless, commonalities have been found within studies that result in the emergence of four distinguishable clusters that speak to older game player motives.

Digital or not, at the heart of any game is the sense of challenge that is taken on by the player. The desire to succeed in a game does not seem to diminish with age and is even an integral component for many older players to enjoy the game. Known as 'interactive motivation', this refers to the fulfilment that comes from a sense of control within the game, overcoming challenges, obtaining mastery, or progressing through levels. In video gaming terminology, these motives are related to game play challenges, as opposed to motivation derived from the audiovisual experience of playing a game.

'Interactive motivation' has been evidenced as a prevailing drive for older players, as the sense of challenge and the development of mastery set the stage for both satisfaction and pride. Losing a game can lead to frustration, but it may also be a springboard for perseverance. This is a fine line within any game, but perhaps more so with older players because of the increased likelihood of encountering challenges that stem from age-related impairments. However, it has been found that perseverance that results in success leads to an intensified sense of accomplishment for the older player (Nap et al. 2009).

The enjoyment that may derive from challenge is not the only motivational factor that entices an older gamer to play. It has been found that they may also be drawn in by 'immersive motives' that are elicited by those elements that are often found within the rich context of a game. Some older players are motivated to play because of the enjoyment that derives from exploring a rich game world, meeting interesting characters, following exciting storylines, playing out a fantasy, and being exposed to the general audiovisual and sensory experience of playing a game.

The strength of an immersive motive may be attributed to the contextually vivid game world of the player. It has been found that older players who interact within such rich environments tend to revel in the beautiful scenery of the game (Pearce 2008), which creates a sense of wonder that stimulates imagination. However, not all games are designed to afford that level of visual stimulation. In one study, although less pronounced, immersive motivation was found to be present among older gamer participants who were allowed to create virtual characters that were based upon family members (Nap et al. 2009). This was also the case when they were given the option to explore digital games that allowed them to revisit, relive and reminisce over former activities (e.g., rally driving while playing DTM Racer) or places visited in their youth (e.g., a trip to Egypt while playing a puzzle game in an Egyptian setting).

A significant component to playing a game derives from the socialization that may occur when playing it. This has been found to be a key motivation for many older players and is not surprising, as opportunities for socialization can wane with advancing age. It is not uncommon for older adults to engage in activities that support and nurture relationships with loved ones, such as family members. Thus, 'social motives' refer to the enjoyment players derive from a sense of competition, cooperation, social interaction, fellowship or camaraderie while playing digital games.

Various studies provide evidence of this motive as the primary reason why older players play. It is not so much the game itself that keeps them returning, but the opportunity to spend time with a partner, children or grandchildren. Digital games should rather be designed to support this motive, but it is a challenge to ensure that these games meet the range of game playing needs, preferences, and capabilities among multi-generational players.

In addition, it must be considered that social motives for older players may alter over time. For example, competition may be a driving force at an earlier stage in life, but this need may decrease over time as other social motives take precedence (Woldberg 2008). Finally, some older players are motivated to play as a means to avoid, support or replace other activities. These 'contextual motives', therefore, function as a means of escapism, relaxation, arousal, passing the time or diversion.

Games can serve as a springboard to launch a player into a realm that allows him or her to momentarily 'live' within an alternate reality. This escape from the real world has been found to be a source of respite for older players, as they are faced with both personal and interpersonal challenges. For example, Nap et al. (2009) described how digital games can function as an escape for older adults whose partners suffered from a medium stage of dementia. These participants reported using digital games as a means to help forget or avoid the sorrow they go through on a daily basis.

In addition to escapism, some older players view games as preferred alternative activity or source of entertainment, such as watching TV. This is significant, as opportunities and viable options for activities decrease with age as impairments increase. Therefore, digital games have the potential to serve as a meaningful activity, provided that it is designed in a way that can accommodate the aging players' abilities. Furthermore, these games can become increasingly meaningful if they reflect a previously enjoyed activity that is no longer feasible.

As well as these motives, there is an underlying fifth motive, that older players playing as a means to facilitate certain positive effects toward their personal life outside of the game. Although this is rarely a primary motive for regular game play, the opportunity to enhance motor or cognitive skills, knowledge acquisition, new social connections, and self-image, is recognized as a potential side benefit. Paradoxically, this motive has been the focus of many games, such as brain-training games, that are now flooding the market.

The cluster of motives presented could also be applied to younger audiences, yet the reason supporting the motive would likely differ. Nonetheless, there are various other dimensions that distinguish older players from their younger counterparts. Thus, the following sections of this chapter will explore how games are tied into the daily lives of older adults, and how differences between them and younger audiences can be identified.

Lifestyle: When Games Become a Hobby

For many people (regardless of age), playing digital games is more than just a hobby: it is a reflection of identity and personality. Being a 'gamer' can be part of a lifestyle. For older adults, games were often in line with pre-existing and meaningful interests that they felt highly passionate about. For example, Pearce (2008) reported that one of her respondents began playing online role-playing games after she learned how the alternative worlds within such games reflected her passion for fantasy fiction. Similarly, Nap et al. (2009) reported how digital game play for two participants, in particular *Flight Simulator*, was part of a deeply-rooted passion for aviation. Copier (2002) supported this stance by describing how playing digital games for many of her participants was a logical evolution of a passion for traditional, analogue games and play in general. Similar to motivational factors that prompt game play, older players are often faced with challenges that accompany age. These challenges may come in the form of declining functional ability or diminishing access to opportunity. Thus, digital games can be a means to connect with an aspect of their identity that would otherwise be neglected.

While games can become part of the identity of older adults when they are tied into meaningful aspects of their lives, it should be noted that the term 'gamer' should be used carefully. The majority of research on the topic indicates that players past the age of 50 have relatively limited knowledge about gaming culture. In fact, Copier (2002), Woldberg (2008) and

Nap et al. (2009) described how their older adult participants did not consider themselves to be actual 'gamers', a term they associate with younger people. Nonetheless, Pearce (2008: 152) did report how some of her participants were 'avid and experienced fans who are highly developer and genre-conscious'. While this quotation is hardly enough to justify referring to older adults as 'gamers', it does again indicate how much variety there exists in the older audience of digital games.

Content Preferences: The Kind of Games They Love to Play

Similar to any other kind of art or entertainment, playing digital games is a highly subjective activity. A game that is adored by one player might be disliked by somebody else. The range of game genres reported in the research on older adults who play digital games is, therefore, a broad one. Even though such heterogeneity in terms of content preferences makes it difficult to draw general conclusions about the older player, there are general commonalities across the studies that focus on this particular topic.

An initial finding suggested that there may be somewhat of an age ceiling on games that require a lot of dexterity and fast response time. For example, Pearce (2008) reported how action- and/or combat-oriented games were only a favourite among those aged from 40 to 65 and not older cohorts. Similarly, De Schutter (2011) reported that older digital game player participants with a preference for action games were significantly younger than their older counterparts, who had a preference for puzzle games, adapted versions of traditional games, and simple web-based games. At first glance, this may seem to be solely attributed to a preference for the genre of the game, yet such games typically require a speedy response time to prompts within the game and sufficient manual dexterity to manipulate the controller. Such considerations are related to the gradual decline of fine motor skills that increase with age. Thus, one's ability to interact within a game can affect game preferences.

While reduced dexterity and reflexes can limit the range of games an aging individual is capable of enjoying, such sensory psycho-motor losses often reduce the amount of possible real-life activities as well. When an older gamer is no longer able to physically participate in a once enjoyed hobby, he or she is more likely to welcome the opportunity to re-enact it via a digital game (Nap et al. 2009). For example, in one instance, an older adult participant wanted to play games that were racing simulations because race-car driving was a long-time ambition for this individual. Likewise, other players prefer games that reflect a childhood hobby, such as reading (Pearce 2008). In this instance, games have the potential to evoke imagination, in the same way as a favoured childhood book series.

A personal-historical perspective may also negatively influence a person's perspective on in-game content. Older generations have experienced or have been exposed to significant turbulent events, such as war and civil disorder. This was one of the explanations provided as to why some older players avoid violent games (Pearce 2008), which is also reflected in older persons' preferences for movies with cheerful or heart-warming content, in contrast to most young adults' preferences for violent and scary movies (Mares et al. 2008). Therefore, it may be of no surprise that many older players are generally not fond of overly violent games.

Another influential factor for game preference is that of socialization. Opportunities for intergenerational play (e.g., Haddon and Silverstone 1996; Khoo and Cheok 2006) were regarded as significant among older players. The nurturing of meaningful relationships tends to be critical for aging adults, and especially so as their perspective of future time diminishes. Therefore, digital games can be approached as an invaluable intergeneration tool for older players (De Schutter and Vanden Abeele 2010).

A final preference found among the participants in these studies centres on the game platform, the hardware and software upon which the system operates. As discussed earlier, PCs, as a professional or communication tool, often prelude digital games. This finding is reflected in the prevalence of PCs for digital gaming, as it was the most cited (preferred) platform among the older adults in each of the studies (see for example De Schutter 2011; Nap et al. 2009; Pearce 2008; Woldberg 2008). On the other hand, console games were noted for affording greater opportunities for intergenerational game play (Voida and Greenberg 2012).

In conclusion, from the literature it seems that an appropriate digital game for an older audience is more likely to be a non-violent PC game that ties into pre-existing interests of the player – preferably activities that they are no longer able to do – and that is designed to take age-related functional constraints into account, and has the option to be enjoyed alongside valued family members and friends.

Time Expenditure: Integrating Games in Daily Life

Playing games can consume a considerable amount of time. While story-driven games can easily take over ten hours to complete (Howlongtobeat. com 2013), others are open-ended or continuously updated (e.g. *Farmville*, *World of Warcraft*, *Flight Simulator*, etc.), and therefore, offer what is known as re-playability. However, not everyone is willing to invest ample amounts of time, as appears to be the case for some of the participants in Pearce's study (2008).

The age of an older player may be an indicator of how much time is spent playing digital games in a single sitting. It has been found that younger-aged cohort players commit more time to game play than older-aged cohorts (De Schutter 2011). This may be attributed to factors such as exposure to and familiarity with gaming technologies, yet it was found in another study that older players feel a greater sense of demand on their time due to occupational and social obligations (Quandt et al. 2009). However, it may also be posited that it becomes increasingly difficult for an aging player to remain engaged in an activity due to physiological and cognitive demand. For example, prolonged sitting and controller manipulation may cause joint stiffness or pain, and extended periods of concentration and visual attentiveness may become more challenging.

Another factor worth noting with respect to the amount of time committed to game play is gender. Among younger audiences, male members spend more time playing, yet this trend appears to reverse in later years (De Schutter 2011). One explanation for this finding could be that older females of these generations are confined or tied to the house more than their husbands. As a result, they will play games more, in particular, short, round two-dimensional puzzle games, adaptations of traditional games, and web-based games (e.g., Nap et al. 2009). Another explanation for the high percentage of older female players is that it reflects the demographics of this population; there are greater numbers of older adult females than males.

The time of day and day of week that participants play has also been found to be a component of this theme (Quandt et al. 2009; Pearce 2008; Nap et al. 2009). Overall, nights and weekends were the preferred time to play digital games. This may be attributed to finding a 'free' moment of unobligated time, as part of a relaxation routine, or an activity to occupy time before going to bed. The younger members of these older adult participants reported a preference for playing after dinner, on weekend days, and immediately after work during the week (Pearce 2008). These trends will need to be monitored in the coming years as the younger members continue to age, as this may have a bearing on game preferences (i.e., a mentally challenging vs. a relaxing game).

As suggested earlier, factors such as occupational obligations tend to influence the amount of time an older person has available or is willing to commit to game play. For example, it has been found that there is a relationship between the amount of time an older player commits to game play and employment status (De Schutter 2011). Persons with a retired status seemed to spend less time playing than those still within the workforce.

However, this perspective is not fully supported, as work demands are cited as an inhibitor to free time (Quandt et al. 2009).

Besides work, educational status and interpersonal/social relationships seem to affect, or at least be an indication of, time availability for digital gaming. One study found that older adult participants with high levels of education commit less time than those with average or lower levels within their educational backgrounds (De Schutter 2011). It is premature at this time to propose why this may be the case and what implications this may have for this niche; thus, additional research is merited. Additionally, finding an agreeable timeslot with a person with whom one may want to play a game can be a source of frustration (Chen et al. 2012; Nap et al. 2009). This finding suggests that if the main purpose for playing is based on social motives, then this may influence the amount of time one spends playing.

Social Context: Playing Games with and around Others

Undoubtedly, social context shapes experiences and can also be a strong determinant for adopting activities in the lives of people, as reflected by the significance of social gaming reported in a number of studies. For example, in one study, younger older adult players cited social aspects as a primary motivator to play online games and 63 per cent of the participants ranked socializing as favourite game activities (Pearce 2008). Based on these findings, it appears that the perceived social interaction within such digital games seems to influence the overall gaming experience of these players.

The social context of play seems to influence not only current game play preferences, but also when the adoption of digital games took place. According to Pearce (2008), 28 per cent of those participants aged 40 to 65 had their first gaming experience in an arcade. Video arcades boomed in the late 1970s and 1980s, where people (including families) played games in a social setting. When arcades were at their peak, it was publically acceptable to play digital games, as it was a reflection of the society's shifting technological culture. However, in the late 1980s until recently, gaming was generally perceived as a youth-oriented activity (Quandt et al. 2009). Traces of this perception remain alive today, as digital game play among older persons is deemed as unusual, both by society and non-gaming peers.

Another social aspect to consider is the significance of the in-game experience for social players. Five studies assessed the preferences of senior players with respect to the identity of the co-player(s) within the game. According to Pearce (2008) and Quandt et al. (2009), older adult game players place special emphasis or preference on like-minded co-players.

Similarly, De Schutter (2011) highlighted that older players prefer to invest in a playing partner they know well, rather than playing with complete strangers. This was evidenced by Nap et al. (2009) when none of the participants in the study reported caring for playing with an unknown person over the internet.

Older players also report less interest in rapid advancement within game rankings. One explanation claims that this may be attributed to a preference among older players to play with those of their own age cohort, suggesting that younger players value speedy advancement (Quandt et al. 2009). Based on the above findings, it can be suggested that older adult co-players should have a mutual background (i.e., compatible interests) and/or are already known to each other. Although it may appear that these players prefer co-players of a similar age, De Schutter (2011), Nap et al. (2009) and Chen et al. (2012) found that older adult players also play with younger counterparts. These younger co-players are often younger family members, such as children and grandchildren. This is done as a means of nurturing that connection, creating a common interest, or simply gaining attention from the younger person. This interaction has the potential to promote quality of life, as Chen et al. (2012) stated that being in touch with children is essential for seniors' health and wellbeing.

Finally, digital game play can be an important and direct means of enhancing a sense of connectedness among co-players or even facilitating meeting new people (De Schutter and Vanden Abeele 2010). According to Pearce (2008) – and contrary to the popular stereotype – online games and game communities may actually serve to expand the social lives of older adults, by providing an additional social venue. Some of the participants of De Schutter and Vanden Abeele (2010) used digital games to meet as many people as possible, because they believed they lacked social interaction. In addition, according to Quandt et al. (2009), computer-mediated interactions have the potential to develop into real-life social relationships. Overall, the findings within the reviewed studies indicated that social context may be a major determinant in an older adults' adoption of digital gaming, the formation of specific co-player identity and the transfer of virtual contacts to substantive relationships.

Conclusion

Actively playing older adults are a highly heterogeneous audience, citing a wide variety of reasons for the adoption of digital games into their lives and motivating factors for continued play throughout old age. Although older players have points of commonality with younger audiences, it is critical to recognize that they are an equally diverse population, yet are often viewed as a homogenous niche with static qualities.

With respect to the vast range of characteristics and preferences among older players, several themes stand out. It is evident that a duality exists between players who take games quite seriously by making it a part of their lifestyle, and those who play more casually. While the former are typically very knowledgeable about the games they play, the latter tend to be more dependent upon others when seeking and learning new games. Nonetheless, for both groups, social context and time expenditure for game play strongly speaks to the significance of the meanings that players attribute to games. This poses a challenge, as gaming is not always a socially accepted pastime for older adults, and sometimes has to be incorporated into a busy schedule.

From the studies it appeared that there is an overall preference among seniors for two-dimensional puzzle games, adaptations of traditional games, and simple web-based games. This could be explained by analysing game characteristics in relation to the functional abilities of the players. First, these preferred games are low in complexity, which may be advantageous for those who have limited gaming technology experience, and also possibly declining cognitive physiological response. In addition, these games do not usually require a lengthy time commitment. Thus, a player is not obligated to spend an excessive amount of time playing per game play session, which can be inconvenient for any number of age-related reasons, such as mental fatigue. Also, these games are designed to allow the player to proceed at his or her own pace (untimed). This may be advantageous for those who experience sensorimotor impairment as evidenced by, for example, a delayed reaction time to a timed prompt within a game.

Additionally, the digital adaptation of traditional games has proven to be popular and could be explained by the fact that the older adult players previously enjoyed or found them (the non-digital version) to be rewarding. This fits with Melenhorst's findings (2002) that indicate how older adults are willing to learn new activities and technologies when the benefits are clear and evident.

With consideration to older adult player studies, there is ample room for further research, as several related studies cite contradictory findings. For example, the age range and gaming experience among participants in Pearce's (2008) sample differed considerably from other studies, thus, resulting in a greater diversity of findings. Another example is the significance and influence of playing behaviour (time allotment) among retired older adults, as Quandt et al. (2009) and De Schutter (2011) reported contrasting results. Furthermore, the studies lack a cohesive theoretical foundation, as research has been carried out in a highly explorative manner, using a quasi-tabula rasa principle within various disciplines.

Despite some varied findings, the commonalities among older adult players should be applied toward the development of digital games that target this audience. Because it is not possible to design a single game that suits the interests, skills and ability levels of all older adult players, developers should consider the characteristics of specific older adult player niches. For example, familiar, self-paced card games have been shown to be popular among select samples of older players. Thus, research may be warranted that explores traditional card games and design the game in a manner that takes normative, and potentially advanced, age-related impairment into account. This includes features such as colours used, font and text size, and the speed of graphics.

Older adult digital game play is a relatively new area of study, yet will burgeon in the coming years as game-savvy Baby Boomers advance into old age. Additionally, younger generations that have incorporated game play into their daily life, and potentially as a component of their identity, will likely want to continue this activity as they age. However, to accommodate the future game playing needs of an individual, additional research is warranted that probes the unique characteristics that exist or will emerge within old age.

Notes

1. It is quite difficult to define the term 'game'. Philosopher Ludwig Wittgenstein claimed that games have common features but no one feature is found in all. For an overview of definitions of the term, please refer to the work of Juul (2005).
2. This chapter focuses on individuals over 50 years of age, who are referred to as 'older adults'.

References

Aison, C., G. Davis, J. Milner and E. Targum. 2002. *Appeal and interest of video game use among the elderly*. Harvard Graduate School of Education (May 2002), i–28. http://www.jrmilner.com.

AppData. 2013. Farmville – Application Info. *AppData – Independent, Accurate Facebook Application Metrics and Trends from Inside Facebook*. Database. Retrieved from http://www.appdata.com/apps/facebook/321574327904696-farmville.

Bailey, S. 1989. *Experimental computer games study at Lowman Home*. Columbia: University of South Carolina, College of Social Work.

Basak, C., W.R. Boot, M.W. Voss and A.F. Kramer. 2008. 'Can training in a real-time strategy videogame attenuate cognitive decline in older adults', *Psychology and Aging* 23(4): 765–77.

Beasley, J.E. 1989. *Innovative computer applications with the elderly*. Columbia: University of South Carolina, College of Social Work.

Chen, Y., J. Wen and B. Xie. 2012. '"I communicate with my children in the game": mediated intergenerational family relationships through a social networking game', *The Journal of Community Informatics* 8(1). Available at http://ci-journal.net/index.php/ciej/article/view/802/892.

Clark, J.E., A.K. Lanphear and C.C. Riddick. 1987. 'The effects of video game playing on the response selection of elderly adults', *Journal of Gerontology* 42(1): 82–85.

Copier, M. 2002. *Ouderen en games: Een kwalitatief onderzoek naar ouderen die digitale spellen spelen*. Heerlen: International Institute of Infonomic in Heerlen; Maastricht: Centrum voor Gender en Diversiteit in Maastricht.

Crawford, C. 1982. *The art of computer game design*. Vancouver: Washington State University. Available at http://www.vancouver.wsu.edu/fac/peabody/game-book/Coverpage.html.

De Schutter, B. 2011. 'Never too old to play: the appeal of digital games to an older audience', *Games and Culture: A Journal of Interactive Media* 6(2): 155–70. doi:10.1177/1555412010364978.

De Schutter, B. and V. Vanden Abeele. 2008. 'Meaningful play in elderly life'. Paper presented at the annual meeting of the International Communication Association 2008. Quebec, Montreal, Canada.

De Schutter, B. and S. Malliet. 2009. 'A new or just an older breed of gamer?'. Paper presented at the annual conference of the International Communication Association, Chicago, USA.

De Schutter, B. and V. Vanden Abeele. 2010. 'Designing meaningful play within the psycho-social context of older adults', in *Proceedings of the 3rd International Conference on Fun and Games*. New York: ACM, pp. 84–93. doi:10.1145/1823818.1823827.

Dogruel, L. and S. Jöckel. 2008. 'Game design for the elderly – an acceptance perspective'. Presented at Meaningful Play '08, Michigan State University, East Lansing, Michigan.

Drew, B. and J. Waters. 1986. 'Video games: utilization of a novel strategy to improve perceptual motor skills and cognitive functioning in the noninstitutionalized elderly', *Cognitive Rehabilitation* 4(2): 26–34.

Dustman, R.E., R.Y. Emmerson, L.A. Steinhaus, D.E. Shearer and T.J Dustman. 1992. 'The effects of videogame playing on neuropsychological performance of elderly individuals', *Journal of Gerontology* 47(3): 168.

Edge Magazine. 2003. 'The modern age – mods have graduated from internet servers to being an integrated part of publisher's marketing strategies and shop shelves worldwide', *Edge Magazine* 126. Available at http://www.edge-online.com.

Entertainment Software Association (1999–2012). 2012. 'Essential facts about the computer and video game industry'. Entertainment Software Association. Available at http://www.theesa.com.

Fromme, J. 2003. 'Computer games as a part of children's culture', *Game Studies: The International Journal of Computer Game Research* 3(1). Available at http://www.gamestudies.org/0301/fromme/.

Gamberini, L., A. Mariano and G. Barresi. 2006. 'Cognition, technology and games for the elderly: an introduction to ELDERGAMES Project', *PsychNology Journal* 4(3): 285–308.

Gerling, K.M., F.P. Schulte and M. Masuch. 2011. 'Designing and evaluating digital games for frail elderly persons', in T. Romão, N. Correia, M. Inami, H. Kato, R. Prada, T. Terada, E. Dias and T. Chambel (eds), *Proceedings of the 8th International Conference on Advances in Computer Entertainment Technology* (ACE '11). New York: ACM New York.

Goldstein J., L. Cajko, M. Oosterbroek, M. Michielsen, O. van Houten and F. Salverda. 1997. 'Videogames and the elderly', *Social Behavior and Personality* 25(4): 345–52.

Haddon, L. and R. Silverstone. 1996. *Information and communication technologies and the young elderly*. Falmer: University of Sussex.

Hagoort, T. and C. Hautvast. 2009. *National gamers survey 2009*. Amsterdam: TNS NIPO, Amsterdam: NewZoo. Available at http://www.gamesindustry.com/company/542/service/1765.

Hollander, E.K. and H.R. Plummer. 1986. 'An innovative therapy and enrichment program for senior adults utilizing the personal computer', *Activities, Adaptation & Aging* 8(1): 59–68.

HowLongToBeat. 2013. 'How long does it take to beat your favorite games?'. Available at http://www.howlongtobeat.com.

IJsselsteijn, W., H.H. Nap, Y.A.W. de Kort and K. Poels. 2007. 'Digital game design for elderly users', in B. Kapralos, M. Katchabaw, J. Raynovich (eds), *Proceedings of the 2007 Conference on Future Play*. New York: ACM New York, pp. 17–22.

Juul, J. 2005. *Half-Real: video games between real rules and fictional worlds*. Cambridge, MA: MIT Press.

Juul, J. 2008. 'What's the casual in casual games?' Presented at the [Player] Conference, IT University, Copenhagen. Available at http://www.jesperjuul.net/cv.html.

Karmali, L. 2012. 'Mists of Pandaria pushes Warcraft subs over 10 million', *IGN*. Available at http://www.ign.com/articles/2012/10/04/mists-of-pandaria-pushes-warcraft-subs-over-10-million (accessed 11 January 2013).

Kern, D., M. Stringer, G. Fitzpatrick and A. Schmidt. 2006. 'Curball — a prototype tangible game for intergenerational play'. Paper presented at the *IEEE International Workshops on Enabling Technologies: Infrastructure for Collaborative Enterprises* (WETICE '06). Manchester, UK: IEEE Press.

Khoo, E.T. and A.D. Cheok. 2006. 'Age invaders: inter-generational mixed reality family game', *The International Journal of Virtual Reality* 5(2): 45–50.

Liszkiewicz, P.A.J. 2010. *Cultivated play: Farmville*. Presented at SUNY Buffalo, NY, USA. Available at http://mediacommons.futureofthebook.org/content/cultivated-play-farmville.

Mares, M.L., M.B. Oliver and J. Cantor. 2008. 'Age differences in adults' emotional motivations for exposure to films', *Media Psychology* 11: 488–511. doi:10.1080/15213260802492026.

Marston, H.R. and S.T. Smith. 2012. 'Interactive videogame technologies to support independence in the elderly: a narrative review', *GAMES FOR HEALTH: Research, Development, and Clinical Applications* 1(2): 139–52.

McGuire, F.A. 1984. 'Improving the quality of life for residents of long term care facilities through video games', *Activities, Adaptation & Aging* 6(1): 1–7.

Melenhorst, A.S. 2002. *Adopting communication technology in later life: the decisive role of benefits.* Doctoral dissertation. The Netherlands: Technical University of Eindhoven.

Miller, G. 2005. 'Society for neuroscience meeting: computer game sharpens aging minds', *Science* 310(5752): 1261.

Nacke, L.E., A. Nacke and C.A. Lindley. 2009. 'Brain training for silver gamers: effects of age and game form on effectiveness, efficiency, self-assessment, and gameplay experience', *CyberPsychology & Behavior* 12(5): 493–99.

Nap, H.H., Y.A.W. de Kort and W.A. IJsselsteijn. 2009. 'Senior gamers: preferences, motivations and needs', *Gerontechnology* 8(4): 247–62.

Nap, H.H. and U. Diaz-Orueta. 2012. 'Rehabilitation gaming', in S. Arnab, I. Dunwell and K. Debattista (eds), *Serious games for healthcare: applications and implications.* Hershey, PA: IGI Global, pp. 50–75.

Neufeldt, C. 2009. *Wii play with elderly people.* Paper presented at the ECSW 2009. Vienna.

Nielsen-Netratings. 2004. *Online games claim stickiest web sites.* Available at http://www.nielsen-netratings.com/pr/pr_040616.pdf.

O'Brien, D., R. Benjamin Knapp, O. Thompson, D. Craig and S. Barrett. 2013. 'An exploration of seniors' motivation to use mobile brain-exercise software', *Gerontechnology* 11(3): 436–44.

Pearce, C. 2008. 'The truth about baby boomer gamers: a study of over-forty computer game players', *Games and Culture* 3(2): 142–47.

Pratchett, R. 2005. *Gamers in the UK. Digital play, digital lifestyles.* BBC.

Quandt, T., H. Grueniger and J. Wimmer. 2009. 'The gray haired gaming generation: findings from an explorative interview study on older computer gamers', *Games and Culture: A Journal of Interactive Media* 4(1): 27–46.

Riddick, C.C., E.B. Drogin and S.G. Spector. 1987. 'The impact of videogame play on the emotional states of senior center participants', *Practice Concepts* 27(4): 425–27.

Schaie, K.W. 1996. *Intellectual development in adulthood: the Seattle longitudinal study.* New York: Cambridge University Press.

Schultheiss, D. 2012. '"Entertainment for retirement?": silvergamers and the internet', *Public Communication Review* 2(2): 62–71.

Shannon, C.E. 1950. 'A chess-playing machine', *Scientific American* 182(2): 45–51.

Tarling, A. 2005. *Older people's social and leisure time, hobbies and games.* Masters Thesis, University of Sussex.

Van Gils, M., J. Derboven and K. Poels. 2008. *The appeal of brain games to the aging individual.* Paper presented at the Meaningful Play 2008. East Lansing, Michigan: Michigan State University.

Vanden, Abeele V., B. De Schutter, J. Husson, G. Vos and J.H. Annema. 2008. *e-Treasure: fostering intergenerational play by means of a digital game.* Paper presented at the Meaningful Play 2008. East Lansing, Michigan: Michigan State University.

Vetere F., M. Nolan and R.A. Raman. 2006. *Distributed hide-and-seek*. Sydney, Australia: ACM, 325–28.

Voida, A. and S. Greenberg. 2012. 'Console gaming across generations: exploring inter-generational interactions in collocated console gaming', *Universal Access in the Information Society* 11(1): 45–56. doi:10.1007/s10209-011-0232-1.

White, G., D. Harley, L. Axelrod, G. McAllister and G. Latham. 2009. *Abstract Wii gaming for older players. Breaking new ground: innovation in games, play, practice and theory.* Proceedings of DiGRA 2009. Brunel University, London.

Williams, D. 2006. 'A brief social history of game play', in P. Vorderer and J. Bryant (eds), *Playing video games: motives, responses, and consequences.* New York and London: Routledge, pp. 197–212.

Wilson, J.L. and R. DeMaria. 2002. *High score! The illustrated history of electronic games.* Berkeley, CA: McGraw-Hill Publishing Co.

Woldberg, Y. 2008. *Gamende vijftigplussers en de game industrie* (Master). Utrecht University, Utrecht, The Netherlands.

13. DIGITAL OWNERSHIP ACROSS LIFESPANS

Wendy Moncur

AS TECHNOLOGY ADOPTION CONTINUES TO increase across one's lifespan, the question of what happens to the resulting digital content at the end of life is increasingly topical. We are embracing opportunities to create and share digital content that has personal significance: photos, emails, blogs, videos and more. This content is superseding the boxes of memory-laden letters and photos which were previously stored in our homes. Digital content has the advantage that it can be created, accessed and shared anywhere, at any time. However, unlike boxes of letters and photos, digital content cannot easily be inherited when its creator dies – especially if it is stored in online accounts. Moreover, ownership itself can be a grey area, with content such as iTunes and eBooks licenced rather than sold to users. Facilities for users to nominate an inheritor for their digital content are largely absent, and (with few exceptions) lack support in law. Inheritors struggle to identify and access online accounts and their content. Internet Service Providers usually refuse to give inheritors access to the deceased's account details, as terms of service commonly stipulate that accounts are non-transferrable. Processes of bequest and inheritance are further clouded because digital and physical death are rarely simultaneous. Users may linger on in a virtual world indefinitely after physical death.

If inheritors gain access to digital content, they are repurposing it. New levels of personalization are being introduced into funerals and memorial services, as digital content is used to evoke the life of the deceased. Online memorial sites provide opportunities for shared grieving and the maintenance of continuing bonds with the dead. Yet if they lack appropriate moderation, these sites may generate further distress when insensitive posts cannot be removed by those most deeply affected by bereavement.

This chapter explores the issues surrounding ownership of digital content across multiple lifespans, and the ways in which digital content lives on after its creator dies. First, we consider what it means to exist in the digital age, before describing the digital assets which people may own, and the challenges which they face in bequeathing and inheriting them. We acknowledge that definitions of lifespans and death are highly complex, and subject to wide cultural variations. The central focus of this chapter is specifically on lifespans in the UK.

Physical, Social and Spiritual Lifespans in the Digital Age

We suggest that the human lifespan in the Digital Age is made up of three main layers: physical, social and digital (Walter et al. 2012). A fourth one may also be present – the spiritual lifespan. These layers do not run in direct parallel. Their start points may be asynchronous, and the time and cause of 'death' will vary. A user can persist digitally long after they have died physically.

For most of us, death will come in old age, after a prolonged physical decline, beset by multiple conditions. By 2030, 86 per cent of deaths are expected to be of older adults (people aged over 65), and 44 per cent of deaths of those will be over 85 (Leadbeter and Garber 2010). Routine bureaucratic processes are associated with physical death. Even death itself is subject to legal definition: in Western medical terms, 'death' generally refers to brain death (Lock 2001). The time, date and cause of death are recorded, and a death certificate issued. The body is disposed of through burial, cremation, entombment or donation to medical research. Reports of the death travel through the deceased's network of relatives, friends and acquaintances by a mixture of word-of-mouth, personal correspondence, computer-mediated communication and death notices in the press.

As people move towards the end of life, it is common for many to become increasingly socially isolated, experiencing a 'withering ... of social identity and social interaction' (Walter et al. 2012: 15). For some, this will lead to social death, 'the final event in a sequence of declining social involvement' (Mulkay and Ernst 1991: 180). This may be hastened by old age, poor health, lack of mobility, spousal death and institutionalization (Gibson et al. 2010; Lawton 2000). Social death may itself play a role in hastening physical death (Timmermans 1998). Unlike physical death, social death is not accompanied by certification or ritual. Rather, it is a gradual fading. Yet if social death is considered to be the death of all social interaction, it may be delayed until long after physical death through the maintenance of continuing bonds by the bereaved (Klass et al. 1996). Through transferred agency, social existence may continue beyond physical death. Prendergast et al. (2006: 889) have previously commented on the role of cremated remains in sustaining the social identity of the deceased, who are rein-tegrated into the 'times and spaces which constituted their life history and social identity' through 'new forms of disposal and memorialization'. Further opportunities to sustain social identity are emerging through digi-tal technologies. For example, LifeNaut offers clients the unsettling facility to download their personality into digital form, for future reanimation at a later date. The product claims the potential to 'create a computer-based avatar to interact and respond with your attitudes, values, mannerisms and beliefs' (LifeNaut n.d.), although this service is yet to be fully implemented.

The advent of medical technology which can sustain physical life has blurred the edges of our mortality further. In the case of irreversible brain damage ('brain-stem death'), an individual may be artificially ventilated for a limited period in order to enable successful organ donation (Haddow 2005). Their physical life is sustained temporarily even after a clinician has signed a death certificate, and they are treated by hospital staff and relatives as 'already dead' because of their inability to respond socially (Sudnow 1967: 74). Thus in this context social life ends, whilst physical life continues.

The question of what makes up a lifespan is further complicated by conditions such as dementia and traumatic brain injury. Both can lead to dramatic changes in the identity of an individual, memory loss and a decline in cognitive abilities. Relatives and friends may well mourn the loss of the person that they knew, their identity, personality and shared history, despite that person's continued physical existence (Sweeting and Gilhooly 1997). There are processes in place which recognize the loss of agency associated with significant cognitive decline. In the UK, a 'Lasting Power of Attorney' (LPA) can even be drawn up in advance by an individual in case they experience incapacity. A Property and Financial Affairs LPA enables a friend, relative or professional to make decisions for that individual about their property and money, whilst a Personal Welfare LPA covers decisions about the person's healthcare and personal welfare (AgeUK n.d.). A deci-sion over whether a Property and Financial Affairs LPA should be invoked is made by a lawyer, whilst a Personal Welfare LPA can be invoked by a medical professional.

After physical death, individuals may expect their existence to continue on in the afterlife, or to be reincarnated into this world in a new form. Such expectation is largely dependent on religious beliefs (e.g. Roman Catholic beliefs in heaven, purgatory and hell) and cultural traditions (e.g. Korean ancestor worship; Prendergast 2005). Where an expectation of an afterlife exists, death is succeeded by rituals to ease the deceased's passage. Communication between the living and the dead may continue, although such communications are proscribed in several religions. In Spiritualism, the relationship across the 'Great Divide' is a 'continuation of the lived one, with the deceased offering support and advice which the living can then either act on or not ... in many cases it is not so much the content of the communications per se that is significant for people, but rather the fact that their loved ones have communicated with them' (Walliss 2001: 142). This relationship is sustained through the intercessory role of the medium.

The Digital Lifespan

An individual's digital life is usually made up of a mixture of official data (such as birth and marriage records), work-related data, and personal data (such as emails, photos, blogs and group memberships). In this chapter, we focus specifically on personal data. Such data is used to build up one or more digital identities – whether identifiable, pseudonymous or anonymous (Foresight Institute 2013). Much like offline identity and reputation (Fine 2001), care is often taken by users in constructing an online representation of self, with varying degrees of accuracy and completeness used to manipulate the impression projected to suit how the user wants to be perceived by others (boyd and Ellison 2007; Moncur et al. 2009).

Digital existence may begin before a user is born – for example, when parents share ultrasound images of their foetus by email. But what defines the end of digital existence? If physical life ends when a heart stops beating, and social life ends with the extinction of social identity and interaction, does digital death occur when internet use ceases?

Is Digital Death Possible?

It is difficult to establish that a user's online activity has ceased entirely. Online activity is comprised of access to many different services, often from multiple devices and physical locations. A user may also adopt many overlapping identities, sometimes detached from their physical identity or location, and express their identities in different ways (Foresight Institute 2013). This makes it extremely difficult to link digital identities with the originating physical user (Black et al. 2012), and to identify a comprehensive pattern of discontinued use. If one online account falls out of use, the user may still be active elsewhere on the internet. They may have forgotten their password or account details, or their work place may have blocked access. Clearly, failure to use a specific account should not signify digital death. In the case of posthumous email services – which store users' emails and send them out in the event of the user's death – some do make this flawed assumption. For example, the default setting for *Dead Man's Switch*[1] is for the service to automatically send emails to a user '30, 45, and 52 days after you last showed signs of life'. If the user fails to respond, posthumous emails are issued on their behalf by the service provider. This paves the way for misunderstandings, embarrassment and potential distress, if errors are made in merging digital and physical layers of existence. It is easy to imagine the messy consequences of a confessional 'posthumous' email sent accidentally. Whether someone should even write such an email in the first place is moot.

Cessation of internet use may stem from a range of reasons. Physical death is clearly one of them – although this may not prevent continued online communication. For example, services such as *Vuture*² will send out posthumous videos via email, Facebook or text message on behalf of a user on specific dates long after their death. A living user may go offline through difficulties with access and cost, or lack of skills, interest and support. This has been observed both amongst 10 per cent of young adults (aged 17–22) in the UK (Eynon and Geniets 2012), and amongst those at the End of Life (EoL). Such difficulties are compounded for those at EoL by declining physical/cognitive abilities, and by organizational barriers created by care providers (Hourizi et al. 2011). Yet these users should not be considered digitally dead, merely dormant. In Western society, death implies finality, while these lapsed users may log on again if the opportunity presents itself. Even when an individual is banned from using the internet for life – as seen in recent US court judgements against paedophiles (Moshirnia 2009) – it is likely that digital traces of that individual will persist online.

An exception to the lack of clarity over digital death exists in computer gaming, where users interact virtually on a regular basis to form communities and relationships. In the context of World of Warcraft, Gibbs et al. find that online environments and experiences are 'integral and contiguous with offline environments and experiences, rather than discrete 'alternate worlds' (2012). Haverinen documents the Second Life funeral conducted to mark the physical death of a player offline (2010). On these occasions, digital and physical death are (almost) synchronous. However, if we consider the internet as a whole, digital death is almost impossible to identify from patterns of user behaviour, without the ability to link all user accounts back to specific people. Early attempts to link virtual and physical identities have begun (Black et al. 2012), which aim to deliver insights into what aspects of real and virtual identity are important, as well as establishing the social acceptability and legal admissibility of linking real and virtual identities.

Process and Persistence

> [T]echnologies are not yet designed to effectively acknowledge – or engage
> with – the inevitable death of their user.
>
> (Massimi and Charise 2009)

As we have described, the notion of digital death is a grey area. The situation is exacerbated by the lack of a standard mechanism for reporting a
user's physical death within the digital world. Internet Service Providers
(ISPs), social networking sites (SNSs) and other online service providers
are inconsistent in their approaches to managing user death. For example:

- Twitter will close down an account, or help family members to take a
  backup of Twitter feeds if they provide a link to a public obituary or news
  article;
- Yahoo! (and by association Flickr and Delicious) will delete an account on
  receipt of a death certificate;[3]
- eBay have no published policy on how the accounts of a deceased user are
  handled – even though a deceased user may have funds in their account;
- Google has a 'lengthy' two-stage process 'with multiple waiting periods'
  through which an authorized representative can apply to obtain the
  contents of a deceased person's Gmail account. The representative must
  provide information including their own ID and a death certificate for the
  deceased person;[4]
- Facebook provides options for 'verified immediate family members' (a
  spouse, parent, sibling, child) or an executor to delete or 'memorialize' the
  deceased's Facebook page. Memorialization limits profile access to existing Facebook friends, who can subsequently write on the user's Wall in
  remembrance.

Facebook has expended more effort on processes to deal with deceased
users than many ISPs, yet most of its estimated 2.89 million users who
died in 2012 will continue to linger on (Lustig 2012). Public awareness
of the options to delete or memorialize a loved one on Facebook remains
limited, and the number of dead users with active accounts continues to
rise (Wortham 2010). As a result, invitations to reconnect or 'Say Happy
Birthday!' will be generated and sent automatically on behalf of dead
users. While many social network members will find these messages upset-
ting, some will welcome them as a way of maintaining a connection with
the deceased (Kasket 2012). Indeed, the persistence of a digital identity
may help the bereaved to mourn (Brubaker and Hayes 2011), an area
which we will address later in this chapter. However, digital persistence
after physical death also presents opportunities for spammers and fraud-
sters to repurpose digital identities for malign and perhaps illegal intent. In

semi-structured interviews which we have conducted with the bereaved, one participant described the distress of getting an email from her husband, asking to her to make a payment on his behalf. Her husband had died three months previously. Her shock and distress at receiving the email were compounded by anger when she tried to close down the hacked account. The service provider lacked the relevant processes to allow her to do this, as she was not the account owner. Ultimately the account was closed, but only after extensive efforts by the widow.

It is a measure of the immaturity of current ICT systems that they cater inadequately for the death of their users, despite their ubiquity. Users are likely to persist digitally long after physical death – perhaps indefinitely. Indeed, there is an expectation amongst some users that the internet serves as 'a repository that cannot die' (Kirk and Banks 2008). Unless this problem is addressed, the living may be outnumbered by the dead and their data in cyberspace. There is potential for this data to be repurposed for commercial value (Moncur 2014), although it is too early yet to predict what form such repurposing will take.

Assets and Their Value

Tangible Assets

Around 30 per cent of UK adults make a will. This lets them bequeath their heritable and movable property to nominated individuals. 'Heritable' property refers to any property which cannot be moved – for example, land and houses. 'Movable' property covers every type of property which is not land or connected with land – such as money, jewellery, books, furniture, computers. While heritable property is subject to the inheritance laws of the country where it is located, movable property is subject to the laws of the country where the owner resided. For those who do not make a will, defaults apply to inheritance based on legal definitions of who is next-of-kin. International legislation exists to resolve uncertainty when assets are distributed across multiple jurisdictions, or questions exist over which country's laws apply to distribution of the deceased's movable property (Conseil des Notariats de l'Union Européenne 2010).

Heritable and movable property can be valuable in a variety of ways. A house has obvious financial value. A cheap brooch may be worth little money, yet be imbued with emotional significance if the deceased wore it often. A filing cabinet laden with paperwork may have informational value, containing vital information to wind up the estate. A completed manuscript may have intellectual value. Any of these items may also serve as repositories for memories and meanings in our lives. Belk identifies that 'photographs, souvenirs, trophies, and more humble everyday objects' serve to 'mark, commemorate and announce our life history' (Belk 1990: 669).

Intangible Assets

Who We Are: Memory, Identity and Reputation

'Our memories constitute our lives' (Belk 1990: 674), yet memories cannot be bequeathed in the same way as tangible artefacts. I may still remember my grandmother sitting at her kitchen table, even if I do not inherit the table. Just as social death lacks the formal processes associated with physical death, so the bequest of memories is informal. Memories can persist after death if they have been shared in life, supported by oral and written histories, photos and artefacts. The act of sharing makes memories dynamic, subject to incremental change as well as to fading away. Entwined in memory are a sense of individual identity and group continuity. These may be sustained beyond death through the transmission of heirlooms, collections or other significant possessions, particularly where there are children or grandchildren who are willing to take over. Identity is also entwined with reputation. Fine observes that 'individuals have the power to shape their own reputations, but even historical figures are burnished or tarnished by interested others' (Fine 2001: 6). Our reputation – whether personal or mass-mediated – may outlast us, and change independently after our death for better or worse. Whilst Galileo was vilified by many during his life, his reputation for scientific discovery grew after his death and continues on. The UK BBC television presenter and charity worker, Jimmy Savile, enjoyed an enormously positive socially constructed reputation during his life. This has been destroyed since his death in 2011 through damning allegations of extensive sexual abuse of children, with journalistic reportage playing an integral part in disseminating the allegations (Lawless 2012).

Digital Assets

We have already observed that it is difficult to die digitally, because of the absence of links between our physical and digital selves, and the lack of a clear process by which the bereaved can declare a loved one digitally dead across all of their online accounts and identities. The awkward question of what happens to personal data after a user dies also lies unanswered. With the exception of three US states – Idaho, Nebraska and Indiana – there is no legal provision for the bequest of data (Yu 2012).

The personal data that makes up users' online identities lies scattered across a virtual landscape comprised of emails, photos, blog posts, financial transactions and more. This data is created, accessed and updated from multiple locations, on multiple devices. It may be stored locally – perhaps on a laptop, smart phone or work computer – or on a remote server via the Cloud. Similar to heritable and movable assets, this data can be imbued with emotional, financial and intellectual significance. Significant quantities of valuable personal data are being generated, as social and business interactions are increasingly conducted online. In Dying in a Digital Age, a 2,000-person survey of UK participants which we co-authored, 80 per cent owned digital assets (Remember a charity 2011). Remarkably few (9 per cent) had considered how they would pass on their digital assets when they die, even though:

- over half stored important domestic and personal details online or on personal computers;
- 74 per cent placed a strong sentimental value on their digital music and photo collections;
- 80 per cent said their digital assets were financially valuable;
- 56 per cent of participants owned a digital music collection. Of these, 45 per cent valued their collection at over £100, and 10 per cent at over £1,000;
- 34 per cent of participants owned Smartphone Apps, with 20 per cent of owners saying their collections were worth over £100.

Even if users do think through which digital assets they want to bequeath, ISPs' terms and conditions will (at best) provide a default for what will happen to personal data after a user dies. At worst, 'instructions for retrieving data after a person dies are [...] non-existent' (Farwell 2007). Given the inevitability of death and the ever-increasing amount of personal data stored online, this situation is unsatisfactory for users, the bereaved and for ISPs. Those who do wish to put their digital affairs in order cannot be sure that their wishes will be actioned if they die. Their inheritors may face an unpleasant and costly legal battle to gain access to the deceased's personal data, especially as users increasingly store their digital assets in the Cloud and via online storage rather than on their home PC.

Discussions over digital assets are made more complex by the question of ownership. Just because a user has data does not mean that they own it – even if they have paid for it. Digital versions of books, films and music are usually sold under licence, in a leasing arrangement where the purchaser has the right to use the item, but does not own it. Whilst users may have invested substantial amounts in Kindle books and iTunes music, they cannot legitimately bequeath either. Second Life accounts can also contain substantial financial value. Linden Lab (owners of Second Life) provides the option for any player to proactively nominate an inheritor of their Second Life account and associated assets. They explicitly emphasize the need for players to give their inheritor's 'legal (real-life) name', rather than a digital identity (Linden Research 2012). Questions of ownership are further muddied by co-ownership and replication (Harper et al. 2011). For example, if a photographer takes a digital photo of a group of five people, and shares it with them, who 'owns' it? If the same photo is copied and circulated across social media, ownership may be diluted to the point of irrelevance. A caveat applies, however, over which debate continues: recent European legislation on 'The Right To Be Forgotten' arguably 'creates a legally enforceable right to demand the deletion of any photos or data that I post myself, even after they've gone viral, not to mention unflattering photos that include me or information about me that others post, whether or not it is true' (Rosen 2012). It is hard to envisage how this legislation can be implemented.

When we consider their values and potential to be inherited, digital assets currently have more in common with memories, identity and reputation than with tangible assets. They may remain unchanged, be forgotten or lost, or content may be augmented by inheritors in ways unforeseen by the deceased.

Bequest of Digital Assets

In the absence of standardized practices for the bequest of data, workarounds proliferate. Executry services are offered by start-up companies and lawyers, serving as Band-Aids over the ever-growing problem.

Options

Digital estate planning services are offered by a number of companies (The Digital Beyond 2011), including AssetLock,[5] LegacyOrganiser[6] and SecureSafe.[7] They can offer a practical solution to the existing problems of digital bequest. These services usually hold an inventory of online accounts on behalf of the user, and may also store a user's last wishes, instructions for their funeral, emails to be sent out after they die, and instructions in case of brain death. It is usually straightforward to update this digital inventory when online accounts are added or deleted, or passwords change. Digital estate planning services can be useful if a user has many different online accounts, changes passwords often, has a complex set of digital inheritors rather than just one person, or wants the executry process to be carried out automatically once third party proof of physical death is provided. However, there are concerns over their legitimacy and longevity. Firstly, it can be difficult to establish the legitimacy of digital estate services. Some service providers list terrestrial business addresses on their websites, and provide company details: some do not. Most offer to store users' online account logon details and passwords securely – including those for bank accounts. Sharing passwords and account details often violates ISP terms of service. In the case of online banking, password sharing also exposes the account holder to the risk that their bank will not reinstate the account and its contents in the event of digital fraud and theft. More cautious users may wish to check that the service provider is legitimate, and not an online fraudster. Secondly, the companies offering digital estate services are young (The Digital Beyond 2011): with two exceptions, they were founded after 2005. Uptake of services is lower than initially projected (Nield 2011). This raises the question of whether the user will outlive the service provider, leaving their inheritors without the intended access to digital accounts.

Some lawyers also offer to maintain a digital inventory on behalf of clients. In this case, it is not so straightforward to update the digital inventory, if online accounts are added or deleted, or passwords change. Lawyers may levy an extra charge to update the inventory. A third option is for users to maintain their own list of online accounts, identities, passwords and web addresses, whilst nominating a trusted friend or loved one as their digital executor (Carroll and Romano 2011).

As Band-Aids on the problem of digital bequest, none of the options which we have described above are water-tight. They all violate common ISP terms of service over password sharing. However, they are useful temporary fixes until a robust and ubiquitous solution is found.

What to Bequeath? Creation, Curation and Identity

If users do want to bequeath some of their digital assets, which will they choose to pass on? It is now so easy to create photos, emails and other digital media that the volume of personal data which we create is rising dramatically. Ready availability of cheap online storage reduces the need for immediate curation. In pre-digital times, pressure on space meant that creation and curation were linked. Once read, unimportant letters were thrown in the bin. The return of photos from the developers triggered a process of curation, as accidental shots of feet and thumbs were weeded out. This limited set of photos served as 'an investment in creating a memory bank' (Chalfen 1987), securing memories and a sense of identity. Now, a small memory card holds thousands of photos, whilst users store a decade or more of emails online, with no intention of deleting them (Kirk and Banks

2008). Creation and curation of digital materials do not go hand-in-hand out of necessity.

Those planning their legacies may face a daunting task in sorting through vast archives of personal data, and identifying those digital assets which are worth passing on. Throwaway comments on Facebook and dull work-related emails will (hopefully) not be worth passing on. Evidence of misdemeanours, affairs or negative opinions about loved ones will be too sensitive. Some assets will be just plain embarrassing, providing Technicolor reminders of events and foolish interactions which are best forgotten (Mayer-Schoneberger 2009). The act of curation allows the user to play an active (but time-consuming) role in the process of negotiating the memories they leave behind – much like the process of impression management that some users undertake on an on-going basis (boyd and Ellison 2007). Conversely, the ability to create limitless copies of data means that all inheritors can potentially get identical copies of data, no matter what material it comprises.

Inheritance and Repurposing

If the deceased has not taken successful proactive steps to manage their digital legacy, inheritors face a complex task to access the personal data left behind. Inheritors may not know what accounts the deceased held online, or what the user ids and passwords are. If the deceased maintained an online address book – for example, in an email contact list – it can even be difficult to notify social network members of the person's death and funeral (Moncur et al. 2012).

As we have already outlined, ISPs do not usually provide the bereaved with access to the deceased's online accounts. Not only is there little profit to be had in providing access (McAlear 2011), there is also a risk of violating privacy. Whilst the dead have no legal right to privacy, there is a risk of violating the privacy of the deceased's still-living correspondents. The decisions taken by Yahoo! in respect of US Marine Corps Lance Corporal Justin M. Ellsworth's personal data are relevant here. Ellsworth was killed in action in Iraq in 2004. After his death, access to the personal data (emails, attachments, diary entries) which he stored with Yahoo! was requested by his father. The ISP's refusal to surrender the data led to a high-profile court case (Farwell 2007; Connor 2012). The judgement went against Yahoo! who subsequently provided his father with the contents of emails sent to Ellsworth. The emails were provided on CDs, and as printouts. However, outgoing emails sent by Ellsworth were not handed over (Tines 2005). The result would have been much like hearing only one side of a conversation.

If inheritors do gain access to digital content, they are repurposing it. New levels of personalization are being introduced into funerals and memorial services, as digital content is used to evoke the life of the deceased. Orders of service incorporate images of the deceased (Walter et al. 2012). PowerPoint is used to co-ordinate the display of photos and video clips during the service, against a backdrop of the deceased's favourite tunes culled from their MP3 player (Moncur et al. 2012). In the longer term, the bereaved are reusing existing digital data to create their own technology-based responses to death and loss, such as online memorials (Hume and Bressers 2009; Nager and Vries 2004). Such repurposing can make a beneficial contribution to the bereavement process. Online memorial sites provide opportunities for shared grieving (Moncur and Kirk 2014). The social media pages of the deceased present opportunities to maintain an on-going (albeit one-sided) conversation with them, and to share memories with others in the social network (Kasket 2012).

Grief has become more public online than it is offline, as the bereaved post comments on memorial sites, and casual visitors add to them. There are many positives to the opportunities to express grief online, especially for young people who communicate through this medium by default (Sofka 2009). However, the lack of accountability over the instantiation, ownership and moderation of online memorials can be problematic. While it is often possible to post inappropriate and insensitive content, it is more difficult for those affected most deeply by loss to remove it if they wish to.

Conclusion

In this chapter, we have described the problems and challenges inherent in digital ownership across lifespans. While many users make the assumption that their valuable data can be passed on to inheritors, this is often not the case. Indeed, they may not even own their data. We have seen how it is extremely difficult even to identify a user's complete set of online assets, let alone take over ownership of them. At this moment in time, a Western user's digital lifespan has more features in common with their social life than their physical one: both digital and social life lack a distinct ending, or processes to mark that end. Much like reputation and memory, a user's data may linger after the user's physical death. Some of it may develop new significance as it is re-appropriated by inheritors, whilst much will surely be consigned to a dusty virtual corner where it will lie forgotten.

As users' digital footprints continue to increase dramatically, it is timely to consider how users want their digital assets to be managed, so that the financial, emotional and informational value embedded in them is not lost.

Acknowledgements

I acknowledge the financial support of the EPSRC, grant no. EP/I026304/1. I am grateful to Professor Tony Walter of the Centre for Death and Society (University of Bath) and Mark Zarb (University of Dundee) for providing constructive comments on the draft of this chapter and for suggesting relevant references.

Notes

1. http://www.deadmansswitch.net/.
2. http://myvuture.com/.
3. http://info.yahoo.com/legal/us/yahoo/utos/utos-173.html.
4. https://support.google.com/mail/answer/14300?hl=en.
5. http://www.assetlock.net/.
6. http://www.legacyorganiser.com.
7. http://www.securesafe.com/en/.

References

Age UK, Powers of attorney. Available at http://www.ageuk.org.uk/money-matters/legal-issues/powers-of-attorney/ (accessed 23 October 2012).

Belk, R.W. 1990. 'The role of possessions in constructing and maintaining a sense of past', *Advances in Consumer Research* 17(1): 669–76.

Black, S.M. et al. 2012. 'SuperIdentity: fusion of identity across real and cyber domains'. Refereed proceedings of ID360: Global Issues in Identity, Texas, April 23–24. Available at http://eprints.soton.ac.uk/336645/.

boyd, d. and N.B. Ellison. 2007. 'Social network sites: definition, history, and scholarship', *Journal of Computer-Mediated Communication* 13(1): Article 11.

Brubaker, J.R. and G.R. Hayes. 2011. '"We will never forget you [online]": an empirical investigation of post-mortem myspace comments', in *Proceedings of the ACM 2011 Conference on Computer Supported Cooperative Work (CSCW '11)*. New York: ACM, pp. 123–32.

Carroll, E. and J. Romano. 2011. *Your digital afterlife*. Berkeley, CA: New Riders.

Chalfen, R. 1987. 'Snapshot versions of life. *Project MUSE*'. Available at http://muse.jhu.edu/books/9780879728748 (accessed 8 November 2012).

Connor, J. 2010. 'Digital life after death: the issue of planning for a person's digital assets after death', *Texas Tech Law School Research Paper No. 2011-02*. Available at SSRN: http://ssrn.com/abstract=1811044.

Conseil des Notariats de l'Union Européenne. 2010. 'Which law applies? Can I choose the law applicable to my succession?' Available at http://www.successions-europe.eu/en/netherlands/topics/which-law-applies_can-i-choose-the-applicable-law-to-my-inheritance/ (accessed 8 November 2012).

Eynon, R. and A. Geniets. 2012. *On the periphery? Understanding low and discontinued internet use amongst young people in Britain*. Oxford: Nominet Trust.

Farwell, J. 2007. 'Death & digital data: what happens to what you leave behind?' *Computers & Electronics* 18(9): 33–35.

Fine, G.A. 2001. *Difficult reputations: collective memories of the evil, inept, and controversial*. Chicago: Chicago University Press.

Foresight Institute. 2013. *The future of identity*. London: Government Office for Science.

Gibbs, M. et al. 2012. 'Game studies – tombstones, uncanny monuments and epic quests: memorials in World of Warcraft', *Game Studies* 12(1). Available at http://gamestudies.org/1201/articles/gibbs_martin.

Gibson, L. et al. 2010. 'Designing social networking sites for older adults', in L. MacKinnon and T. McEwan (eds), *BCS '10*. British Computer Society, pp. 186–94.

Haddow, G. 2005. 'The phenomenology of death, embodiment and organ transplantation', *Sociology of Health & Illness* 27(1): 92–113.

Harper, R. et al. 2011. 'What is a file?' *research.microsoft.com*. Available at http://research.microsoft.com/pubs/154539/MSR-TR-2011-109.pdf (accessed 29 August 2012).

Haverinen, A.E. 2010. 'Digitalization of death rituals: how attitudes towards virtual mourning are transforming in Finnish context'. Paper presented at the Nordic Network of Thanatology, Aalborg, Denmark.

Hourizi, R., W. Moncur and T. Walter. 2011. 'Digital participation at the end of life', in *Proceedings of Digital Engagement 2011*. Newcastle, UK. Available at http://de2011.computing.dundee.ac.uk/wp-content/uploads/2011/10/Digital-Participation-at-the-End-of-Life1.pdf.

Hume, J. and B. Bressers. 2009. 'Obituaries online: new connections with the living – and the dead', *Journal of Death and Dying* 60(3): 255–71.

Kasket, E. 2012. 'Continuing bonds in the age of social networking: Facebook as a modern-day medium', *Bereavement Care* 31(2): 62–69.

Kirk, D. and R. Banks. 2008. 'On the design of technology heirlooms', in *Proceedings of the International Workshop on Social Interaction and Mundane Technologies* (SIMTech '08).

Klass, D., P.R. Silverman and S.L. Nickman. 1996. *Continuing bonds: new understandings of grief*. Washington, DC: Taylor & Francis.

Lawless, J. 2012. 'Jimmy Savile myth in ruins one year after lavish funeral', *Huffington Post*.

Lawton, J. 2000. *The dying process: patients' experiences of palliative care*. New York and London: Routledge.

Leadbeter, C. and J. Garber. 2010. *Dying well*. London: DEMOS.

LifeNaut, n.d. Bina48 Social Robot with Lifenaut.com | LifeNaut. Available at https://www.lifenaut.com/bina48/ (accessed 1 November 2012).

Linden Research. 2012. *Linden Lab Official: death and other worries outside Second Life*, Second Life Wiki. Available at http://wiki.secondlife.com/wiki/Linden_Lab_Official:Death_and_other_worries_outside_Second_Life (accessed 8 November 2012).

Lock, M. 2001. *Twice dead: organ transplants and the reinvention of death*. Oakland, CA: University of California Press.

Lustig, N. 2012. '2.89m Facebook users will die in 2012, 580,000 in the USA'. Available at http://www.nathanlustig.com/2012/06/06/2-89m-facebook-users-will-die-in-2012-580000-in-the-usa/ (accessed 2 November 2012).

Massimi, M. and A. Charise. 2009. 'Dying, death, and mortality: towards thanatosensitivity in HCI', in *CHI '09 Extended Abstracts on Human Factors in Computing Systems* (CHI EA'09). New York: ACM, pp. 2459–68.

Mayer-Schoneberger, V. 2009. *Delete: the virtue of forgetting in the digital age*. Princeton, NJ: Princeton University Press.

McAlear, A. 2011. 'Policy vs. reality', *The digital beyond*. Available at http://www.the-digitalbeyond.com/2011/03/policy-vs-reality/ (accessed 9 November 2012).

Moncur, W. 2014. 'Faceless Facebook reps help bereaved families look back, in The Conversation'. Available at https://theconversation.com/faceless-facebook-reps-help-bereaved-families-look-back-23741 (accessed 27 February 2014).

Moncur, W. et al. 2012. 'From death to final disposition: roles of technology in the post-mortem interval', in *Proceedings of the SIGCHI Conference on Human Factors in Computing Systems* (CHI'12). New York: ACM, pp. 531–40.

Moncur, W. and D. Kirk. 2014. An emergent framework for digital memorials. In *Proceedings of the 2014 Conference on Designing Interactive Systems* (DIS '14). New York: ACM, pp. 965–74.

Moncur, W., J. Masthoff and E. Reiter. 2009. 'Facilitating benign deceit in mediated communication', in *Proceedings of the 27th International Conference Extended Abstracts on Human Factors in Computing Systems* (CHI EA '09). New York: ACM, pp. 3383–88.

Moshirnia, A. 2009. 'Internet amputation and digital death: are decade-long internet bans constitutional? | Citizen Media Law Project', in *Citizen Media Law project*. Available at http://www.citmedialaw.org/blog/2009/internet-amputation-and-digital-death-are-decade-long-internet-bans-constitutional (accessed 2 November 2012).

Mulkay, M. and J. Ernst. 1991. 'The changing profile of social death', *European Journal of Sociology* 32: 172–96.

Nager, E.A. and B. De Vries. 2004. 'Memorializing on the world wide web: patterns of grief and attachment in adult daughters of deceased mothers', *Omega: Journal of Death and Dying* 49(1): 43–56.

Nield, B. 2011. 'Who's afraid of the digital reaper?' *CNN.com*, Digital Bi. Available at http://edition.cnn.com/2011/TECH/web/01/13/digital.death/index.html?hpt=C2.

Prendergast, D. 2005. *From elder to ancestor: old age, death and inheritance in modern Korea*. Folkestone: Global Oriental.

Prendergast, D., J. Hockey and L. Kellaher. 2006. 'Blowing in the wind? Identity, materiality, and the destinations of human ashes', *Journal of the Royal Anthropological Institute* 12(4): 881–98.

Remember a charity. 2011. 'Millions of pounds at risk as people overlook "digital assets"'. Available at http://www.rememberacharity.org.uk/news.php/67/millions-of-pounds-at-risk-as-people-overlook-digital-assets (accessed 8 November 2012).

Rosen, J. 2012. 'The right to be forgotten', *Stanford Law Review Online* 64: 88.

Sofka, C.J. 2009. 'Adolescents, technology and the Internet: coping with loss in the digital world', in David E. Balk and Charles A. Corr (eds), *Adolescent encounters with death, bereavement, and coping*. New York: Springer Publishing Company, pp. 155–74.

Sudnow, D. 1967. *Passing on: the social organization of dying*. Englewood Cliffs, NJ: Prentice-Hall.

Sweeting, H. and M. Gilhooly. 1997. 'Dementia and the phenomenon of social death', *Sociology of Health & Illness* 19(1): 93–117.

The Digital Beyond. 2011. 'Digital death and afterlife online services list. Available at http://www.thedigitalbeyond.com/online-services-list/ (accessed 3 October 2011).

Timmermans, S. 1998. 'Social death as self-fulfilling prophecy: David Sudnow's Passing On Revisited', *The Sociological Quarterly* 39(3): 453–72.

Tines, C.V. 2005. 'Family gets GI's e-mail', Detroit News. Available at http://www.justinellsworth.net/email/detnewsapr.htm (accessed 4 February 2013).

Walliss, J. 2001. 'Continuing bonds: relationships between the living and the dead within contemporary spiritualism', *Mortality* 6(2): 127–45.

Walter, T. et al. 2012. 'Does the internet change how we die and mourn? An overview', *Omega: Journal of Death & Dying* 64(4): 275–302.

Wortham, J. 2010. 'As Facebook users die, ghosts reach out', *The New York Times Technology*. Available at http://www.nytimes.com/2010/07/18/technology/18death.html?_r=1&scp=1&sq=ghosts reach out&st=cse.

Yu, R. 2012. 'Digital inheritance laws remain murky', *USA Today*. Available at http://www.usatoday.com/story/tech/2012/09/19/digital-inheritance-law/1578967/ (accessed 16 November 2012).

NOTES ON CONTRIBUTORS

Arlene J. Astell is Ontario Shores Research Chair in Community Management of Dementia and Professor of Health Services Research in the Centre for Assistive Technology and Connected Healthcare (CATCH) (University of Sheffield). She leads COBALT (Challenging Obstacles and Barriers to Assisted Living Technologies), a collaborative project to increase adoption of ALTs and has recently established the THAW (Technology for Healthy Ageing and Wellbeing) network to look at supporting good mental health in later life. Arlene is UK lead of three international projects: AAL-WELL, investigating novel technologies to support people living with mild cognitive impairment; In-Touch, exploring the potential of iPads for people living with dementia; and IN-LIFE a H2020 project rolling out ICT for people living with dementia across Europe.

Rebecca Berman has been a researcher at the Leonard Schanfield Research Institute at CJE SeniorLife since 2006. Previously she co-directed (with Dr Madelyn Iris) ASSERT (Assistance, Services and Support for Evaluation Research Training), a project to build the capacity of social service organizations for conducting evaluation research at Northwestern University's Buehler Center on Aging, while serving as Research Assistant Professor. In 2005, Dr Berman received the Part Time Faculty Recognition Award from the Association of Gerontology in Higher Education while on the faculty of the MA in Gerontology Program at Northeastern Illinois University. Since receiving her doctorate in Anthropology in 1988 from Northwestern University, she has integrated her experiences as evaluator, researcher, educator and consultant into a passion for facilitating the ability of non-profit and human service organizations to engage in and benefit from meaningful evaluation, research and outcomes measurement.

Julie A. Brown is an Assistant Professor of Gerontology in the Department of Social and Public Health in the College of Health Science and Professions at Ohio University (Athens, OH). She earned her doctoral degree from the Graduate Center for Gerontology at the University of Kentucky. With a specialization in gerontechnology, her research focuses upon a life course perspective of digital gaming and technology use among older populations.

Bob De Schutter is a C. Michael Armstrong Professor at the College of Education, Health & Society and the Armstrong Institute for Interactive Media Studies, and a Research Fellow of the Scripps Gerontology Center at Miami University (Oxford, OH). His research and teaching interests include game design, the older audience of digital games, and the use of digital games for non-entertainment purposes. He has been invited to teach in Europe, North America and Asia, and his work has been published in leading publications of several academic fields. Bob has served industry as an independent consultant, web developer and entrepreneur, is a lifetime member of the International Game Developers Association, and has founded and chaired the Gerontoludic Society, and the Flemish chapter of the Digital Game Research Association. Prior to joining Miami University, Bob was the lead designer of the e-Media Lab of the KU Leuven (campus Group T).

Sarah Delaney is a Senior Research Consultant with the Work Research Centre in Dublin. She holds an undergraduate degree in Social Anthropology from Queen's University Belfast and a Masters degree in Applied Social Research from Trinity College Dublin. Sarah specialises in researching eHealth as it is applied to chronic disease management, mental health and psychiatry of old age. She is also experienced in the development and application of innovative approaches to research and evaluation.

John Dinsmore is Health Innovation lead and Deputy Director at the Centre for Practice and Healthcare Innovation based at the School of Nursing and Midwifery, Trinity College Dublin and CEO of PILO Health Ltd. Dr Dinsmore's research focuses on the design and development of assistive technologies, health psychology and behavioural change to improve the quality of life and quality of care of individuals living with chronic illnesses and disability as part of an enhanced user experience model. Working on various collaborative national and international projects, his research also examines the need for primary care and health service re-design to adopt technologies to assist in the treatment and management of chronic and debilitating conditions. A particular focus of his work is the creation of assistive software platforms and content (primarily in mHealth) to enable individuals with chronic illness and disabilities to self-manage at home, build social connections and learn about their condition.

Chiara Garattini is an anthropologist working as part of the Health & Life Sciences group at Intel. Prior to this, she worked in the field of ageing, technology, independent living and chronic illnesses as postdoctoral researcher and ethnography lead at the Technology Research for Independent Living (TRIL) Centre, University College Dublin. Her expertise revolves mainly around health, technology and user experience (UX) research. She has a particular interest in exploring the way in which people understand and interact with technologies, and the challenges faced when technology is translated from the lab to the real world.

Trisha Greenhalgh is a GP and Professor of Primary Care Health Sciences at University of Oxford. Her research interests lie at the interface between medicine, sociology and innovation. She uses innovative interdisciplinary approaches, drawing on narrative, ethnographic and participatory methods, to explore complex, policy-related issues in contemporary healthcare.

Caroline Holland is a Research Fellow in the Faculty of Health and Social Care at The Open University, UK. Originally a geographer by discipline and following a career in social housing management, over the last twenty years she has researched aspects of the physical, social, technological, emotional, and political environments of later life. Taking a generally qualitative and often participative approach to research, she has explored aspects of mainstream and specialized housing; social interactions in public places; everyday age discrimination; hairdressing as a medium for presenting the ageing identity; the transition to care homes for people with dementia; and how older people do or do not engage with new technologies.

Simon Holland is Creator and Director of the Music Computing Lab at The Open University, UK. He is co-investigator on the E-Sense Project, and the Older People and Technological Inclusion ESRC Seminar Series. He has devised numerous human-centred computing innovations, including the Haptic Bracelets, the Haptic Drum Kit, AudioGPS, Harmony Space and Direct Combination. He was awarded the 2011 PyrusMalus Mobile Human Computer Interaction Award in Stockholm for the most influential paper in Mobile HCI over the period 2001–2011. He is currently collaborating with neuroscientists and physiotherapists on applications of the Haptic Bracelets to rehabilitation for Stroke and Parkinson's disease.

Jonathan Hughes is a Lecturer (Access and Curriculum) in The Open University's Centre for Inclusion and Collaborative Partnership. His PhD ('The premature end of lifelong learning? The impact of policy discourse on older learners') focused on how policy discourses about learning in later life impact on the provision of such learning and the use of computer technology by older people. He is interested in later life learning as an area with important, although often neglected, implications for wellbeing, social inclusion and civic engagement in later life. This interest has led to involvement in The Open University's Research into Age Discrimination and Older People and Technology (OPT-In) Projects. In September 2012, Jonathan became chair of the Association for Education and Ageing.

Madelyn Iris is former director of the Leonard Schanfield Research Institute (now retired) at CJE SeniorLife in Chicago. She is an Adjunct Associate Professor in the Department of Medicine, Feinberg School of Medicine, Northwestern University. Dr Iris received her PhD in Anthropology from Northwestern University, and holds a Master's Degree in Medieval Studies from the University of Toronto. From 1989 until August 2005, she was an Associate Professor in the Department of Medicine and at the Buehler Center on Aging, Feinberg School of Medicine, Northwestern University. Dr Iris' research focuses on several topics, including elder self-neglect, elder abuse and neglect, and cultural beliefs and values related to Alzheimer's disease. Dr Iris is a fellow of the Gerontological Society of America and the Society for Applied Anthropology, a Past President of the National Association for the Practice of Anthropology and the Association for Anthropology and Gerontology, and serves on the editorial boards of the *Annals of Anthropological Practice*, the *Journal of Cross-Cultural Gerontology* and the *Journal of Elder Abuse and Neglect*.

Christina Leeson is a PhD researcher in the Department of Anthropology at the University of Copenhagen. Her PhD project focuses on a new type of social robot developed by Japanese researchers to be tested in the Danish care for older and disabled people. Christina did her Master Thesis at the Department of Anthropology, the University of Copenhagen in 2010 on the development and use of the social robot, PARO, in the care for older people in Japan. After that and before starting her PhD, she was employed by the Health and Care Administration in the Municipality of Copenhagen to develop and implement strategies for 'welfare-technology' in the health-care system.

Daniel López is Associate Professor in the Department of Psychology and Education at the Open University of Catalonia. His PhD was an ethnographic study of the socio-material construction of 'independent and safe aging' in a telecare service in Catalunya. His research interests are the biopolitical and technoscientific construction of later life and the production and maintenance of mundane care arrangements as grass-root innovations. He is currently working on the emergence of collective arrangements of care such as senior co-housing projects and peer-care networks.

Wendy Moncur is a Reader in Socio-Digital Interaction at the University of Dundee. She is also a Visiting Fellow at the Centre for Death and Society at the University of Bath, and a Key Technology Partner Visiting Fellow at the University of Technology Sydney, Australia. Intrinsically interdisciplinary, Wendy's research programme focuses on the design of technology to support being human in a Digital Age. Grounded in computing, her research draws on insights from many other fields, including anthropology, psychology and literature. Wendy is Principal Investigator on the EPSRC-funded *Charting the Digital Lifespan*, and concurrently, holds an EPSRC Post-Doctoral Fellowship (Cross Disciplinary Interfaces) for *Digital Inheritance*.

Henk Herman Nap has an MSc in Cognitive Ergonomics and a PhD in Gerontechnology. He worked as a post-doctoral researcher on senior gamers at the Game Experience Lab in Eindhoven (TU/e). He published journal and conference papers and is active as a reviewer of both. He worked as a research scientist and project coordinator for Smart Homes in serious gaming and assisted living projects. He currently works as a senior project leader at Vilans – the Dutch expertise centre on long-term care – in eHealth and serious gaming implementation projects.

Louis Neven obtained his PhD at the University of Twente on how designers and engineers represent older technology users. He subsequently worked for Lancaster University, on a project on ageing and sustainable technologies, and for Utrecht University on a project on micro/nanotechnology and ageing. He currently works as Lector ('research professor') in Active Ageing for Avans University of Applied Science. Louis is broadly interested in the way in which technology and ageing are co-constructed and in how the match between (geron)technologies and the wants, needs, practices and identities of older people can be improved.

Mayumi Ono is a Senior Assistant Professor at the Center for Global Partnerships and Education, Okayama University, Japan, specializing in cultural anthropology. Her dissertation is about the international retirement migration of Japanese older adults to Malaysia. Her research interest includes transnationalism, international retirement migration in Asia, lifestyle migration of Japanese people in Asia, long-stay tourism, medical tourism and transnational mobility of patients seeking care.

David Prendergast is a social anthropologist and a Principal Investigator in the Intel Collaborative Research Institute for Sustainable Connected Cities with Imperial College and University College London. He also holds the position of Visiting Professor of Healthcare Innovation at Trinity College Dublin. His research over the last fifteen years has focused on later life-course transitions and he has authored a number of books and articles on ageing, health, technology and social relationships. During his career David has been involved in several major research projects including: a multi-year ethnography of intergenerational relationships and family change in South Korea; the provision of paid home care services in Ireland; a three-year ESRC study into death, dying and bereavement in England and Scotland; and Intel's Global Ageing Project which explored the expectations and experiences of health and ageing around the world. After receiving his PhD from Cambridge University, Dr Prendergast held research posts at the University of Sheffield and Trinity College Dublin.

Rob Procter is Professor of Social Informatics in the Department of Computer Science at Warwick University. His research is strongly interdisciplinary and focuses on socio-technical issues in the design, implementation, evaluation and use of Information Communication Technologies (ICT), with a particular emphasis on ethnographic studies of ICT systems in diverse use settings, including the workplace and the home, computer-supported cooperative work and participatory design. He has made a significant contribution to methodologies for user-centred, participatory design, with an emphasis on the co-production ('co-realization') and co-evolution of ICTs with and by users.

Tomás Sánchez-Criado is currently Lecturer in Social Sciences in the Psychology & Educational Sciences Department, Open University of Catalonia. He holds a PhD in Social Anthropology ('The logics of telecare: the fabrication of "connected autonomy" in telecare for older people', Universidad Autónoma de Madrid, 2012), having undertaken an ethnographic project on home telecare devices for older people in the region of Madrid (Spain), focusing on the practices of implementation and use of such devices and services through which certain articulations of users, care relations and spaces emerged. He is currently doing ethnographic research on different practices of participatory, collaborative and activist design for independent living and urban accessibility, analysing the political role of infrastructures of everyday life in care relations.

Rachel Singh is an anthropologist with a passion for exploring how people shape technology use. She began her career in design research at Intel Labs Europe within the Health Research and Innovation Group where she conducted ethnographic research in order to understand how existing technology and design developments can be swiftly integrated into health and social care systems. She is currently based in London where she works on multidisciplinary teams, for both the public and private sectors, to help continuously connect the people who design products and services with the people who will use them.

Claire Somerville is a Medical Anthropologist. She teaches the Masters of Development Studies qualitative methods course at the Graduate Institute of International and Development Studies (Geneva). Dr Somerville is an independent research consultant in health, development and technology, working in collaboration with international organizations and industry/ business partners. Previous appointments have been as Senior Social Scientist at the Technology Research for Independent Living (TRIL) Centre, Trinity College Dublin, Research Fellow at the Centre for Primary Care and Public Health at Barts and the London, Queen Mary University London, and Lecturer at the University of Newcastle, Australia. She has a PhD from the University of Cambridge, and a Masters degree in Medical Anthropology from the School of Oriental and African Studies.

Philip B. Stafford directs the Center on Aging and Community at the Indiana Institute on Disability and Community, at Indiana University in Bloomington. He is a senior consultant with the AdvantAge Initiative, a national project that has supported community planning for ageing in over twenty-six US communities. Stafford has chaired a statewide committee entitled 'Hoosier Communities for a Lifetime', and he manages a statewide 'Lifetime communities contract for the Grantmakers in Aging', funded by the Pfizer foundation. He is a founding board member of the Memory Bridge Foundation and the author of numerous articles on culture and dementia, participatory research and planning and the meaning of home for older people. He is the editor of *Gray areas: ethnographic encounters with nursing home culture*, 2003, SAR Press. His recent book, entitled *Elderburbia: aging with a sense of place in America*, was published by ABC-Clio in October 2009.

Paul Sugarhood is an occupational therapist at East London NHS Foundation Trust, London, and a Visiting Research Fellow at the Centre for Primary Care and Public Health, Queen Mary, University of London. He has worked in a variety of acute and community settings. His research interests focus on older people, particularly ageing in place, active ageing and environmental interventions to support these.

Josie Tetley has been a nurse for over twenty-seven years. She is Professor of Nursing at Manchester Metropolitan University. Prior to this she was a Senior Lecturer in nursing at The Open University, working in the Faculty of Health and Social Care. Over the last eighteen years she has undertaken a wide range of research projects with older people and family carers. Using primarily participatory ways of working, she has focused in her research on active ageing, the use of new technologies in health and social care and lifelong learning. Josie's commitment to participatory working is evidenced through work which has included joint conference presentations and co-authored publications with project participants.

Verina Waights is a Senior Lecturer and member of the Centre for Aging and Biographical Research at The Open University. She has over twenty-five years' experience in education and research and is the OU lead for the EU funded DISCOVER project, which aims to develop digital skills of carers' and the older people they care for to enhance their wellbeing and social inclusion; she is also a co-investigator on the ESRC-funded seminar series: 'Older People and Technological Inclusion'. Previously she has worked with Birmingham City Council, UK on the EU funded NET-EUCEN scenario, concerned with building digital skills for carers. Recently, she was a member of the CARICT (ICT for caregivers) expert validation workshop, developing recommendations for future EU policy and research. Her research focuses on older people's use of new and emerging technologies and the role of technologies in improving their quality of life.

Stephanie Warren is a retired headteacher and chairperson of Senior Voice, an organization that champions the needs of older people in Milton Keynes. She was awarded the Sheila McKechnie 'Take Action' award in 2012 for her campaigning work to retain the cheque guarantee card. Stephanie was also awarded the 'Golden Wonder' person for her voluntary work in Milton Keynes. She has taken part in a number of lifelong learning activities and has shared her experiences through contributions to conference presentations and publications.

Joe Wherton is a Senior Research Fellow at the Centre for Primary Care and Public Health, Queen Mary, University of London. His research focuses on the user-centred design of technologies and services for older people with assisted living needs. He uses qualitative and participatory design methods to inform the development of solutions that meet the needs of older users in real domestic settings.

INDEX